Editor of the catalogue
DR MYRTALI ACHEIMASTOU-POTAMIANOU

Design and production of the catalogue
RACHEL MISDRACHI-CAPON

English translation
DR DAVID A. HARDY

Editorial advisor
DIANA ZAFIROPOULOU

Artistic advisor
MOSES CAPON

Publication assistant
EVANGELIA VAMVACOPOULOU

Colour photographs

BYZANTINE MUSEUM OF ATHENS	
M. SKIADARESIS	1-6, 8, 9, 12, 14-18, 23-25, 27, 28, 30-51, 53-66, 68, 71, 72, 74, 78-80
G. BALIS	29, 75-77
I. PATRIKIANOS	7
DUMBARTON OAKS COLLECTION	13
THE ART MUSEUM, PRINCETON UNIVERSITY	
C. FIORI	67
THE MENIL COLLECTION	73
THE METROPOLITAN MUSEUM OF ART	52
THE WALTERS ART GALLERY	
S. TOBIN	19, 26, 70
S. TOBIN	21, 22, 69

Type-setting	Stripping
S. PANAGOPOULOS	G. PAPAPANAGOPOULOS
FOTOGRAMMA LTD	(colour plates and cover)
	P. PAPADOPOULOS
Colour separation	Print
MICHAILIDES BROS.	A. PETROULAKIS
	Binding
	G. SGARDELIS

Cover illustration: Cat. no. 48
Printed and bound in Athens, Greece, 1988

HOLY IMAGE, HOLY SPACE
ICONS AND FRESCOES FROM GREECE

Greek Ministry of Culture
Byzantine Museum of Athens

The Walters Art Gallery, Baltimore, Maryland
The Trust for Museum Exhibitions, Washington DC

THE EXHIBITION IS SPONSORED BY

THE TRUST FOR MUSEUM EXHIBITIONS
and THE PARTICIPATING MUSEUMS

Support for this exhibition
and its interpretative programs
has been given by
THE NATIONAL ENDOWMENT FOR THE HUMANITIES, A FEDERAL AGENCY

The GREEK AIR FORCE made an aeroplane available for the transportation of the exhibits

Assistance for transport costs has been received from
OLYMPIC AIRWAYS

HOLY IMAGE, HOLY SPACE
ICONS AND FRESCOES FROM GREECE

THE WALTERS ART GALLERY, BALTIMORE, MARYLAND
August 21 - October 16, 1988

CENTER FOR THE FINE ARTS, MIAMI, FLORIDA
November 14, 1988 - January 8, 1989

KIMBELL ART MUSEUM, FORT WORTH, TEXAS
February 6 - April 2, 1989

THE FINE ARTS MUSEUM OF SAN FRANCISCO, SAN FRANCISCO, CALIFORNIA
April 25 - July 15, 1989

THE CLEVELAND MUSEUM OF ART, CLEVELAND, OHIO
September 6 - October 22, 1989

THE DETROIT INSTITUTE OF ART, DETROIT, MICHIGAN
November 19, 1989 - January 14, 1990

LIST OF LENDERS

ATHENS Byzantine Museum of Athens; Benaki Museum; City of Athens Museum; Kanellopoulos Museum; 2nd Ephorate of Byzantine Antiquities (Kyklades); R. Andreadis; P. Kanellopoulos; Family of I. Yannoukos; Private Collections. **CRETE** 13th Ephorate of Byzantine Antiquities, Iraklion; Church of St. Matthew Sinaiton, Iraklion. **ELASSON** Metropolis of Demetrias and Elasson; Monastery of the Olympiotissa. **IOANNINA** Metropolis of Ioannina; 8th Ephorate of Byzantine Antiquities. **KASTORIA** Archaeological Collection. **KERKYRA** Antivouniotissa Museum. **LARISSA** 7th Ephorate of Byzantine Antiquities. **PATMOS** Monastery of St. John the Theologian; Monastery of Zoodochos Pigi, Chora; Church of Ayios Georgios Aporthianon (or Dimarchias), Chora. **PATRA** 6th Ephorate of Byzantine Antiquities. **RHODES** Metropolis of Rhodes; 4th Ephorate of Byzantine Antiquities. **SKOPELOS** Church of Zoodochos Pigi, Livadi. **SPARTA** 5th Ephorate of Byzantine Antiquities. **SYROS** Metropolis of Syros, Tinos, Andros, Kea and Milos. **THESSALONIKE** 9th Ephorate of Byzantine Antiquities; Monastery of Vlatadon. **TINOS** Sacred Foundation of the Evangelistria. **VERIA** 11th Ephorate of Byzantine Antiquities. **ZAKYNTHOS** Zakynthos Museum; Metochion of the Monastery of St. Catherine Sinaiton.

USA Private Collections. **BALTIMORE** The Walters Art Gallery. **HOUSTON** The Menil Collection. **NEW YORK** The Metropolitan Museum of Art. **PRINCETON** The Art Museum, Princeton University. **WASHINGTON DC** Dumbarton Oaks Collection.

COMMITTEE OF HONOUR

HIS EMINENCE ARCHBISHOP IAKOVOS
GREEK ORTHODOX ARCHDIOCESE OF NORTH AND SOUTH AMERICA

HER EXCELLENCY MADAME MELINA MERCOURI
Minister of Culture, Athens

THE HONOURABLE PAUL SARBANES
United States Senator, the State of Maryland

HIS EXCELLENCY GEORGE PAPOULIAS
Ambassador of Greece to the United States

HIS EXCELLENCY ROBERT KEELEY
Ambassador of the United States to Greece

MANOLIS CHATZIDAKIS
of the Athens Academy

KURT WEITZMANN
Professor of Art and Archaeology, Emeritus,
Princeton University

THE HONOURABLE JOHN BRADEMAS
President, New York University

ORGANIZING COMMITTEE

MANOLIS CHATZIDAKIS
of the Athens Academy
Chairman

NIKOS ZIAS
Director of Byzantine and Post-Byzantine Monuments
Greek Ministry of Culture

MYRTALI ACHEIMASTOU-POTAMIANOU
Director of the Byzantine Museum of Athens

NANO CHATZIDAKIS
Professor at the University of Ioannina

GARY VIKAN
Assistant Director for Curatorial Affairs / Curator of
Medieval Art, The Walters Art Gallery, Baltimore, Maryland

THALIA GOUMA-PETERSON
Professor of Art History, The College of Wooster,
Wooster, Ohio

WILLIAM TRONZO
Associate Professor of the History of Art, The Johns Hopkins
University, Baltimore, Maryland

EUTHYMIOS TSIGARIDAS
Ephor of the 10th Ephorate of Byzantine Antiquities

LASKARINA BOURAS
Curator of the Byzantine Collection of the Benaki Museum,
Athens

ANASTASIOS MARGARITOFF
Inspector of Conservation, Greek Ministry of Culture

STAVROS BALTOYANNIS
Inspector of Conservation, Greek Ministry of Culture

SAMUEL SACHS, II
Director, The Detroit Institute of Arts, Detroit, Michigan

EDMUND P. PILLSBURY
Director, Kimbell Art Museum, Fort Worth, Texas

HARRY S. PARKER, III
Director, Fine Arts Museum of San Francisco
San Francisco, California

EVAN H. TURNER
Director, The Cleveland Museum of Art, Cleveland, Ohio

ROBERT H. FRANKEL
Director, Center for the Fine Arts, Miami, Florida

ROBERT P. BERGMAN
Director, The Walters Art Gallery, Baltimore, Maryland

A GREETING FROM
THE GREEK MINISTER OF CULTURE

Byzantine painting, a brilliant and revealing art with which the Western world has become acquainted only in recent years, now sets out through this series of exhibitions to conquer the USA. Byzantine art, of course, is not unknown to specialists and scholars in American universities and research centres. The broader art-loving public, however, has not previously had the chance to get to know this painting, which has succeeded in making an aesthetically perfect image of religious faith, of hope in redemption and victory over death.

Icons had a double meaning for the Byzantines, as they still do for the Greek Orthodox Christians of today: objects with a religious purpose, they are at the same time works of art: of a painting with strong, clean colours, with a clear outline, a painting stylized and abstract – that is, with elements closely akin to the perceptions of modern art.

Those who know Greece only from the classical beauty and symmetry of the Parthenon, or the harmonious mean of ancient sculpture, may well be unprepared for and astonished by this very different, intensely expressive art.

Though anthropomorphic like every Greek expression, it is nonetheless an art with a fascination of its own, which one discovers little by little. The more familiar with it one becomes, having first overcome the initial difficulties of approach, the more one becomes bound up with it: captivated.

It is the fascination of this different expression of Greek creativity that I hope our American friends will feel. And I am very happy and proud that the opportunity is being offered to them during the time that I have responsibility for the Ministry of Culture. Thanks are due to Mr Yannis Charalambopoulos, Vice-president of the Greek Government and Minister of National Defence, for making an aeroplane available for the transportation of the exhibits. I would also like to thank everyone, both American and Greek, who has contributed to the mounting of this exhibition which, because of the nature of the objects involved (works of art on wood), has created many special technical difficulties. Happily, however, all these difficulties have been overcome by our desire to bring to the New World the new message transmitted by this old ageless art.

MELINA MERCOURI
Greek Minister of Culture

PREFACE

In the history of world cultures, images have often played important roles. Among the cultural traditions of Western civilization perhaps at no time was that role more critical than during the millennium-long reign of the Byzantine Empire. And within the orbit of Byzantium no images were more potent or more vital than icons.

The Byzantine icon (literally translated as 'image') functioned as intercessor between the earthly and divine realms. Such works, particularly in their portable, painted variety, resonated with such power that in the eighth century the imperial power issued decrees banning these supremely spiritual images. The power of the icon – and, by extension, that of the Church – had to be restricted by the emperor. This movement – Iconoclasm – succeeded temporarily in limiting the creation of icons, but after the lifting of the ban in the ninth century, an unprecedented burst of icon-making ensued that lasted until the end of Byzantium in 1453 and, in lands associated with the traditions of Orthodoxy, continues to the present day.

The painted icon is to medieval Greek culture what the *kouros* and *kore* are to Greek antiquity, an exemplary embodiment of the aesthetic and spiritual aspirations of an entire age. Yet while the statuary of Greek antiquity can be quickly called to mind by many individuals, the same may not be said for the Byzantine icon. The modern view of icons in fact derives from exposure to them not in their true Byzantine variety, but as emanating from primarily derivative and often later traditions in Italy and Russia. It was the so-called *maniera greca* of early Italian painting, so disparaged by Renaissance writers, that conditioned our view of icons and, until recently, failed to allow a proper understanding of the Byzantine accomplishment. This approach, coupled with the fact that very few of these perishable wood panels have come down to us, explains why the Byzantine icon has remained an enigma to scholars and critics and virtual *terra incognita* to the public.

In the past twenty-five years great strides have been made in scholarly research on the Byzantine icon. The present exhibition for the first time presents to the American public a representative number of true Byzantine icons (some in the medium of fresco). The power and presence of these images are conspicuous. The rigour of their aesthetic tradition and their spiritual nature are quickly intuited by the modern observers. Seemingly so distant from the experiences of the twentieth century, the icons' immediacy of impact is testimony to their universality.

The Walters Art Gallery, responsible for the organization of the American exhibition, The Trust for Museum Exhibitions, the project's initiator and organizer of the American tour, and the five other American museums that will present this unprecedented exhibition to the American public, are proud to have forged with the Greek Ministry of Culture and the Byzantine Museum of Athens a partnership on behalf of so important a project. For their exceptional generosity, we extend our deepest gratitude to the many talented individuals who have made possible this exhibition and its superb catalogue, and most particularly Her Excellency Madame Melina Mercouri; her special advisor for exhibitions, Mr. Spyros Mercouris, the Ministry of Culture of Greece; Dr Myrtali Acheimastou-Potamianou, Director of the Byzantine Museum of Athens; Dr Gary Vikan, Assistant Director of Curatorial Affairs and Curator of Medieval Art, The Walters Art Gallery; and the Greek Organizing Committee. We are deeply indebted to all who have worked tirelessly to make this important cultural partnership between the Greek nation and the United States a reality.

We would also like to express our deep appreciation to His Eminence, Archbishop Iakovos, Primate of the Greek Orthodox Church in the Americas, who has supported this endeavor from its earliest stages and has lent his assistance to us in countless ways. We are particularly pleased that this exhibition will be touring in the United States during 1989, the thirtieth anniversary of his Enthronement as Archbishop of the Greek Orthodox Archdiocese of North and South America, and we look upon the Tour as a fitting celebration for this distinguished Ministry.

Finally, we would like to express our gratitude to the National Endowment for the Humanities, whose generous grant made the exhibition possible, and to the six American museums without whose co-operation the exhibition would never have been realized.

May this exhibition serve to awaken in the American public a heightened awareness of an essential legacy of Western civilization's spiritual and artistic history – the Byzantine icon.

ROBERT P. BERGMAN
Director, The Walters Art Gallery

ANNE VAN DEVANTER TOWNSEND
President, The Trust for Museum Exhibitions

CONTRIBUTORS

M. A.-P. : M. ACHEIMASTOU-POTAMIANOU
Cat. nos. 17, 18, 29, 39, 50, 54, 66, 69

Ai. B. : AI. BAKOUROU
Cat. no. 7

Ch. B. : CH. BALTOYANNI
Cat. nos. 53, 63, 74

M. B. : M. BORBOUDAKIS
Cat. nos. 76, 77

L. B. : L. BOURAS
Cat. nos. 47, 71, 72, 79, 80

S. A. B. : S. A. BOYD
Cat. no. 13

M. C. : M. CASANAKI
Cat. no. 73

M. Ch. : M. CHATZIDAKIS
Cat. nos. 2, 3, 4, 5, 6, 8, 9, 37, 43,
48, 51, 55, 75

N. Ch. : N. CHATZIDAKIS
Cat. nos. 14, 30, 40, 41, 42, 44, 45,
46, 57, 58, 60, 61, 62, 78

E. M. Ch. : E. M. CHOULIA
Cat. no. 1

K. Ph. K. : K. PH. KALAFATI
Cat. no. 49

G. K. : G. KALAS
Cat. nos. 19, 26, 52

Ch. M.-T. : CH. MAVROPOULOU-TSIOUMI
Cat. no. 24

D. M. : D. MOURIKI
Cat. no. 64

Th. P. : TH. PAPAZOTOS
Cat. nos. 12, 16, 28, 38

N. T. : N. TETERIATNIKOV
Cat. no. 67

A. T. : A. TOURTA
Cat. nos. 23, 25

D. D. T. : D. D. TRIANTAFYLLOPOULOS
Cat. no. 65

E. N. T. : E. N. TSIGARIDAS
Cat. nos. 15, 31, 32, 33, 34, 35, 36

M. V. : M. VASSILAKES
Cat. nos. 27, 56, 59, 70

G. V. : G. VIKAN
Cat. nos. 10, 11, 20, 21, 22

P. L. V. : P. L. VOCOTOPOULOS
Cat. no. 68

CONTENTS

* Reprinted from the Exhibition Catalogue, From Byzantium to El Greco, Greek Frescoes and Icons, Athens 1987

GLOSSARY

Akra Tapeinosis. Man of Sorrows or Christ of Pity. A predominantly liturgical type of icon inspired from the passion ritual. It depicts the death of Christ's human nature and the liberation of the divine one.

Anapeson. A type of reclining Christ Child prefiguring Christ on the Cross. It was inspired by Byzantine hymns.

Bema doors. Cf. Sanctuary doors.

Chiton. Undergarment or tunic.

Comnenian. Byzantine dynasty reigning from 1081 to 1185.

Deesis. The prayer for intercession. Deesis compositions consist of Christ between the supplicant figures of the Virgin and St. John the Baptist. The Great Deesis also includes portraits of the twelve Apostles.

Dodekaorton. A set of twelve icons representing the major feasts of the Orthodox Church (Annunciation, Nativity, Presentation in the Temple, Baptism, Trasfiguration, Raising of Lazarus, Entry into Jerusalem, Crucifixion, Resurrection, Ascension, Pentecost, Dormition of the Virgin). These icons form a frieze on top of the iconostasis beam.

Eleousa. The Virgin of Mercy.

Emmanuel. Variant of Pantocrator, where Christ is represented young and beardless.

Epistyle. Architrave, the iconostasis beam.

Glykophilousa. The Virgin of Tenderness. An iconographic type in which the faces of the Mother and Child touch each other.

Himation. Outer garment.

Hodegetria. The most popular type of Virgin Mary holding the Christ Child and pointing to Him as a way to salvation. It is thought that the archetype which was painted by St. Luke, was kept in the Hodegon Monastery in Constantinople, and was invoked for the protection of the city.

Iconostasis. The screen separating the sanctuary from the nave. From the late 11th century the central doors (sanctuary doors) are flanked by icons of Christ and the Virgin. Above these icons is the epistyle, often decorated with icons of the Great Deesis and/or of the twelve feasts. On top of the screen stands the cross between two small icons of the lamenting Virgin and St. John (the 'lypira').

Kardiotissa. An epithet of the Virgin usually referring to a variant of the Virgin Glykophilousa, particularly popular in Crete. It is thought to derive from a highly venerated icon kept in Karyes of Mount Athos.

Katholikon. The main church in a monastery.

Koimesis. The Dormition or 'falling asleep' of the Virgin, or any other saint, at the moment of death.

Lypira. Cf. Iconostasis.

Maphorion. Woman's cloak with fringes lifted at the back of the neck and used as a hood.

Melismos. The representation of Christ Child in a chalice, accompanying the officiating bishops in the church apse from the 13th century onwards.

Omophorion. The principal characteristic of the liturgical dress of bishops. A band of cloth looped around the neck and marked with crosses.

Palaeologan. Byzantine dynasty reigning from 1259 to 1453 (fall of Constantinople).

Pantanassa. The queen of all. An epithet of the Virgin.

Pantocrator. The Almighty: the most usual type of Christ holding a gospel in one hand and blessing with the other.

Peribleptos. Epithet of the Virgin meaning 'looked at from all sides, admired or honoured by all observers'.

Phelonion. It corresponds to the chasuble of the Western Church and is usually decorated with crosses.

Platytera. Representation of the Virgin and Child; it occupies the church apse as a symbol of the Incarnation.

Proskynetarion. Stand for icons exposed to public or private veneration.

Prothesis. The northern part of the sanctuary where the offerings for the divine liturgy are deposited.

Sanctuary doors. The central doors of the iconostasis which give access into the sanctuary (also Bema doors)

Sticharion. A bishop's undergarment. A long tunic, related to the *albe* of the Western Church.

Triptych. Portable icon comprising a central panel and two folding wings.

Virgin of the Passion. Representation of the Virgin and Child with two archangels carrying the symbols of the Passion.

Zoodochos Pigi. The life-giving source. A type of the Virgin emerging from a chalice-shaped fountain which was inspired by Byzantine hymns.

A collection of Byzantine paintings has travelled from Greece to distant, boundless America, for the first time. It comprises select items, wall paintings and icons, dating from the tenth to the seventeenth centuries: a long period in Greek history, which begins at a time when the territory of the modern Republic of Greece was part of the Byzantine Empire. It continues in the years after the capture of Constantinople by the Crusaders (1204) when various Greek areas gradually became Frankish possessions. The Franks were followed by the Turks who, from the middle of the fourteenth century began to subdue the northern regions, bringing the conquest to completion after 1453.

During this period the Greek and other Christian peoples who dwelt in the areas under foreign domination remained true to Orthodoxy. Like the population of the free areas of the Empire, they continued to produce works of art with a similar unshakeable faith in Byzantine style and iconography, only slightly, or sometimes not at all influenced by the art of their Christian conquerors.

After the fall of Constantinople in 1453, Hellenism was clearly divided into two areas, each with a different cultural character. Crete and a few islands continued under Venetian occupation, and its art therefore had fertile contacts with that of Western Europe, while mainland Greece was subject to the Turks; the art of this area, though still vigorous and varied, is more conservative.

The exhibition has been assembled with a view to demonstrating the variety and quality of the artistic currents that predominated in the entire area from Macedonia to Crete during this long, unbroken span of time, covering the Byzantine and Post-Byzantine periods. Wall paintings of exceptional quality, dating from the tenth-eleventh and thirteenth centuries, from Central Greece and the islands, and fine icons of the same period, hitherto known only to scholars, give the exhibition its particular emphasis. In the following period, attention is concentrated on the artistic production of Crete in the fifteenth and sixteenth centuries: as a result of the historical conjunctures, the island had become the chief artistic centre of Hellenism, as regards both painting and wood-carving. At the same time, local workshops developed in the areas occupied by the Turks, whose activities extended to the neighbouring Orthodox countries; for the large churches on Mount Athos and at Meteora, however, painters were summoned from Crete, indicating that all the Greeks of the region shared the same tastes.

The works presented here have only recently become known, from investigation in the field and in museum laboratories. They attest to the high technical and artistic level of this enchanting art, that retains the warmth of faith and worship. A number of icons from the same region now housed in American museums has been added to the collection from Greece, thereby facilitating the realization of the aims of the exhibition.

A great responsibility was shouldered by those who took the decision to allow these select, old works, to be transported, and to entrust them to the care of their colleagues in the USA, and the latter have an equally great responsibility. The decision was made easier by the experience gained from the organization of exhibitions with a similar content in places closer to Greece, in Florence (1986) and London (1987): on the one hand, no damage was suffered by the works of art, and on the other, they met everywhere with a warm reception, both from the broader art-loving public, and from the specialists. Everyone appreciated the value of the spiritual message brought by this collection from the southern corner of Eastern Europe. And the message continues to be a new one, since this is the first time that an exhibition of Byzantine and post-Byzantine icons and wall paintings has been seen in a number of American cities on this scale, in terms of the number of exhibits, the wide-ranging origins of the paintings, and the chronological period they represent. This noble message will undoubtedly be received by the American art-loving public, thereby justifying this bold venture.

MANOLIS CHATZIDAKIS
of the Athens Academy
President of the Organizing Committee

The works presented in this exhibition of Byzantine and post-Byzantine religious painting, which is touring the United States of America, represent a small but select proportion of those that survive in Greece, once the southern province of the Byzantine Empire, the most brilliant and powerful empire in Medieval Europe. Despite its insignificant political status – with the exception of the area around Thessalonike, which was always of importance –, the province of Greece was the backbone of Byzantium throughout its almost one thousand years of history, as bequether and transmitter of the Greek spirit, the Greek language, and ancient Greek culture. Later Greece was the natural heir to the intellectual and artistic estate of the Byzantine Empire, the importance of which for the history of European civilization has still fully to be assessed.

The Greek character of Byzantine art, which is one of its outstanding features, can clearly be seen in all its creations. It manifests itself primarily in the use of man as the measure, dictating forms and sizes, determining the scale and defining the harmony of the proportions. It is perpetuated by the dominating position occupied by the human figure: sanctified and elevated to the sphere of the divine and radiating the ethos and light of Christian humanism, this regulates every aspect of the art, whether the painted decoration of churches, or the more restricted composition depicting a particular sacred event. It can be detected in the styles, the inherited techniques and artistic manners. It can be recognized in the order, rhythm and decorum that usually characterize Byzantine art.

These works of Byzantine art were the products of deeply held belief and piety, created for the most part by anonymous artists; they reflect the decorum of the kingdom of heaven, at the same time revealing the good taste of their recipients. Through their structure and unchanging principles, they give tangible form to the conception of the divine as perceived by Orthodox doctrine; as true works of art, however, they also reflect, through the changes, variations and modifications of types and form, the meaning and fluctuations of their times, and the distinctive values, joys and suffering of the men whose worship they served.

The double-sided icon from the Monastery of Vlatadon in Thessalonike (cat. no. 23) is an interesting and rare example of the continuity of honour and worship paid to Byzantine icons. A fourteenth-century icon, of great artistic value and high theological meaning, it was set in the centre of a later icon dating from the end of the fifteenth century, and thus continued to serve a religious end; the decoration on both sides of the later icon was adapted to the iconographic content of the inlaid Byzantine work. The double-sided icons (cat. nos. 17 and 18) are examples of another tactic more frequently pursued by following generations to preserve important Byzantine icons. These remained in churches for centuries in their original form, and when they required renewal, it was carried out with the proper respect for the older work; a new representation was painted on their second side, with the same subject and the same iconographic type, covering the original depiction without damaging it, as has become clear in recent years from the removal of the later paintings.

The long retention of Byzantine icons in worship is merely one aspect of the preservation of the Byzantine artistic tradition in the areas of mainland and island Greece that were subject to the Ottoman Turks, the Venetians and the Franks. The preservation of the Byzantine tradition more generally, however, as a dynamic source of religious independence, national self-awareness and resistance to foreign influences and intervention, did not prevent the formation and development of post-Byzantine art, and especially of painting, which is of interest here: this was based on tradition, and found the appropriate styles and expressive manners demanded by the changed conditions and new ideas. The leading role in the formulation and dissemination of these styles and manners was played by Crete where, under Venetian rule, conditions were favourable.

Until its conquest by the Turks in 1669, Crete, with its numerous painters and organized artistic workshops, was the most advanced, pioneering centre of painting; its influence extended far beyond the boundaries of modern Greece, to the entire eastern Mediterranean, and its works were destined for recipients who were not confined to Orthodox Christians but belonged to a wide variety of circles. The perfection attained by the art of Crete is amply demonstrated by the many Cretan icons in the exhibition. These were the work of fine painters of the fifteenth to the seventeenth centuries, both known and anonymous; commissioned by Orthodox clients, and also by Catholics, whether Hellenized or not. They also illustrate the rich 'dowry' bestowed by the island of Crete in the second half of the sixteenth century on one of its distinguished scions who chose the road to the West – Domenikos Theotokopoulos (see cat. nos. 71 and 72), later known as El Greco, who conquered the lofty peaks of European art. It is worth recalling that about three centuries earlier another distinguished Byzantine painter, Theophanes, had left Constantinople for distant Russia, where he achieved greatness and was similarly remembered as Theophanes the Greek.

Outside Crete, other idioms were developed in mainland Greece especially in the areas of Macedonia and Epirus, either with or without the influence of Cretan painting. These idioms, some less significant than those of Crete, some of equal vigour, plasticity and importance, are those of an authentic art, pulsating with the contemporary rhythms of artistic expression. Its influence was felt throughout the northern areas of the Balkans and it played an equally definitive role in the formation and development of post-Byzantine art in the following centuries. Icons cat. nos. 16B, 17b, 23A-B, 38 and others, are examples of this art.

In concluding this note, we would like to extend our warm thanks to The Walters Art Gallery in Baltimore and the other American museums that are playing host to this exhibition, and to The Trust for Museum Exhibitions. In particular we wish to thank Dr Gary Vikan, Assistant Director and Curator of Medieval Art of The Walters Art Gallery, and the President of The Trust for Museum Exhibitions, Mrs Ann Townsend and their colleagues, for the great efforts they have taken in co-operation with their Greek counterparts to ensure the proper organization of the exhibition, and for their equally great enthusiasm.

Many thanks are also due to Dr Nicholas Oikonomides, Professor at the University of Athens, to Dr Nano Chatzidakis, Professor at the University of Ioannina, and to Dr Euthymios Tsigaridas, Ephor of Byzantine Antiquities, who wrote some of the texts accompanying the exhibition; to the archaeologists in the Ministry of Culture, Mr Isidoros Kakouris and Mrs Evangelia Ioannidaki; to the chemists Mr Kostas Asimenos and Mrs Eleni Mangou-Andreopoulou, the conservators Mrs Irini Tsengi and Mr Nicholas Minos; to our colleagues at the Byzantine Museum, Athens, and especially to the archaeologists Mrs Chrysanthi Baltoyanni, Mrs Maria Mavroidi, Dr Angeliki Mitsani and Miss Phaidra Kalaphati; to the conservators Mrs Thalia Papageorgiou, Mrs Aliki Simandoni, Mrs Irini Bali, Mr Spyros Varotsis, Mr Georgios Balis and the many others in the Museum laboratories, who worked under the direction of Mr Stavros Baltoyannis; to the secretary Mrs Evi Frangaki and others who have contributed in a wide variety of ways to the organization of the exhibition and the publication of the catalogue; and to the skilled conservator of the 1st Ephorate of Byzantine Antiquities, Mr Stavros Papageorgiou and his colleagues, who detached the wall paintings from the Church of Ayios Nikolaos in Veria, Lakonia, and undertook the difficult and delicate task of reassembling them in the impressive group of a small church (cat. no. 7).

The exhibition would have been almost impossible to organize without the kind and generous support of the various Ephorates of Byzantine Antiquities, the museums, the local ecclesiastical authorities, monasteries and churches, and the private collections who made the works available, to whom an enormous debt of gratitude is owed. Particular mention should be made of the Ecumenical Patriarchate of Constantinople, which readily gave its approval to the inclusion in the exhibition of the three wonderful Byzantine icons from the Monastery of Vlatadon in Thessalonike (cat. nos. 19, 20 and 24), on the recommendation of the Monastery; of the Monastery of St. Catherine on Sinai, which consented to make available two important icons attributed to Michael Damaskinos, from its metochion in Iraklion, Crete, the Church of St. Matthew Sinaiton (cat. nos. 76, 77); and also of the Monastery of St. John the Theologian on Patmos, which, though celebrating nine hundred years of unbroken activity since its foundation, graciously agreed to deprive its own celebrations of three outstanding Cretan works (cat. nos. 48, 51 and 55). The thought of the Greeks resident in America will undoubtedly have been of some weight in the decision taken by all these to make their precious works of art and sacred treasures available for such a journey, long in both distance and time.

This exhibition of Byzantine and post-Byzantine art from Greece brings to the United States a special message, and with it an invitation to form a deeper acquaintance with our country. To the Greeks of America it also brings something very precious: the colours, sounds and fragrances of the sacred figures from the country of their origin, the 'distant mother, the unfading rose' of Odysseas Elytis's poem 'Axion Esti'. And it is properly dedicated to them.

MYRTALI ACHEIMASTOU-POTAMIANOU
Director of the Byzantine Museum of Athens

For several generations of American art historians, whose graduate education in the 1940s, 50s, and 60s brought them to Princeton University, medieval art was Byzantine art, and Byzantine art *was* Kurt Weitzmann. Though of course, Kurt would deny that, and justifiably, since his immense learning and scholarship range far wider – from Late Antiquity to the High Middle Ages, from the Greek East to the Latin West. But still, it was Kurt Weitzmann, as much teacher as scholar, who first introduced so many of us to Byzantium – a culture which initially seemed, to me at least, more alien than exotic.

My own first exposure to Byzantium was at Princeton nearly twenty years ago, when Kurt had just recently returned from the last of several research expeditions to St. Catherine's Monastery at Mount Sinai. He had gone there to photograph and document its extraordinary collection of Byzantine icons, and I remember still, as many of others must, the excitement of seeing for the first time the slides he brought back. Though 'confusion' might be a better word, for we had come to know Byzantine art mostly through its (much more plentiful) manuscripts and ivories, and so these imposing panels were totally new and unexpected. They were so fragile, and so few had survived. Yet here was the gentle grace of Duccio and the emotional power of Cimabue – great artists by then so familiar to all of us – but in paintings by much earlier Byzantine masters of whom no one had ever heard, much less studied or written about. This made no sense; somehow it seemed as much an injustice to them as a distortion of art history.

Of course 'Holy Image, Holy Space' cannot, by itself, right that wrong. And in any event, Kurt Weitzmann has himself done much over the last two decades to introduce the icon to a broader public – most notably, through his popular 1979 monograph, The Icon. But still, this exhibition represents a unique opportunity to bring some of Byzantium's finest surviving panel paintings before a public which otherwise could never hope to visit Mount Sinai – or, for that matter, the many remote Greek collections, large and small, from which it has been assembled. Moreover, they will experience the icon in ways that even Kurt could not fully have anticipated twenty years ago. This is true in large measure because of recent discoveries by Greek scholars, who have succeeded in tracing the tradition of Byzantine panel painting well beyond the Fall of the Empire (AD 1453). The great master Angelos, active at mid-15th century, and the impressive early career of Domenikos Theotokopoulos (El Greco) on his native Crete, have come fully to light only in the 1980s – as have a surprising number of fine icons in this exhibition, including the huge Three Church Fathers panel in the Byzantine Museum. For this, specifically, we owe thanks to Greek conservators, who have been able to remove layers of obscuring overpaint, and thereby – much like archaeologists – 'discover' masterpieces hidden underneath. Certainly no other branch of

Byzantine art history is changing as rapidly – or with more exciting and unexpected results – than is that of the icon.

But this is only half the story. For while it is true that those of us involved with 'Holy Image, Holy Space', both Greek and American, had the initial goal of introducing Byzantine panel painting as 'good art' – as art-historically significant art – we had a second, even more ambitious aim. Namely, we hoped to present the icon of its own terms, not simply as art, but as sacred art – as a uniquely Byzantine achievement born of equal measures of art and spirit. Many can recall the powerful impact of visiting Chartres or some other great cathedral for the first time: once having entered such a church, one feels and understands 'Gothic' as one never could before. And the same is true of the icon. The experience it offers – in a sense, demands – is intensely personal and immediate. And it must take place 'in person'. For it is only when standing face-to-face with a great icon that one can fully appreciate, understand, and be touched by Byzantium's achievement. And if this exhibition, in some measure, succeeds in creating an atmosphere where that can happen, then it, too, will have accomplished much.

GARY VIKAN
Assistant Director for Curatorial Affairs / Curator of Medieval Art
The Walters Art Gallery, Baltimore, Maryland
Guest Curator, 'Holy Image, Holy Space'

BYZANTIUM
AND ANCIENT GREECE

The visitor who comes from viewing the Elgin Marbles in the British Museum to the exhibition of Greek icons at the Royal Academy may well feel nonplussed. Has he stepped into a totally different world, separated from classical Greece by an unbridgeable gulf? The difference is real enough. The men who built the Parthenon would be just as disconcerted could they visit the exhibition. Byzantine artists were not slavish copyists of models from a distant past. They had their own traditions, their own values, their own ideals. Yet they and the society in which and for which they worked were linked by a complex web of continuity with Greek antiquity, and their work cannot be fully understood unless we bear in mind these links.

First among them comes the Greek language. Like other languages it changed over the centuries. But the rate of change was slow if we compare it with that which led from Anglo-Saxon to modern English. And the literary language of the Byzantines remained close to that of classical and post-classical antiquity. The literature of Classical Greece, of the Hellenistic world, and of the Fathers of the Church was instantly accessible to any educated Byzantine. And with the literature he absorbed the ideas and values which it expressed. He might well take a critical stance towards some of these. He might sometimes misunderstand them. But he was not cut off by a language barrier from the world of his ancestors, as was the medieval Italian or Frenchman, to say nothing of his English or German contemporary.

The Byzantines, too, possessed and were aware of a political and institutional continuity with the past which the West lacked. In Italy, France, Spain, Britain, Germanic kingdoms had established themselves on the ruins of the Roman Empire. The Byzantine state *was* the Roman Empire, and its citizens called themselves Romans. Their rulers were the direct successors of Augustus, Trajan and Constantine. Their institutions had changed over the centuries by evolution rather than by revolution.

They looked back with familiarity to classical Greece. In their schools they read Homer and Sophocles, Demosthenes and Aristotle, while generations of schoolboys practised composing speeches to put in the mouth of Pericles or Alexander. However, the long centuries of Hellenistic and Roman Greece were closer to the Byzantines than was classical Athens, both in time and in empathy. Lucian and the Greek novelists, Ptolemy and Galen were more readily accessible to them than were Aeschylus or Herodotus. It was in large measure through Hellenistic eyes that they perceived Classical antiquity.

This was the world in which the Christian Church grew and spread. It was the world in which that synthesis of Hellenic and Judaeo-Christian culture was worked out, which has marked the civilization of Europe through the centuries. This fusion took place in a society of Greek culture, through the medium of the Greek language, from St. Paul through Clement of Alexandria to the great Fathers of the fourth and early fifth centuries: Athanasius, Gregory of Nazianzus, Basil of Caesarea, Gregory of Nyssa, John Chrysostom, Cyril of Alexandria.

A result of this creative fusion of two originally distinct traditions was that very many elements of classical Greek culture became integral parts of Christian Byzantine culture. These ranged from proverbs and anecdotes to a philosophical view of the world to which Plato and Aristotle, the Stoics and the Sceptics, and the Neoplatonists of late antiquity had all made substantial contributions. These classical elements, of course, included much that was only superficially, if at all, reconcilable with Christian doctrine – magic, astrology, popular rites and celebrations. In 692 a Church Council fulminated against those who consulted fortune-tellers, clairvoyants and sorcerers, or who took part in peasant mummery in which the false gods of the Hellenes were invoked. Five centuries later a learned churchman observed sadly that such practices were still prevalent. At the end of the fourth century John Chrysostom denounced from the pulpit those mothers who hung coins of Alexander the Great from their children's necks as amulets. A thousand years later Greek mothers were still doing just that.

At the other end of the spectrum the austere Elements of Theology of the pagan Neoplatonist Proclus, with its view of the universe as an uncreated and timeless emanation from the primal One, was preserved, copied and read for a thousand years after Christianity had become the sole permitted religion. In the twelfth century a scholar-bishop wrote a refutation of it because of the growing interest it aroused among his contemporaries. In the last years of the Byzantine Empire it inspired Gemistos Plethon's grand Platonic vision of the world, in which Christianity found no place. The lectures which Plethon gave in Florence in 1438 fired the imagination of the early Italian humanists, and led eventually, ten years after Constantinople had fallen to the Ottoman Turks, to Marsilio Ficino's translation into Latin of all Plato's dialogues, which provided the essential foundation of Renaissance Platonism. Ficino's portrait bust by Andrea Ferrucci da Fiesole still stands in Florence cathedral. Plethon's mortal remains were brought from Mistra in the Peloponnese by Sigismondo Malatesta in 1464 and reburied in a sarcophagus in the outer wall of the Tempio Malatestiano in Rimini. These two Renaissance monuments are a testimony to the persistence with which the Byzantines preserved the philosophical heritage of their ancestors.

Byzantines were always conscious that their civilization had two roots, Hellenic and Christian, and often referred to them. A man – or an epoch – might lay more emphasis on the one or the other, but neither could be totally rejected or denied.

Elements of both are constantly found side by side, as a kind of cliché of Byzantine thought. An eleventh-century archbishop makes a trivial moral point by quoting from Homer and the Psalms. The emperor Alexius Comnenus justifies the seizure of church plate at a moment of crisis to pay his troops by citing the examples of David, who gave the consecrated bread from the temple of the Lord to his soldiers, and Pericles, who took ten talents of silver from the temple of Athena 'for a secret purpose' during the revolt of the Euboeans.

During their long membership of the Roman Empire the Greeks learned to transcend the narrow local patriotism which often marked them in the Classical period. As one of them remarked in a somewhat idealistic panegyric of Rome, Roman citizenship did not belong to a single city but was a common nationality for the whole civilized world. This sense of the importance of belonging to a greater political unity than a man's native city was strengthened when the Roman Empire became the Christian Roman Empire, the unique instrument of a divine plan for the salvation of mankind. While Western Europe dissolved into a kaleidoscopic mosaic of statelets which might grow, flourish and wither away within a single lifetime, the Byzantine Empire, though its frontiers might expand or contract, remained a powerful, durable, stably administered state of unequivocal legitimacy, alone of its kind in medieval Europe, and engaging the unquestioning loyalty of the great mass of its citizens. It naturally inherited many elements of Roman political tradition. The greatest of these was law. Justinian's Code and Digest in Greek translation, and with various adaptations, remained authoritative sources of substantive law to the end. In the West Roman law had to be rediscovered by the Doctors of Bologna in the eleventh century. In the East it was never lost. Byzantine society, for all its occasional violence, in principle lived under the rule of law, not of arbitrary decree or feudal custom. And its law was a direct heritage from the classical world.

These are some of the elements of continuity that marked the Byzantine world, a continuity that involved creative use of a rich tradition to meet new needs. The Byzantines did not preserve classical tradition unchanged, in a kind of deep freeze, until the West had need of it. It was their own heritage, which they used for their own ends.

Historians will explain in more detail and with more discerning expertise how Byzantine artists treated the legacy of antiquity at different periods. I will confine myself to a few general considerations. First, it would never have occurred to any Byzantine to build a replica of the Parthenon. That was left to the citizens of Edinburgh in 1822 – 'and they ran out of money after erecting twelve columns' – and of Nashville, Tennessee in 1920. But they had all round them far more examples of Classical and Hellenistic art than we possess. Their way of looking at them changed with centuries. At first their connection with pagan culture endowed these monuments with sinister and threatening overtones. The statues in the Hippodrome at Constantinople were believed to be inhabited by potentially dangerous spirits. In the course of time, however, artists turned to copying, both in iconography and in style, the naturalistic art of antiquity, which they gradually fused with Christian artistic traditions largely of Near Eastern origin. One need only look at the sixth-century liturgical vessels from Riha and Stuma in Syria (now divided between the Archaeological Museum in Istanbul and Dumbarton Oaks in

Washington), or the superb seventh-century David plates from Cyprus (now divided between the National Museum of Cyprus and the Metropolitan Museum of Art in New York) to see how early and with what distinction this adaptation of Classical art to Christian purposes began. The classicizing illustrations in the manuscript of Gregory of Nazianzus executed for the emperor Basil I *c.* 880 (Paris gr. 510), or the tenth-century Paris Psalter (Paris gr. 139), or the contemporary Bible of Leo the Patrician (Vat. Reg. gr. 1) show how profound the influence of antique models on Byzantine art had become by the age of the Macedonian emperors. Even such conservative art forms as the mural decoration of churches and the painting of icons were not immune to the artistic currents of their time.

A less obvious channel of classical influence, which has only recently begun to be explored, is the use made by Byzantine artists of earlier literary descriptions. This applies in particular to the graphic and vivid descriptions of Biblical scenes and events by the fourth-century Fathers, who had all been trained in the sophisticated techniques of rhetorical description. But it may well go much further: the description of a natural object, a landscape, or a work of art was one of the exercises prescribed on the school-books from which the Byzantines learned the art of self-expression, and for which they looked to classical models. Whether artists themselves read books – which were costly objects in the Middle Ages – or whether literary influences were mainly transmitted via their patrons, is an interesting question, to which we do not yet know the answer.

The third channel of influence is a more abstract one. Plato was deeply moved by art, and at the same time feared it for its power. He banished it from his ideal state because it was at two removes from the true reality, the world of ideas, of which physical objects were but imperfect copies. The problem of the nature of artistic representation preoccupied his later followers, whom we call Neoplatonists. The greatest of these, Plotinus (third century AD), ventured to correct his master and to suggest that an artist might well see beyond the physical object which was his model to its ideal nature. In other words he recognized that art could be a creative activity and not a mere manufacture of facsimiles. This view of the status and activity of the artist contributed to the arguments used by the defenders of icons during the great iconoclast dispute which rent Byzantine society in the eighth and early ninth centuries. In this way the attitude of the Orthodox Church and Orthodox society towards the artist and his work was in part determined by a philosophical discourse which originated in classical Greece. In no domain of Byzantine art was this more important than in that of icon painting.

ROBERT BROWNING
Emeritus Professor, University of London

BYZANTINE GREECE

During its one thousand years' history, the Byzantine Empire, the Christian state of the Roman East, embraced a variety of different civilizations and formed an amalgam of diverse creeds and cultures. Byzantium, a state of human nations had its capital at Constantinople, the meeting point of Europe and Asia. Though firmly attached to the political and social institutions of the Later Roman Empire, it evolved the new ecumenical religion, Christianity, spoke the Greek language, and adopted Greek education.

In order to trace the boundaries of Greece under the Byzantine Empire, we have to bear in mind that the word 'Hellas' is a historical term, without any specific geographical content. The geography of Byzantine Hellenism coincides neither with the wider borders of the Empire, nor with the narrower borders of modern Greece. Within the constantly changing borders and the varied ethnic composition of the Empire, the formation of Greece as an independent region was influenced by the administrative organization, the military organization, and the nature of communications.

During the Early Byzantine period, the Greek lands, which formed part of the broader administrative framework of the state, were assigned to the 'praefectura' of Illyricum and divided between the provinces of 'Macedonia' and 'Achaea' or 'Hellas' they were far removed from the centre, where the decisions of great moment were taken. With the exception of Macedonia and its capital Thessalonike, which occupied an important position on the major arteries of communication between East and West, the Greek lands occupied a position of secondary importance. During this transitional period, events of great importance hastened the end of the ancient world. The proclamation of Christianity as the official religion of the state marked the beginning of the Early Christian civilization that flourished in the fifth and sixth centuries. The Greek mainland and islands are full of brilliant, richly decorated monuments. This building activity suggests economic prosperity. The Early Christian basilicas are sometimes built over pagan temples, sometimes close to famous pagan shrines, and sometimes on the tombs of martyrs, as in the case of the large basilica of St. Demetrius in Thessalonike, the basilica of the Ilissos in Athens and the basilica at Lechaeum near Corinth.

The natural disasters in the middle of the sixth century – the earthquakes of 522 and 551 – and more importantly the incursions of the Avars and the Slavs from the end of this century onwards, caused major upheavals. Urban life went into decline and economic activity diminished. This was the beginning of the critical years of the 'μέγιστον χάσμα' ('great chasm') in the historical record and the cultural evolution. The root causes are to be sought in the colonization by the Slavs and in events of a more general nature that were happening in the Empire, such as the consolidation of the naval power of the Arabs in the Mediterranean, and the consequent collapse of the Byzantine supremacy at sea. The disturbances of the seventh century signalled the failure of the Greco-Roman political, economic and intellectual system.

Between the end of the seventh century and the first decades of the ninth, the provincial administrative system of the Empire was reformed by the introduction of a new administrative institution, the 'theme'. The reassertion of the authority of the state was to mark a gradual revitalization of the area, despite all the difficulties it had to face as a result of the invasions by the Arabs and the Bulgars during the ninth and tenth centuries. The economic and demographic recovery can be detected in the revival of the earlier urban centres and the founding of new settlements. Local industry flourished, and the quantity of currency in circulation increased. In the countryside, the powerful landowners occupied great estates. At the same time, the Church was reorganized and there was a revival in religious and monastic life. The cultivation of letters and art was a feature of the period from the beginning of the ninth century onwards.

The disturbance of the international balance of power in the Mediterranean, the decline of the naval power of the Arabs, and the expansion of the Western powers into the East ushered in a new period. The Norman raids against Greek lands at the end of the eleventh century were to be repeated more savagely in the twelfth. The abandonment of the Byzantine Mediterranean to the maritime cities of Italy was one of the main features of the last centuries of Byzantine history. The Latin economic penetration that accompanied the domination by Western trade led to the decline of Byzantium. The political and economic sovereignty of the West culminated in the dissolution of the Byzantine Empire in 1204. The Latin feudal states – the kingdom of Thessalonike, the Duchy of Athens, and the Principality of Achaea – were erected on the ruins of the Byzantine state. The Venetians installed themselves at points that would secure control of communications by sea: the Ionian islands, Modon and Coron in the Peloponnese, Crete and the Cyclades became Venetian possessions. In 1204, the unity of Byzantine Greece came to an end. The efforts of the Byzantine emperors and the despots of Epirus and the Morea resulted in the reconquest of the lost territories, but the end of the fourteenth century saw the beginning of the gradual expansion of the Ottoman Turks, and the conquest of Greek lands. In 1460, the Despotate of the Morea fell into the hands of the Turks and the last remnant of Byzantine authority in Greece was finally dissolved.

ANNA AVRAMEA
Professor at the University of Crete

THE GREEK WORLD
AND THE LATIN DOMINATION

If the division of Christendom into two hostile worlds constitutes one of the most important chapters in the history of Europe, the events following the Fourth Crusade were as decisive as the fall of Constantinople for the history of Hellenism. The capture of Constantinople by the Crusaders in 1204 and the establishment of Latin domination over the territories of the dismembered Byzantine state marked the end of the Byzantine Empire as an entity; at the same time, what Nicetas Choniates described as the 'μέγιστον χάσμα διαφορᾶς' ('great chasm') was finally created between the Christian East and the Christian West.

The history of the population of the Eastern Empire after the Western world had prevailed passed through three phases: first, there was resistance to Latin influence, then adjustment to the new situation and contact with Western civilization and the more developed Western economies, and, finally, acceptance of the institutional framework of foreign sovereignty. This threefold reaction, the expression of a culture whose main hallmark was the vitality stemming from its powers of assimilation, enabled the Greek element to take advantage of the favourable conditions created by Western rule, and at the same time led it to define its social and ideological orientation.

To refer to the territories of the Byzantine Empire, the Latins used the term 'Romania', a word of popular origin, synonymous in the Byzantine sources with the Βασιλεία τῶν Ρωμαίων ('Kingdom of the Romans'). The Latin empire of Constantinople was thus called 'Imperium Romaniae', the Doge of Venice added to his titles that of 'dominus quartae partis et dimidiae totius Imperii Romaniae', the codification of feudal institutions in Greece was given the name of 'Assises de Romanie', and Nauplion is referred to throughout the period of Latin domination as 'Napoli di Romania'. The Venetians distinguished between 'Romania bassa' (the Peloponnese, Euboea, Crete, and the islands) and 'Romania alta' (Macedonia, Thrace, and the Bosphorus). For the chronographer Salimbene, thirteenth-century Greece was a province of Romania ('Grecia ... est provincia Romaniae'). And the very document by which the territories of the Byzantine Empire were distributed amongst the Crusaders is known as the 'Partitio terrarum Imperii Romanie'.

Divided into Frankish and Venetian possessions, the Greek regions experienced differing fortunes from the thirteenth to the end of the eighteenth centuries, involving varying periods of Latin sovereignty, and one or more foreign lords. Some areas passed directly from the Byzantine administration to Venetian sovereignty, others became fiefs, in accordance with Western practice, and yet others passed through a feudal phase before becoming Venetian possessions. The historical climate affecting the population of each region thus varied according to the specific local conditions. Even before the Fourth Crusade Cyprus had come under the domination of the French Lusignans, who ruled over the island for about three hundred years, until the establishment in 1489 of Venetian authority, which lasted until 1570. From 1211 until 1669 Crete was the most important colony of the naval power, Venice, in the eastern Mediterranean. Attica, Boeotia and the Megarid initially came under French sovereignty, the first Duke being the Burgundian Otto de la Roche; they were subsequently ruled by the Catalans, the Navarrese and the Florentines. The Principality of Achaea was one of the most important Latin areas in Greece, and under the Villehardouins occupied a unique position in the feudal world of the east. The Ionian islands were governed by the Angevins, Orsini, Tocchi, Venier and other Latin rulers, until they were annexed to the colonial system of Venice. Euboea, having initially been granted as a fief to three nobles from Verona, who governed it as a triumvirate ('terzieri'), also became a Venetian possession. Venetian possessions in the Peloponnese included Modon, Coron and later Nauplion, Argos and Monemvasia. The islands of the Aegean became the Duchy of the Archipelago, and were divided as fiefs amongst Venetian nobles (Sanudi, Querini, Barozzi, Dandolo, Ghisi etc.). Chios and Lesbos were Genoese trading posts, while Rhodes, under the Knights Hospitallers of St. John became the centre of a considerable state that served as an ideal base of operations against Turkish attacks.

The new order of things established in the Greek world in 1204 not only signalled the end of a political situation but also brought about significant changes in the structure of Greek society. The introduction of the feudal system into Romania gradually produced a diversified regime compounded of former Byzantine institutions, local customs and Frankish practices. Belief in the eastern creed, which, along with the language, distinguished the native element from the foreign, came to be the line that divided the Latin Catholic conqueror from the Greek Orthodox conquered. The result was that religious belief began to be confused with the national sentiments of Hellenism, and gradually came to coincide with national identity.

A long time was to elapse before the tensions between the two Christian communities of Latin Greece relaxed, their differences diminished and a common way of life was established that finally enabled the two disparate religious communities to coexist in the same geographical region. The coexistence of Greeks and foreigners in the same area was the result of two parallel historical phenomena that can be observed during this period: on the one hand, the Latins slowly but surely came under the influence of the natural and human environment and began to be assimilated into Greek culture, and on the other the Greeks, despite retaining their religion, language and traditions, and attempting to preserve their identity and personality, began nonetheless to infiltrate and participate in the social and economic structures of the conquerors. However, although a cultural gap could be detected between Greeks and foreigners in the first centuries of Latin domination, Hellenism later came under the influence of the Renaissance and absorbed the values of Western civilization. Contact between Western and Greek forms found its finest expressions in Crete. Cretan craftsmen and artists, while remaining true to the Byzantine tradition, succeeded in using new expressive means to interpret Renaissance models of architecture and painting.

Although foreign domination undoubtedly had its painful aspects, the Greeks succeeded through their own abilities in finding a new cultural path and in opening up new avenues of creativity.

CHRYSA MALTEZOU
Professor at the University of Crete

BYZANTINE
WALL PAINTING
IN GREECE

Byzantine painting, especially mural painting, though pre-eminently a conservative art form, is nonetheless a living art, which responds to the changing demands of official church doctrine and of popular belief. To understand this more fully, it should be remembered that the dynamic of painting is the result of two counterbalanced tendencies. On the one hand stand all the elements that lead to unity of place and continuity in time, and on the other those that lead to differentiation and evolution. The first tendency embraces the constant, unchanging ideological values that find their expression through the iconography of an Orthodox church and belong to the level of doctrine, history, devotion and ritual. These values undergo very few fluctuations through time, with only the occasional shift of emphasis. They are constants, firmly linked with the notion of accuracy in matters of history and doctrine, and with the demand for likeness, not only in the portrayal of the saints, but also in a more general sense: they constitute an essential precondition if the decoration of a church is to find acceptance as authentic from the point of view of Orthodox iconography. Those who drew up iconographic programmes and the painters themselves naturally solved the problems with which they were faced by concentrating strictly on models whose authenticity was indisputable: miraculous icons, earlier wall paintings, illustrated manuscripts, sketch books, descriptions and so on. Amongst the conservative elements should be included the techniques of mural decoration, whether we are talking of mosaics, or frescoes, or of a mixture of fresco and tempera that derived from Greco-Roman painting. The styles of painting, too, continued to the end to exhibit the basic variations within the main trends that had already emerged in late antiquity. It should be added here that one of the constant preconditions making for the unity of artistic expression was its anti-realistic and transcendental character, though it nonetheless respected the human figure and the basic shapes of objects.

Within this constant framework, presented here in a very simplified form, there were countless variations during the thousand years, or more, of vital creative activity: sometimes these were determined by non-artistic factors, such as the historical circumstances of the time, the social classes to which the patrons of art belonged and the local economic conditions. Drastic intervention by the political authorities, as in the case of Iconoclasm, was rare. At the artistic level, in explaining the variety of expression we also have to take into account the local tradition and the personal contribution of the artist, which was not as insignificant as it might seem.

Given this background, we are in a position better to understand the difficulties involved in determining the common characteristics of the painting of a particular region in the Byzantine period, such as the region now occupied by the Republic of Greece. The first difficulty is that this region formed only part of a wider area in which Greeks lived and worked during the Byzantine period, and may not therefore be regarded as a separate geographical entity. Secondly, the main body of Greece is divided by high mountains, and fragmented into numerous islands, large and small, scattered around the mainland: this produces distinct regions between which communication is not easy and which, moreover, in different periods, depended to differing degrees on the main Byzantine centres of Constantinople and Thessalonike. In this context it was not possible for painting, even in the area of modern Greece, to acquire a unified character that would set it apart from that of other regions outside Greece.

It is possible, however, to distinguish certain more general characteristics deriving from precisely those non-artistic factors that we have noted. One of the most indicative is the comparative numbers of wall paintings decorating monuments. Throughout Greece no less than two thousand cycles of wall paintings, dating from the seventh to the fifteenth centuries, have survived, often superimposed one upon another. This is not the final count but it is greater than that for all the surviving cycles in all the other Byzantine regions in Europe and Asia Minor, or in the neighbouring Orthodox states. Moreover, differences can be distinguished in the density of monuments in different parts of Greece. They are much more densely concentrated in Greece south of Olympus one of the reasons for this difference being that in the area north of Olympus the majority of monuments are to be found in the relatively large towns. In Thessalonike alone we know from documentary sources that there were more than a hundred churches and monasteries, and the layers of painting that will have covered the walls of these sacred buildings will have been much greater in number. Most of them disappeared, however, during the long centuries of Ottoman occupation. In the south of Greece, by contrast, with the exception of a few towns like Mistra and Yeraki, most of the known Byzantine monuments are to be found in the countryside, outside the relatively small fortified towns that were located in the safer mountain regions.

The consequence for art of this distinction is that the art of the northern region has an urban character, since it was fostered within the relatively sophisticated cultural environment of the city. This does not mean that all the monuments in the south were non-urban in character. First, there were large monastic foundations, built and dedicated by the Emperors, or by secular and religious rulers, who brought to the peripheral areas the means to construct works of a high artistic level, if not of the level of luxury represented by marble revetments and mosaics. Secondly, because works like these, which are 'imported' in character, might influence the local production, which (to use a modern Greek image) always stood to them in the relationship of a visual 'demotic', or popular language, to the 'pure' literary language, or *katharevousa*.

Other local peculiarities include iconographical archaisms, such as the representation of the founders or of the prophets in the sanctuary apse, or the manner of painting the Pantocrator, in the dome, with otherwise unknown variations, both in the overall composition and in the secondary figures included. A preference for non-figurative decoration can also be observed in Greece, especially in the islands, from the period of Iconoclasm onwards. This is a very interesting phenomenon, whose full extent has yet to be determined.

These phenomena, however, are not unique, or exclusive, and were not part of an autonomous evolution. To different degrees, according to place and to period, they are related to developments in the major centres and in the neighbouring regions such as Asia Minor and Italy.

The links with the West, for which Byzantine painting always served as a model and a teacher, became closer after the Fourth Crusade, which resulted in the dissolution of the Byzantine Empire (1204). A large part of southern Greece, including Crete, the islands of the Aegean and some parts of the Peloponnese, remained under Latin domination until the Ottoman conquest. What is remarkable is that throughout these centuries the Orthodox population continued to 'see' and to paint in a purely Byzantine mode. The inevitable foreign influences were very few, affecting mainly the subject matter and to a much lesser extent the style.

Another, equally remarkable phenomenon can be detected in this region at this period. In Crete, 95% of the surviving Byzantine wall paintings – about 900 in all – which vary greatly in quality, were painted in the fourteenth and fifteenth centuries – that is, during the Venetian period. A similar phenomenon can be observed in the other regions occupied by the Franks. It can be explained to some extent by the change in the social rank of the patrons, and also by comparison with what was happening in the Byzantine area.

For, in the same period, at the end of the Byzantine Empire, there was a general flowering of art, with important centres in Thessalonike, Mistra, Arta and Mount Athos producing work of a high quality whose influence was widely felt. These centres now rivalled Constantinople, even though they were still dependent on it.

Palaeologan painting succeeded in creating pictorial compositions that frequently give expression to complex theological ideas relating to the burning problems of the period. This painting was distinguished by its mastery of the full range of traditional techniques, using the rich repertoire of Orthodox iconography. By these means it created a new style that was to have its influence on the West.

This final flowering of the spiritual world of Byzantium was to live on in the art of the Greeks after the capture of Constantinople.

MANOLIS CHATZIDAKIS
of the Athens Academy

THE CULT OF ICONS

An Orthodox church is unthinkable without its icons in front of which candles are lit, incense burnt and other acts of devotion performed. In this respect the Orthodox differ from Christians of other denominations: Roman Catholics admit in their churches both statues and painted images, but do not, on the whole, address to them much in the way of veneration; Protestants of the more fundamentalist variety eschew all images; while Syrian Jacobites are equally content to worship with or without them.

When we enquire why it is that the Orthodox are so attached to their icons, we discover that this practice has no foundation either in Holy Scripture or in the theology of the early Fathers. Its origins must be sought in historical tradition and its detailed justification is contained in the Acts of the Seventh Council held at Nicaea in 787 as well as in the so-called Synodikon of Orthodoxy of 843. These enactments represent the reaction of the Eastern Church against Iconoclasm, introduced by the Emperor Leo III in 730; and Iconoclasm, in turn, was a reaction to what was regarded in some quarters as an idolatrous veneration of images for which the Almighty had delivered the Christians to chastisement at the hands of their enemies. In other words, the Eastern Church in 843 restored what had been general practice before 730; and since the whole question was definitely settled there and then, that is still where it remains today. The Orthodox Church is a Church of tradition.

We try, therefore, to cast our minds back to 730 (and earlier) and what do we find? Religious images are everywhere, in churches, in private houses, on public monuments, in books, on utensils. Some are 'narrative' images in the sense that they represent an incident, and these may be arranged in a sequence to tell a story either from the Bible or from the life of a saint. They serve to instruct the illiterate in the truths of Christianity or act as reminders of sacred events. Other images, however, are simply portraits and do not convey any action or message other than a 'presence'. They may, if seldom, represent a saint who is still alive, more often a saint of the past – a martyr, an apostle, the Virgin Mary, Jesus Christ himself. It is the portrait icons that attract veneration. They are prayed to and work miracles. Occasionally they speak or weep. They bleed if stabbed by an unbeliever. They float across the sea without getting wet. Like palladia they are carried into battle by armies. They serve as guarantors of contracts. A particle of paint or plaster taken from an icon may be ingested and cure a disease. In short, an icon is perceived not merely as a likeness, but as a vehicle of supernatural power, as the 'double' of the saint represented on it or the 'shell' in which he dwells.

There can be no doubt that such practices were extremely widespread in the sixth and seventh centuries. At the time it was affirmed that icon painting was as old as Christianity itself and was an 'unwritten tradition'; that St. Luke had painted a portrait of the Virgin Mary and that Christ, after impressing his features on a towel had sent it to King Abgar of Edessa. The latter (along with several others) was an image 'not made by hand' (*acheiropoietos*) and demonstrated divine sanction for the existence of icons. Today we no longer believe that icon painting went back to apostolic times. We know from archaeological evidence that the early Christians before *c.* AD 300 cultivated – if they did so at all – an art that was symbolic rather than literal; that portraits of saints began to appear rather timidly at about the time of the Emperor Constantine and that some churchmen did not approve of them. As for the cult of icons, we cannot trace it much before the middle of the fifth century. Speaking historically, what the Orthodox Church has perpetuated is the situation that prevailed in the sixth and seventh centuries.

It is easy to describe the cult of icons as crass superstition and explain its growth as the result of the spread of Christianity to rural populations that had been pagan from times immemorial and were incapable of adopting a spiritual religion without a physical focus of devotion. The Iconoclasts, although they lacked our historical perspective, clearly regarded it as idolatry. So did contemporary Jews. Yet the problem is not quite that simple. Why is it that subtle theologians like St. John Damascene, like St. Theodore the Studite and the Patriarch Nikephoros, who were certainly aware of what strike us as superstitious practices, felt compelled to defend in many hundreds of pages both the existence and – under certain safeguards – the cult of icons, not as unqualified worship (*latreia*), that can be addressed only to the Divinity, but as 'honorific' or 'relative worship' (*timetike* or *schetike proskynesis*)? Why were they convinced that the banning of icons struck at the very heart of the Christian message? I shall not do them the disservice of re-stating their arguments in terms they would have found alien, but shall permit myself one observation. To them as to most other Byzantines the relation of an image to its model (or 'prototype') was not the same thing as it is to us. If pressed on this point, we would say that the production of a likeness is a matter of artistry, that it depends on a configuration of line and colour which captures the lineaments and expression of an individual, not a generalized human face. A Byzantine would not have put it in those terms. To him the relation was more intimate like that of a signet to its impression, different as to substance, but identical as to form or 'person'. That is why he rejected the statement that an icon of Christ or of a Christian saint was an idol. How could it be an idol if it represented Christ? An idol was the picture of a false god, who was really a demon, say Apollo or Artemis. An image of a holy personage was not a mere object: it partook of his nature. And since we worship Christ who was made man and, therefore, ought to be represented so as to make manifest the plenitude of his manhood, it follows that we must do homage to his image just as, on a lower plane, we offer respect to the image of an emperor.

'Most people today', if I may quote Edwyn Bevan, 'would feel that pictures and images are religiously indifferent: they would neither share the Iconoclastic passion against them as idolatrous nor the Orthodox passion for them as an essential element in the Christian cult. We value pictures on grounds quite other than the specifically religious, as giving us an aesthetic pleasure, when they are good art, not as giving us religious uplift'. We are free to enjoy Byzantine icons as good art, but in so doing we miss their deepest meaning.

CYRIL MANGO
Professor at the University of Oxford

BYZANTINE ICONS

The portable icon occupies an important place in the painting predominantly of a religious nature, which was a notable feature of Byzantine culture. While its origins were in Greco-Roman portraiture the icon was an authentic product of Byzantine civilization and came to play a leading role in religious ritual, becoming the supreme cult object of the Orthodox Church. The rich decoration of the Byzantine church with mosaics and wall paintings gave visual expression to the ideology of the Church, triumphant and didactic, through the hierarchically organized space into a microcosm of the religious universe. Above all it was the icon that acted as the catalyst of the mystical communion between the faithful and the world of the transcedental. The icon was the immediate recipient of the prayers directed to the subject of the portrait, and, through prayer, it served as the channel of spiritual exaltation, moral strength and salvation of the soul. The belief in the existence of icons made without the intervention of human hands, and of icons of the Virgin painted by St. Luke, the subtle theological positions and distinctions formulated by the Fathers of the Church on the question of the relationship between icon and prototype, the serious religious, social and political disputes prompted from time to time by the excessive worship of icons culminating in the great crisis of Iconoclasm – all these demonstrate the value and power of icons in the Byzantine world, especially amongst the lower classes of the population.

For icons were to be found not only in churches and other religious institutions, but everywhere, in public buildings, in private houses and in the Palace, in royal 'proskynetaria' and in the imperial treasury, where they were exhibited with the other treasures in the sumptuous Hall of the Chrysotriklinos on days when official audiences were held for foreigners. Talisman and object of worship of the faithful, the icon was an integral part of the public and private life of the Byzantines. Icons accompanied military expeditions and royal embassies. They formed part of the triumphal entry of the emperor into Constantinople on his return from victorious wars. They were used to consecrate fortresses and protect cities. They were carried in procession, with great pomp, on feast days, after natural disasters, or when the city was under siege. The brilliance of the processions in honour of miracle-working icons is captured in a late thirteenth-century wall painting, unique from this point of view, preserved in the Monastery of Vlacherna at Arta, the capital of the Despotate of Epirus. This depicts in detail the procession in which the famous icon of the Virgin Hodegetria was carried in accordance with a prescribed ritual every Tuesday in Constantinople, before hosts of worshippers, and corresponds with descriptions given by foreign travellers.

Icons were made from a wide variety of materials, depending on the purpose for which they were designed; some took the form of mosaics, or were painted or carved in wood or marble; other were made of precious metal, enamel, and so on. Wall paintings sometimes took the place of portable icons on the iconostasis where this was built in masonry. Icons might be adorned with delicate silver and gold leaf, with elaborate frames, with enamels, ivory, pearls and precious stones. The majority of those that have survived – and these will have been the greater number – are painted on wood in accordance with traditional techniques: with encaustic painting, a technique found mainly in the Early Byzantine period, in which the pigments were mixed with the melted wax, or more usually with egg tempera, on a ground prepared with gesso, or gesso on canvas, and more rarely with parchment instead of canvas. As for the different kinds of icon and their use, there were icons that adorned the iconostasis, icons destined for the epistyle with the Dodekaorton and the Great Deesis, and other, double-sided icons, which were usually intended to be carried in procession, reliquaries, diptychs and triptychs. In terms of their subject matter, they can be divided into cult icons of Christ, the Virgin and the saints, and those, mainly of a didactic character, depicting scenes from the Old and New Testaments, the life of the Virgin, the lives and martyrdoms of the saints, and other complex subjects like the Last Judgment. Many icons tell the story of the Dodekaorton; that is, they represent the twelve mainly evangelical scenes whose content was of great doctrinal importance and which adorned the epistyle of the iconostasis from the Middle Byzantine period onwards.

The processes that governed the production of icons in Byzantium are not known in any detail. They were normally anonymous works of piety, and their creation was subject to the limitations of the doctrine requiring a good likeness of the object or person depicted, which guaranteed the authenticity of the religious work. The unchanging iconographic features of holy persons and sacred events were insured by reference to models supplied by miraculous, cult and other icons, by sketch books, and by written descriptions such as those of Ulpius the Roman from the ninth-tenth centuries, or the post-Byzantine Painter's Manual by Dionysius of Fourna.

Stylistically icon painting was influenced by, and influence, mural painting and miniature painting, but with certain decisive differences: the most obvious are those stemming from the norms of the more detailed, precise and disciplined art of the easel; from the limited size and shape of the icons; from the gold background, which was an essential factor in the abstract-transcendental character and the air of luxury of the portable icon; and from their comparatively conservative, hieratic tone, particularly in the case of cult icons. These, with their 'ordained' adherence to ancient models, did follow, albeit in a more restrained fashion, the changes and shifts in preferences and tendencies brought about by the occasional 'renewals' and other currents in art, running from the centre to the periphery and vice versa.

The task of locating the artistic worskshops in which the icons were produced is difficult, since save in a very few instances, the written evidence does not exist, and the icon was an easily transported item. The exceptionally high quality and sensitivity of many of them suggests that they should be attributed to workshops in the capital, which was the leader and focal point of the different artistic currents, a position that enabled it to direct the processes regulating the production and distribution of icons. Thessalonike too, the second largest city in the Byzantine Empire, in which social and other activity was always of the liveliest order, and which had Mount Athos close by, played an important role in the development of the art. Here there were some undoubtedly important workshops producing icons and directing the production of other local workshops in the wider area influenced by the city (Kastoria, Mount Athos and Ochrid). Cyprus, from which important examples of local production are known, was probably a centre for the production of the so-called Crusader icons of the thirteenth century, many of which survive on the island and in the Monastery of St. Catherine on Mount Sinai.

The Monastery of Sinai possesses the largest collection of Byzantine icons now in existence. Many icons have also survived in Greece, in Kastoria, Veria, Thessalonike, Mount Athos, the Byzantine Museum of Athens, and elsewhere. Large numbers of Byzantine icons have, of course, been lost as a result of natural disasters and looting. Others still await discovery, and many that have been damaged have retained their religious function, since they were painted over in the Post-Byzantine period. It is always a great source of delight when a hitherto unknown Byzantine icon is discovered or, as happens not infrequently, is revealed in the conservation laboratory underneath the more recent painting covering it. For every new discovery, whether the painting on it is of a high quality or merely of routine craftsmanship, not only furnishes new evidence for scholarship but also preserves the memory of Byzantium, which kept the Greek idea alive in Europe during the Middle Ages, and conveys something of the spiritual odour of Byzantine art. For this was an art dressed in official religious attire which, thanks to its solid intellectual foundation and its Hellenistic roots, thanks to its adoption of eastern decorative skills, and the way in which it reflected the very structure and fortunes of the Byzantine Empire, sustained a high level of poetic power, vitality and relevance.

MYRTALI ACHEIMASTOU-POTAMIANOU
Director of the Byzantine Museum of Athens

THE ICONOGRAPHY OF THE ICON

In the Painter's Manual, preserved on Mount Athos, the icon-Master advises him who aspires to become an icon painter to pray before the icon of Christ and that of the Mother of God, because the art of painting comes from God, who alone can guide the painter's hand to give form to the mysteries of God. For the first icons were the *acheiropoietoi*, made not by human hands. These were the Mandelion of Edessa on which Christ's face was miraculously imprinted and sent to Abgar, the toparch of Edessa, and the icon of the Theotokos, made by St. Luke. This was painted after the Pentecost, after the apostle received the illumination of the Holy Ghost.

The themes appearing on the icons, and the way they are represented, i.e. their iconography, are related to the theological meaning of the icon, which is to bear witness to the redemption of matter in all creation, as declared by the Incarnation. Referring to the Transcendental, the themes cannot be changed and their mode of depiction must lead the onlooker to the world of Divine Reality.

Both the tradition of miraculously-created icons and actual examples (the earliest have survived in the Monastery of St. Catherine on Mount Sinai) show that the first icons to come into existence were 'portraits'. In fact, the basic theme of the icon is the 'holy portrait'; i.e., the portrait of a person not represented in the corruptible state of the flesh but in a state revealing his partaking of divine life. The need of the faithful to communicate personally with the sanctified man made the authenticity of the portrait of great importance. In most cases, however, authentic portraits did not exist and types were created, which became part of the living Tradition of the Church. The fixation of the type meant that everything ephemeral was removed so that the transcendental quality of the image could be revealed.

Among the various types of Christ, the most predominant on icons has been the bearded Christ, with dark, thick hair, parted in the middle, with a slight wave, falling like 'the streams of a river' usually over his left shoulder. Known as the Pantocrator, the Almighty, this type differs from the humble Jesus of the gospels;

it reveals the God-Man who fills everything. It is He, as Theophilos of Antioch says, who holds and embraces everything. This face manifests the Glory of God, of which Paul (II. Cor. 4.6), Cyril of Jerusalem and others speak.

Types cannot by any means render visually the essence of God, which for man remains unapproachable. They can only suggest that which is revealed to man in the person of Christ. Epithets are often cited next to the image, such as, for example, Christ the Redeemer, or Christ the Wisdom of God, which, combined with inscriptions on the gospel-book held by Christ, indicate to the faithful the energies of God, the gifts of Christ to man.

Similarly, numerous types were established for the image of the Mother of God, the Angels, and the celestial hierarchy (most important among them is the archangel Michael), and apostles and saints, whose earliest portraits are those of ascetics and of military saints – all relating to the doctrine of redemption. Mary is distinguished by the dignity of her appearance. Her deep purple veil, falling over her head and shoulders, bears three star-crosses, symbols of the Trinity, whose instrument was Mary for the Incarnation of the Son of God. Her commonest type is that of the Hodegetria, named after the most venerated icon in Constantinople, that was found in the Monastery of the Hodegon. It was the palladium of the city, carried in processions and in the battlefield. According to tradition, it was painted by St. Luke and was sent to Constantinople from Jerusalem by the Empress Eudocia. It depicted Mary holding the Christ Child in her left hand.

Mary's types reflect the piety of the people, and their personal perception of her. A gamut of human feelings is manifested: calm grandeur, melancholy serenity, tenderness, suffering, compassion. Here too, epithets give another dimension to the type. While, for example, the Hodegetria shows her son who is the way, representing therefore a Christologic doctrine, the Eleousa or Glyko-philousa and their variants such as the Virgin Kardiotissa or the Virgin with the Playing Child, stress Mary's maternal side. But all of the themes, each in its own way, exist still on another level. Dionysius, the author of the Painter's Manual mentioned above, addressing the Theotokos, says that he wishes her icon to be reflected incessantly on the mirror of the beholder's soul, to keep that soul pure, to lift those who bend down, and to give them hope, for they contemplate the eternal prototype of beauty. Such concepts were to find their way into the poetry of one of the greatest masters of twentieth-century poetry, Rainer Maria Rilke.

But the repertory of icon painting is not limited to the 'Holy Portrait', belonging in essence to the cult icons displayed on the proskynetarion or the iconostasis. The great events of the Christ, whether his life on earth and that of his saints, their sufferings, or the 'sacred histories', taken from the Old and New Testaments with a didactic character (another aspect of the meaning of the icon) have a place among the themes. They all belong to the great theme of Christianity, the Incarnation of God.

The Incarnation as such was revealed in the icon of Christ and of his Mother; its great mysteries were told in the twelve Great Feasts, beginning with the Annunciation and normally ending with the Dormition. Their iconography, based on the doctrine of the Church and shaped under the impact of the Church-Festival cycle and the liturgy, was fixed by the tenth century, but not in an absolute manner. If one compares, for example, the renderings of the Dormition of Mary on a thirteenth-century icon to that on a sixteenth-century icon, one sees that in the earlier rendering the theme is reduced to its essentials, with the three bishops Dionysius the Areopagite, Ierotheos and Timothy, who according to the Tradition, are present at Mary's Falling Asleep, given an eminent place. In the later icon, many narrative details are added, such as the 'apostles taken up from every corner of the earth and carried upon clouds by the order of God', and the Virgin is shown already in her glory in Paradise. Or we can see the icon by Theotokopoulos on the same theme in which Christ is receiving the soul of his mother, bending over her, as if to bid her a tender farewell. Similar comparisons can be made with other themes that belong to the 'sacred histories'.

The mysteries of the Incarnation were re-enacted in the Divine Liturgy in the church to which the icon belongs by its own nature. In general, all icons reflect the impact of the Divine liturgy. However, there are icons whose themes depend on liturgical interpretations or hymns. For example, liturgical poetry, which is related to the Passion cycle, found one of its pictorializations in the theme of the Akra Tapeinosis (Man of Sorrows), which develops into different iconographic types. The arms folded over the chest in the earlier renderings, since the late fifteenth century are crossed on the wrist, an iconographic feature of Italo-Greco rendering of the subject.

The few suggested examples indicate that although the themes are prescribed, no two icons are alike. The iconographic repertory is constantly enriched. This was particularly true in the fifteenth century in Crete. The Masters follow the tradition without considering it an obstacle in their creative powers. They depict freely the iconographic types which they had inherited without abandoning the prescribed processes and forms. By altering the rhythm in the composition, the contours, the thickness or thinness of lines, or the colour distribution, they managed always to innovate and to give a personal character to the traditional figures.

The manuals were no substitutes for the living tradition and could not guarantee the painting of an icon. The artists believed that it was God who guided their hands and this was why they noted on the icon that it was made 'by the hand of...', the hand being the instrument of the Holy Ghost. This particular concept, the backbone of the Orthodox iconography, was disseminated through the Greeks everywhere in the Orthodox world and found a place in the poetry of Rainer Maria Rilke. The monk of the *Stunden-Buch* says that the artists cannot paint God in their own way:

> We do not paint you in our own ways,
> Thou Twilight out of Which the morning rose.
> We haul out of ancient colour-bowls
> The same strokes and the same radiant light
> With which the Holy worked, thy beauty to enclose.

If it was not for the Tradition, the icon would have been only a religious picture, not making present the Holy.

All of these themes and the elements they are composed of are subjected to the spiritual. The artists could show the Mother of God with three hands, a martyr holding his own head in his hands or simply depicted next to him, Adam's skull placed at the feet of the Cross, the world personified as an old king, St. John the

Baptist acquiring wings like an angel. In fact, on icons everything acquires wings, becomes heavenly. The weight and shadows of matter disappear. Thin gold lines like rays of divine energy enter the represented bodies, all that belong to the earthly, and dematerialize them. The disfigurement of the physical anatomy does nothing else but to stress man's transfigured state. The icon painter moves and works in a celestial holy space which has nothing to do with the concept of dimension of volume seen by the physical eye. Everything is represented in a way that reveals the joyful beauty of a new creation, the world returning to its original glory (Rom. 8.21). And while the represented themes may seem to be static or immobile, this 'immobility' declares that everything lives within. This is the 'immovable motion' of the mystics, the 'well of the living water'. The themes and the way they are represented reveal 'the hidden man of the heart, in that which is not corruptible' (I. Peter 3.4).

Within this iconography, as unchangeable as the Church of Christ is, which is expressed in this art, the artists are masters of composition. They are poets and cantors who create their poetry and sing their chants with colours, taking their lights from the Holy Ghost that creates through the hands of God's humble, unworthy servant the icon or the Kingdom of God. He who contemplates on the icons will hear within himself the cherubic hymn chanted on Holy Saturday: 'Let all mortal flesh be silent; let us stand in fear and trembling, having no earhtly thought'.

GEORGE GALAVARIS F.R.S.C.
Professor of Art History, McGill University

RELICS AND ICONS

In the ninth century St. Theodore the Studite, one of the most articulate defenders of the cult of sacred images, used the metaphor of a signet ring impressed into various sealing media to help demonstrate the insubstantiality of the icon: 'The impression is one and the same', he wrote, '... yet it would not have remained identical unless it were entirely unconnected with materials... [and] the same applies to the likeness of Christ, irrespective of the material upon which it is represented'. His point was that the icon as a palpable 'thing' effectively disappears as it becomes a mediating devotional vehicle (a 'door') between the venerating beholder and the deity or saint represented. And, by implication, it is solely from the icon's representational identity with its model (the impression with the signet's intaglio) that its sanctity and sacred power derive. Thus Christ, in his icon, is to be revered (solely) 'by virtue of similitude'.

In earlier centuries, however, the nature of icons was often perceived to be quite different. Indeed, literary and material evidence leave no doubt that between the reign of Justinian (d. 565) and Iconoclasm (730), the period during which the cult of sacred images was growing most rapidly in both breadth and intensity, there was an intimate relationship between image and substance, between icon and relic; images were believed sacred, as often as not, because their material was believed sacred.

St. Theodore's signet-ring metaphor, if taken literally, allows for two variant scenarios whereby a sacred object (deity, holy man or relic) could engender a sacred image: either the forming agent (the signet ring) could itself be holy, or the impressed medium (the wax or clay) could be holy. In either case, the resultant icon would be inseparable from its sanctified substance, and necessarily, the nature of the veneration directed toward it could be confused. The first scenario – that of the 'sacred agent' – is best represented by the many well-known *acheiropoietoi* (icons 'not made by human hands') of the period, of which the Mandelion of Edessa is the most famous example: Christ wipes his face with a towel, and the towel miraculously retains his image. It is an icon, because of that image, but it is also a relic, because of Christ's contact. The second scenario – that of the 'sacred medium' – is best represented by the many types of pilgrim *eulogiai* ('blessings') that were then becoming popular. Usually these were small portions of earth, wax, oil or water which had been sanctified by contact with a relic or holy person, and then mechanically impressed with a stamp (into the solid material itself, or onto the vessel containing the liquid) with an appropriate image of whatever or who-ever had done the sanctifying. They are icons, because of that image, but they are also relics, because of sacred contact. Of this category of relic-icon the most characteristic representatives are Symeon Tokens – hardened bits of earth from the 'Miraculous Mountain' of St. Symeon Stylites the Younger (d. 592), sanctified by direct contact with his column and stamped with an image of the saint atop his column.

The surprising thing about the Edessa Mandelion and the Symeon Tokens, however, is that both are known to have existed first (or, in the case of the tokens, alternatively) simply as sacred objects, without images. Averil Cameron has brilliantly demonstrated that the Edessa palladium (at first, just a letter from Jesus to King Abgar of Edessa) quite literally 'acquired' its sacred image in the later sixth century, long after it had become a popular and potent aniconic relic. And as for Symeon Tokens, one need only read the saint's *vita* to discover the high frequency with which his miracle-working sacred earth was being dispensed without its stamped icon. For both towel and token, images were partners to sacred power, but partners after the fact. Apparently, relics without images were good, but relics *with* images were even better. Why?

One senses an answer in the intimate link which, from the earliest years of the cult of relics, associates miraculous imagery with the almost mystical 'relic experience'. St. Jerome's account of Paula's first encounter with the wood of the True Cross (*c.* 400) is typical: 'she fell down and worshipped ... as if she could see the Lord hanging on it'. Proximity to a holy object evoked in her a profound spiritual experience, and that experience had a strongly visual dimension. One even suspects that Paula's 'vision' was somehow instrumental to her conjuring up the physical presence of the deity – a presence which was certainly implicit, but perhaps not fully realized, in the relic itself.

The evidence from Symeon's 'Miraculous Mountain', two centuries later, is much more explicit. Chapter 231 of the saint's *vita* describes the misgivings of a father who is told to return home with his still gravely-ill son to await Symeon's cure. 'The power of God ... is efficacious everywhere', assures the saint. 'Therefore, take this *eulogia* made of my dust, depart, and when you look at the imprint of our image, it is us that you will see'. The father is here being offered two distinct assurances that his son will eventually be saved: the blessed earth – a well-known relic material whose powers he must already have been well aware of – and the saint's image. Somehow, when they return home and gaze on that image, father and son will, in effect, be confronted with a vision of the saint himself. But why should that be reassuring? The answer comes later in the same story. The man's third son falls ill, and naturally, he asks to be taken to the 'Miraculous Mountain'. But his father recalls the words of the saint and assures him that Symeon will come to visit him there, at home, and he will be healed. With this the young man gasps and calls out, 'St. Symeon, have pity on me'. He then turns to his father and cries, 'Get up quickly, throw on incense, and pray, for the servant of God, St. Symeon, is before me...'. At this point Symeon appears in a vision, attacks the daemon that has tormented the youth, and saves him.

Other Symeon miracles, though in less detail, suggest the same scenario – namely, that a vision of the saint was instrumental in making effective the miraculous powers of his earthen *eulogia*, and that the vision could be induced by a man-made image. Similarly, as incubation (sleeping near relics) was instrumental to miraculous healing at early Byzantium's many 'Holy Doctor' shrines (e.g., those of Cosmas and Damian, Cyrus and John, and Artemios), so a dream-like vision of the saint was instrumental to successful incubation. And this vision seems most often to have been induced by icons of the saint set up around the shrine. The shared phenomenon is clear: seeing the saint (through his image) ensured his presence, and his presence ensured the miraculous efficacy of his relic. In other words, the power of the relic was being 'triggered' and released by the saint's icon. This helps to explain why, over time, images would be added to relics.

And it also helps to explain the next development – namely, the gradual disassociation of the icon from the relic-icon. For very soon, the 'trigger' image begins to appear alone; yet, surprisingly, it is still believed to possess the miraculous power it had when in the company of its associative relic. That this is true is clear from the many early Byzantine amulets that bear images originally developed for and popularized with pilgrim *eulogiai*. The blessed earth of the Symeon Token is gone, but the saint's image remains, though now simply impressed onto an 'unblessed' disk of gold or lead or glass, to become a piece of amuletic jewelry. Side by side, the pendant amulet and earthen *eulogia* may look much the same, but what has happened to distinguish them is profound in its implications for the cult of sacred images. For the sanctity and miraculous power formerly thought transferable only through physical contact (of saint to column to earth) is now believed transferable simply by iconic verisimilitude (of image to saint). The implicit theology is made explicit in Chapter 118 of Symeon's *vita*. A hemorrhaging woman from Cilicia (far from the 'Miraculous Mountain', and with no earthen *eulogia*) invokes Symeon's aid with the words, 'If only I see your image I will be saved'. How can this be? Because 'the Holy Spirit which inhabits Symeon covers it [the icon] with its shadow'.

Now it is simply enough that the saint be 'present' in his image; he can perform his miracle without the aid of sacred material. For by virtue of a 'sacred infusion' comparable to that of the Incarnation, Symeon's icon is now believed to be on the same miracle-working level with the saint himself, and with his earthen contact relics. The physical bond to the shrine has been broken, and the 'trigger' rationale of the relic-icon has been obviated. Relics have given birth to icons, and those icons – now totally 'insubstantial' – are free to develop on their own, in full conformity with St. Theodore the Studite's iconophile theology.

GARY VIKAN
Assistant Director for Curatorial Affairs / Curator of Medieval Art
The Walters Art Gallery

ICON PAINTING IN CRETE
DURING THE FIFTEENTH
AND SIXTEENTH CENTURIES

After the fall of Constantinople in 1453, Crete, which had been under Venetian occupation since 1204, took its place as the most important centre of art in the Greek world.

The concentration in Candia (Iraklion) of a group of artists of outstanding talent established the authority of Cretan art, which spread throughout the Greek world, the influence of Cretan painters being particularly pronounced in the major centres of Orthodoxy, on Mount Athos, at Meteora, on the island of Patmos and at the Monastery of Sinai. The Cretan painters, who frequently visited Venice, naturally developed close ties with the Greek community there, which was 5,000 strong in the sixteenth century.

There is documentary evidence for the movement of painters from Constantinople to Crete even before the fall of the city, and during this same period Cretan painters such as Angelos Akotantos travelled to the capital from Crete. The establishment in Crete of painters from Constantinople that seems likely to have taken place after 1453 was therefore a continuation of earlier links between the island and the capital.

Wall paintings in churches of the first half of the fifteenth century, like those painted by members of the Phokas family, display strong affinities with works from a Constantinopolitan atelier, such as those in the Church of the Peribleptos at Mistra (second half of the fourteenth century). The art in these paintings is of a very high quality, and has none of the provincial character to be found in other churches from this period on the island. Only a few icons now dated to the early part of the fifteenth century are included in this exhibition. Despite the differences of style between them, they were all produced in a highly cultured environment. The Dormition from the Kanellopoulos Museum (cat. no. 42), with its erudite iconography, refined drawing and subdued colours, can only be the work of a painter who had learned his art in the Byzantine capital. The Nativity in the Peratikos Collection (formerly Volpi Collection) is closer to the superb ensembles of wall paintings at Mistra. The icon depicting St. Marina from the Byzantine Museum of Athens (cat. no. 41) is an example of the adoption of the Palaeologan style in Crete.

These wall paintings and icons form an integral part of the Palaeologan tradition; at the same time they display those features that gave Cretan painting its distinctive character: the precise outlines, the modelling of the flesh with dark brown underpaint and dense tiny highlights on the cheeks of the faces, the bright colours in the garments, the geometrical treatment of the drapery, and, finally, the balanced articulation of the composition. All these are hallmarks of late fifteenth- or early sixteenth-century Cretan painting, which was to acquire a rather academic character. At the same time, features from Italian painting were assimilated and harmoniously adapted to the austere Byzantine tradition with a quality not encountered in earlier wall paintings influenced by Italian art.

The art of the painter who signs his work ΧΕΙΡ ΑΓΓΕΛΟΥ (the hand of Angelos) clearly reveals the impact of the Palaeologan tradition and the assimilation of secondary features from Italian painting; the emergence of a new artistic vocabulary can also be detected at a different level in each of his works. This painter is probably to be identified with the Angelos Akotantos known from the testament he drew up in 1436 before setting out on a journey to Constantinople; the identification, however, does not solve all the problems related to the variety of styles that are discernible in his signed works.

The chronological framework in which may be set the activity of the most important painters, such as Andreas Ritzos and his son Nikolaos, Andreas Pavias and Nikolaos Tzafouris, rests on documentary evidence. These painters had ateliers and considerable numbers of apprentices, and created icon-prototypes with a new iconography. The Virgin, in the types of the Hodegetria, Glykophilousa or the Virgin of the Passion, warrior saints, St. Nicholas and St. Anthony, scenes from the Dodekaorton such as the Nativity, the Entry into Jerusalem, the Resurrection, the Annunciation and the Dormition of the Virgin, and finally subjects like the Hospitality of Abraham, the Noli Me Tangere and the Dormition of various hermits, were among the most popular subjects copied from such common iconographical models.

An important group of icons can now be dated from the middle of the fifteenth to the beginning of the sixteenth centuries; these have their own particular character, a distinguishing feature of which was the superb technical execution. The painters of these works, masters of a technique inherited from Palaeologan art, frequently displayed an eclecticism that enabled them to include elements from Italian art in their paintings.

The acquaintance with the Italian style of painting is much more apparent in another group of icons produced on Crete. These icons, which reveal an unusual knowledge of the Late Gothic art and are in a refined style, were painted by Nikolaos Tzafouris (cat. nos. 52 and 53), Andreas Pavias, Andreas Ritzos and other famous artists. They were probably commissioned by Catholic customers, and their iconography follows typical Italian models, such as the Madre della Consolazione (cat. no. 53), the Pietà (cat. no. 56) and the Man of Sorrows (cat. no. 55). These Italo-Cretan works are retrospective rather than conservative in character. They reflect the tastes of the clientele which helped to define and disseminate this unique iconography and style through icons that often have a hybrid character, like the icon with the Samaritan Woman (cat. no. 57), which was profoundly influenced by Tuscan painting of the quattrocento.

The Cretan icons of the fifteenth and early sixteenth centuries will also have had a decisive influence on the work of the Cretan painters of the following generation. Theophanes, a Cretan painter active at Meteora and on Mount Athos (1527-1558) followed the earlier tradition and enriched it with more recent Italian features. In 1542, the painter-priest Euphrosynos produced icons in Crete for the Monastery of Dionysios on Mount Athos, following the precepts of the strictly traditional art of Angelos and Ritzos.

In the middle and latter half of the century, the personalities of Michael Damaskinos and Georgios Klontzas helped to 'modernize' Cretan painting. Their work is often dominated by mannerism, as in the icon of St. Justina and two other saints on Kerkyra, which is influenced by the art of Paolo Veronese. It should be noted, however, that in some of their other works, these painters followed the conservative style that drew upon the austere Byzantine tradition.

Their ability to handle different styles must have been a consequence of the way in which the fifteenth-century painters worked. This dual ability is discernible in the early works of Domenikos Theotokopoulos, who served his apprenticeship in Crete in a milieu at once rooted in tradition, yet open to the artistic aspirations of the time. The degree of assimilation of, or resistance to, different artistic styles corresponded to the state of the relationship between the two worlds that coexisted on the island. This direct contact of the Cretan painters with the world of their day is perhaps one of the most valuable aspects of their art.

NANO CHATZIDAKIS
Professor at the University of Ioannina

TASTE AND THE MARKET
IN CRETAN ICONS IN THE
FIFTEENTH AND SIXTEENTH CENTURIES

In Crete during the last two centuries of Venetian rule (from the mid-fifteenth to the mid-seventeenth century) the most important commercial activities were concentrated in the major economic centres of the island: the capital, Candia (now Iraklion), and other cities, such as Chania and Rethymnon. In these centres the urban middle and upper classes became the main bearers of culture. The development of intellectual life followed, and bore fine fruit in literature (Crete produced a number of examples of Renaissance poetry and drama), and in the visual arts, particularly painting, for which the island remained the most important centre after the fall of Constantinople.

The character of this period is well documented by the surviving archival sources. For painting, a wealth of information is furnished by the archives relating to the Venetian administration in Crete (now preserved in the State Archives in Venice). Notarial documents, in particular, yield valuable information on the sources of demand for and supply of Cretan icons, the conditions of icon production, the organized market in Cretan icons and their dissemination in the Mediterranean world and northern Europe through the export trade, the relationship between patrons and painters, and the changing attitude of the public towards painting.

Among the sources of demand for Cretan icons, merchants, both Greek and Italian, held a significant position. The merchants, a special group of customers of Cretan painters, acted as intermediaries between Cretan artists and Western markets, and often expressed collective aesthetic preferences. Their written contracts constitute a considerable proportion (about 15%) of the surviving commissions placed with painters active in Crete.

Documents involving commercial orders for large quantities of Cretan icons reveal that these works were mass produced for export. A vast number of icons were commissioned in 1497 by a Venetian dealer from a Cretan painter. The paintings were to be put up for sale in Europe, notably in Flanders. Half of them had already been disposed of, with great success, in the Western markets by May 1498. The constant demand for these icons is demonstrated by the dealer's insistence that the other half of the order be completed as quickly as possible.

An order for hundreds of icons of the Virgin was placed in 1499 by two dealers, one from Venice and the other from the Peloponnese, with three painters living in Candia, each of them being dealt with separately. The restrictions set by the merchants as to the iconography and style of the paintings (*in forma greca* or *in forma a la latina*), the explicit instructions regarding the colours of the Virgin's garments, and the obligatory use of predetermined models, all reflect the demands of the foreign market, which influenced art production in Crete. The large number of the pieces commissioned (seven hundred) and the short delivery period (forty-five days) attest to the efficiency of Cretan workshops, which can in fact be regarded as production units with a considerable output. Five hundred of the icons commissioned were to be in the style of Late Gothic painting, and the remaining two hundred in the Byzantine tradition, apparently following the demands of an audience with differing aesthetic preferences. Cretan painters, experiencing particular historical and social circumstances, were versatile. Their relationship to the art of the dominating political power, Venice, and to other Western influences, combined with the taste of their mixed public (which included both Greek Orthodox and Roman Catholic, with a broad social and cultural range), led them to an obvious eclecticism, as a result of which they were capable of producing icons in different traditions.

Documents of the above kind attest not only to the mass production of fifteenth-century Cretan icons, but also to the repetition of certain iconographic types, according to the usual practice of medieval workshops. Surviving fifteenth-century icons, both signed and unsigned, illustrate this repetitive use of successful and established iconographic models. On the other hand, they reveal the high level of technical competence and artistic skill of the men who painted them.

It was within this framework that the trade in art was developed in Crete. Paintings were treated as merchandise and the production of icons became part of the system of supply and demand. Besides painters and their assistants, other professionals, such as wood-carvers and carpenters, were also connected with the art trade. Paintings produced under these conditions may have been lacking in originality, but this was offset by their technical perfection, which guaranteed the fine quality of the works and secured the good reputation of the Cretan painters. In fact some of the best known fifteenth-century Cretan masters often added the name of their native town to their signature on paintings destined for exportation: for example, *Andreas Riço de Candia pinxit*; *Andreas Pavias pinxit de Candia*.

The vast production of fine icons in Crete is also attested by the testimony of a French traveller, Jacques Le Saige, who visited Candia in 1518: 'et il se fait aussy à la dite ville [de Candie] largement de belles ymaiges de nostre dame encloses de tableaux de ciprès'.

The flourishing trade in Cretan icons which is manifested towards the end of the fifteenth century does not seem to have continued into the sixteenth. Documents suggest either the failure of commercial enterprises or a lack of interest on the part of the merchants in the market in icons. A contract drafted in 1509 in Candia registers the beginning of an attempt to trade in small triptychs which, however, never came to fruition. In 1556 a merchant placed an order for a specific number of icons with two painters established in Candia. Although the commission was carried out, the merchant exhibited obvious indifference to the delivery of the icons he had ordered, apparently owing to lack of sufficient demand.

The different picture to be derived from sixteenth-century documents may be interpreted as the result of some radical changes in the demand for and distribution of Cretan icons in the West. The art trade in Crete had most likely been affected by a shift in the taste of the public. The deprecatory remarks made by G.B. Armenini (1587) about Greek icons which he had seen in northern Italy were perhaps the result of a shift of this kind; he describes 'pitture delle sacre imagini, le quali erano la maggior parte quadretti di certe figure fatte alla greca, goffissime, dispiacevoli e tutte affumicate' ('paintings of sacred images which were for the most part pictures of certain figures done in the Greek manner, most uncouth, unpleasing and smoky').

In the sixteenth century the predominant artistic fashions were those of the Renaissance and Mannerism, and these overshadowed the earlier enthusiasm for painting in the Byzantine or Late Gothic traditions, although *madonne candiotte* and *quadri dorati de nostra donna alla greca* continued to figure among the valuable possessions of late sixteenth-century wealthy Venetian households.

Not only can this new turn in artistic taste be detected in the attitude of the Italian and the Cretan public; it is also demonstrated by the enrichment of the existing traditions of iconography which was attempted, within the limits of religious painting, by a number of Cretan artists. Suffice it to mention here the names of three sixteenth-century masters, the young Domenikos Theotokopoulos (later the famous El Greco), Michael Damaskinos and Georgios Klontzas, who all adopted a fresh approach to the treatment of traditional subjects, involving the use of Western elements, and often signed their works in new and original ways. Their iconographic innovations were undoubtedly held in esteem by certain social circles, such as the members of the literary society of the *Accademia degli stravaganti* of Candia.

A further development is the appearance, from the beginning of the sixteenth century onwards, of private collections that included icons amongst the Italian and Flemish paintings and pieces of sculpture owned by Cretans and by Venetian noblemen and the wealthy bourgeoisie of Candia. Icons were now regarded as works of art with their own intrinsic aesthetic value, and were judged to be 'precious things for Greek painting' (*cose pretiose per pittura greca*).

By the second half of the sixteenth century large commercial commissions and the mass production of icons belonged to the past, but a new concept of painting and a more favourable attitude towards painters and their work had emerged in Renaissance Crete.

MARIA CONSTANTOUDAKI-KITROMILIDES
Teaching fellow at the University of Athens

MONUMENTAL PAINTING
IN GREEK MACEDONIA
DURING THE FIFTEENTH CENTURY

The artistic production of Macedonia in the fifteenth century is scarcely known. What little information we have to date relates mainly to the painting of the final quarter of the fifteenth century, and is owed to the publications of A. Xyngopoulos and S. Pelekanidis on the monuments of Servia and Aiani, near Kozani, of Kastoria, and of the area of Prespa, near Florina.

As a result of the researches of the last fifteen years, we are today in a position not only to follow the artistic production of Macedonia throughout the entire fifteenth century, but also to determine in detail the artistic currents and workshops operating in this area.

The artistic production of Macedonia in the fifteenth century was smaller than that of the previous period. It was confined mainly to Central and Western Macedonia, and extended throughout the entire fifteenth century, with a concentration in the first and last quarters. This is an indication that despite conditions during the Turkish occupation, which are scarcely known, political and economic conjunctures arose in some of the urban centres and regions of Macedonia that encouraged not only the renewal of the painted decoration of already existing churches, but also the erection and decoration of new ones. This historical and artistic phenomenon can be observed in the surviving monuments of Kastoria, Veria, Mount Athos and the Macedonian hinterland, though not of Thessalonike.

The churches constructed and decorated at this period were usually small, unpretentious, single-aisle, wood-roofed basilicas. The small dimensions of the churches, together with the need to portray the basic subjects of the iconographic programme in a single-aisle basilica, led to the adoption of small-scale scenes, the reduction of the size of the human figure, and the restriction of the number of people to those absolutely necessary in each subject. The result was the disappearance in the fifteenth century of the large-scale compositions and monumental painting characteristic of some of the Macedonian monuments of the end of the thirteenth and beginning of the fourteenth century (the Protaton on Mount Athos, the katholikon of the Monastery of Vatopedi, etc.).

In detail, the artistic production of fifteenth-century Macedonia is as follows:

In the churches of Thessalonike, which finally passed into Turkish occupation in 1430, the prevailing view is that nothing has survived of fifteenth-century wall painting. However, some of the wall paintings of full-length saints on the pillars of the south colonnade in the Church of Ayios Demetrius, and the Crucifixion preserved in the narthex of this church, may be regarded as works of the first quarter of the fifteenth century. The iconographic types, the plastic modelling of the faces, and the palette used in these wall paintings can be recognized in the wall paintings of Rešava in Yugoslavia (1418), which are attributed to artists who came from or were influenced by the artistic environment of Thessalonike.

A few years after the fall of Thessalonike to the Turks (1430), there is evidence that the decoration was undertaken of the katholika of the Monastery of Konstamonitou (1433), the Monastery of Ayios Pavlos (1447) and the Monastery of Thessalonikeos (1451). All this decoration is now lost, with the exception of a fragment of a wall painting preserved in the Monastery of Ayios Pavlos, with the head of St. Athanasios. This fresco is of particular importance, since, coming as it does from an ensemble accurately dated to 1447, it reflects painting trends of the first quarter of the fifteenth century in Macedonia, which were characterized by a return to the models of the so-called 'Macedonian School'. A composition in the narthex of the katholikon of the Monastery of Chilandari (1431) also dates from the fifteenth century.

In recent years, fifteenth-century wall paintings have been identified in the chapel of the Panayia of the Monastery of the Pantocrator, and in the cell of Ayios Prokopios in the Monastery of Vatopedi. And a detached wall painting of Christ Pantocrator, now preserved in the cell of Molyvokklisia near Karyes, may also be assigned to the fifteenth century. Of these, the wall paintings preserved in the cell of Ayios Prokopios are of particular interest. The figures in these have an aristocratic nobility and spiritual serenity that makes them works of high art, echoing the idealistic trends of Byzantine art during the first half of the fifteenth century.

Wall paintings survive from the second half of the fifteenth century in the refectory of the Monastery of Xenophon. Despite the damage and repainting they subsequently suffered, these wall paintings comprise an interesting ensemble dated to 1496/97. Their main features, which distance them from the tradition of works by the Cretan School, are the complete absence of beauty and spirituality in the figures portrayed, and of nobility and elegance in their poses. Here it is possible to detect a deliberate unattractiveness, that goes together with the static inactivity of the persons depicted. These features assign the wall paintings from the refectory of the Monastery of Xenophon to an anti-classical trend, the continuation of which can be seen on Mount Athos in the work of the painter Antonios. The latter, as M. Chatzidakis has demonstrated, worked on Mount Athos at the same period as the great Cretan painter Theophanes, on the decoration of the cell of Ayios Prokopios (1537), the katholikon of the Monastery of Xenophon (1544), and the chapel of Ayios Georgios (1552) in the Monastery of Ayios Pavlos.

During the fifteenth century, Kastoria, which came under Turkish occupation as early as 1386, developed into the most important artistic centre in Macedonia. It may be noted that, despite the Turkish occupation, new churches were erected and decorated at the turn of the fourteenth and fifteenth centuries, demonstrating the vitality of medieval Hellenism in Macedonia. The churches in question are: Prodromos, in Omonoia Square, Kastoria; Ayioi Treis; the Panayia Rasiotissa (1411?); Ayios Andreas tou Rousouli (c. 1430); and the Panayia in the village of Zevgostasi, near Kastoria (1432). With the exception of the fifteenth-century layer of painting in the Panayia Rasiotissa, the wall paintings in these churches represent a continuation of the artistic trends formulated in Kastoria in the second half of the fourteenth century; the expressive power of these trends was almost exhausted by the first half of the fifteenth century. In contrast, the fifteenth-century frescoes in the Panayia Rasiotissa clearly have the basic characteristics of the workshop that was to emerge fully formed in Kastoria during the last quarter of the fifteenth century.

The emergence of this workshop was the most important artistic phenomenon of the fifteenth century in Macedonia. Its activity was confined within a thirty-year period (1483-1510), and works produced by the workshop itself and artists influenced by it have been identified in Meteora, in Western Macedonia, and in the countries in the Balkan peninsula bordering on Greece.

The output of this workshop covers an unexpectedly large geographic area for the period, and reveals a trend towards the revival of fourteenth-century Byzantine painting. The anonymous painters who worked in it aspired to enrich the traditional iconography of their subjects by introducing elements drawn from the daily life of the period (the dress worn by the minor figures, the form of vessels and furniture) and from Eastern weaving (the motifs of the richly woven fabrics). They were also influenced by the realism of Late Gothic art in their rendering of buildings and landscapes, and in adopting realistic expressions that make their figures unattractive. At the same time, it is clear that the workshop was in contact with the trends and manners of fifteenth-century Italian painting, and also with the mannerism of late Comnenian art (end of the twelfth century).

In its extreme expression, however, the painting of this workshop resulted in the icon losing its spiritual content in favour of an expressive realism inappropriate to the idealistic character of Byzantine art. An immediate consequence of this was that the workshop gradually gave place to the tendency to return to established models, which was represented at this period by the Cretan School, and which constituted the renewed expression of the art of the Orthodox Church during the Post-Byzantine period.

In Kastoria itself, which is thought to have been the artistic centre in which this workshop emerged, the decoration of four churches is attributed – in whole or in part – to artists of the workshop: Ayios Nikolaos tis monachis Eupraxias (1485/86), Ayios Nikolaos tis archontissas Theologinas (c. 1490-1500), Ayios Spyridon (c.

1490-1500) and Ayios Nikolaos tou Magaleiou (1505). The wall paintings of the Church of the Ayioi Anargyroi in Servia (1510), near Kozani, have also been attributed to the workshop. To it may also be assigned the unpublished wall paintings of the Church of the Panayia at Torniki (Grevena), those on the east wall of the sanctuary (1498) of the Church of the Panayia Chaviaras in Veria, and some of the wall paintings in the Church of Ayios Demetrius in the neighbourhood of Eleousa in Kastoria.

Of these wall paintings, those in the Church of Ayios Nikolaos tis monachis Eupraxias are of particular interest: not only do they form an almost intact ensemble of the period, but they represent one of the most important works, in classical style, of the workshop which is now generally agreed to have been centred on Kastoria and whose artistic activity extended throughout the Balkan peninsula.

By contrast, the artist to whom the wall paintings (1495/96) on the outside of the west wall of the Church of the Panayia Koumbelidiki are attributed was not influenced by this workshop in Kastoria; at the end of the fifteenth century he follows a conservative artistic trend that looks back to fourteenth-century art for its models.

The wall paintings on the outside of the south wall of the Taxiarchis tis Mitropoleos are an interesting, isolated phenomenon in the fifteenth-century artistic production of Kastoria. They contain portraits of noblemen of Kastoria, wearing sumptuous clothes, who were buried in the church in the first half of the fifteenth century, according to the inscriptions accompanying them (1436 and 1439). These wall paintings, which render the individual characteristics of the people depicted, and are of some interest as portraits, form valuable evidence for the art and society of the city during the first half of the fifteenth century.

The frescoes of Ayios Nikolaos at Vevi, near Florina, were painted shortly after the middle of the fifteenth century, in 1460. These are small-scale compositions and follow a simple iconographic scheme. From a stylistic point of view, the figures are small, slender, almost fleshless, with flat, linear drapery on a monochrome background. The modelling of the faces is painterly, and on occasion summary, loose and flat. A number of iconographic elements link this monument with the monumental painting of Kastoria of the second half of the fourteenth century, and some of the technical and stylistic features can be recognized in monuments dating from the second half of the fifteenth century in Macedonia.

Veria finally fell into the hands of the Turks in 1430, but despite the Turkish occupation, new churches were built and adorned with wall paintings throughout the fifteenth century, and the decoration of existing churches was renewed. Unfortunately, with the exception of the earliest layer of painting in the Church of the Panayia Chaviaras (1498), the wall paintings in the churches of Veria are not securely dated.

Two very interesting ensembles preserved in Veria date from the turn of the fourteenth-fifteenth centuries: the wall paintings of the Church of Ayios Georgios Mikros, and the wall paintings removed from the Church of Ayia Photida, which was demolished in 1938. The wall paintings of the Church of Ayios Georgios belong to the artistic current of the second half of the fourteenth century, which was influenced by the artistic tradition of the early fourteenth century. In contrast, the wall paintings of Ayia Photida, which were not the work of a single craftsman, represent – apart from the scene of the Last Judgment – the expression of an anti-classical tendency in Byzantine art, with an expressionistic character, rather like that of the wall paintings of Zemen in Bulgaria and at Koporin in Yugoslavia (1405-1410).

Some of the earliest fifteenth-century wall paintings preserved in Veria are those in the west wall of the Church of Ayia Anna. The main features of these wall paintings, which were the work of at least two artists, are the simplicity of the compositions; the elongated proportions of the figures, which have width of body but are without volume, and have small heads; the rendering of the volumes of the face without resort to stylization; the predominantly linear treatment of the drapery; the restricted palette; and the attractiveness of the faces, which are expressionless. These wall paintings belong to an anti-classical trend in painting, to which can also be attributed the wall paintings in the Church of the Panayia Kontariotissa in Pieria, and those in the Churches of Ayios Minas at Velvendos and of Ayioi Theodoroi at Servia, near Kozani (end of the fifteenth century). Another feature shared by the painting of these three monuments is the stylized treatment of the landscape, which has a geometric, flat character; the extreme example of this is the landscape in the Church of Ayios Minas at Velvendos. It should also be noted that in two of the monuments from this group, the Church of the Panayia Kontariotissa, and the Church of the Ayioi Theodoroi at Servia, it is possible to recognize a number of iconographic elements that connect the decoration of these churches with the workshop of Kastoria in the last twenty years of the fifteenth century.

The wall paintings of the Church of the Panayia Eleousa at Prespa (1408/9) may be regarded as a provincial expression that moved in the periphery of this artistic tendency. In these wall paintings, which were the work of the monk Ioannikios, certain iconographic elements can be recognized that link them with the artistic tradition of Kastoria in the second half of the fourteenth century.

The demolished Church of the Panayia Kyriotissa in Veria was decorated with a number of wall paintings probably dated to the second third of the fifteenth century. These wall paintings are the product of an artistic trend that can also be recognized in other churches in Veria. The wall paintings of the Church of the Panayia Kyriotissa are probably the earliest work of this trend in Veria, the distinguishing features of which are the simple, flat compositions, the fleshless figures, the linear treatment of the drapery on a monochrome background, and the stylized rendering of the volumes of the faces. This artistic trend was formulated in Veria during the last decades of the fifteenth century in a workshop whose work can be recognized in the earliest layer of paintings preserved in the Churches of the Panayia Gorgoepikoos Panagouda, the Panayia Paleophoritissa, and in the wall painting with the representation of St. Nicholas in the Church of Ayios Nikolaos in Gourna. The activity of this workshop in Veria may be set against the background of a more general artistic trend, of an anti-classical character, in the fifteenth century, the expressions of which can be identified in other monuments, and also in icons, within the broader area of Macedonia, as at the Matka Monastery (1496/97) near Skopje in Yugoslavian Macedonia.

A different fifteenth-century workshop probably produced the layer of painting preserved in the Churches of Ayios Nikolaos at Gourna and Ayios Patapios at

Veria. A number of common iconographic types, and related technical and stylistic characteristics can be recognized in the painting of these two monuments that makes it possible to assign the painting of them to the production of the same artistic workshop. The wall paintings of these two monuments of Veria have fleshy, though rather flaccid, expressionless faces, with spots of red on the cheeks, which differ from the previous trend in their avoidance of the use of outlines for the volumes, and follow artistic trends that can be recognized in wall paintings in Cyprus from the last quarter of the fifteenth century.

An isolated, extreme example in Macedonia of a work of an expressionistic character is furnished by the wall paintings of the Church of Ayios Andreas in the parish of Ayios Georgios in Veria, in which the faces are unattractive: prominence is given to the decorative role of the wrinkles, the treatment of the hair is stylized and the meeting eyebrows are strongly emphasized. A similar trend, which was also revived in the seventeenth century, can be recognized in monuments in Yugoslavian Macedonia, such as the wall paintings of the Church of Prophitis Ilias at Dolgaec (1454/55) and also in Velestovo (1444).

The variety of the artistic idioms that were developed in Veria in the second half of the fifteenth century also finds expression in the wall paintings of this period preserved in the Churches of the Panayia Peribleptos, Ayioi Theodoroi, Ayios Kyrikos and Ioulita, and Ayia Paraskevi.

The wall paintings from the end of the fifteenth century preserved in the Churches of Ayios Andreas in Veria, in the parish of Kyriotissa, Ayios Georgios at Prespa, and the Archangel Michael at Aiani, near Kozani, all move in the margins of the artistic trends of the period, and are characterized by their eclecticism. It is possible in the wall paintings in Ayios Georgios at Prespa to recognize a number of elements deriving from the workshop in Kastoria during the last twenty years of the fifteenth century, and the entire group is distinguished mainly by the stocky, rigid, expressionless figures, which in some cases are singularly unattractive, almost cartoon-like.

To recapitulate, we may say that despite the Turkish occupation, which began in Macedonia in the last twenty years of the fourteenth century, artistic production in this area continued without interruption. During the first period, which in Macedonia should be regarded as the period from 1386 to 1430, the year of the capture of Thessalonike by the Turks, painting was conservative in character, and influenced by the artistic trends of art of the second half of the fourteenth century. It is possible to detect, that is, the phenomenon of the adoption of iconographic types, and also manners, connected with Macedonian painting of the end of the thirteenth and beginning of the fourteenth centuries, as known from the Church of the Protaton on Mount Athos, that of Christos in Veria, that of Ayios Nikolaos in Thessalonike, and others.

At the same period the anti-classical trends in painting were strengthened, and given a variety of style and character. These trends, which were to make their mark on the painting of Macedonia throughout the entire fifteenth century, were accompanied by a gradual decline in the quality of the painting. An exception is formed, during this first period, by the wall paintings of the cell of Ayios Prokopios on Mount Athos, the quality of which makes them the last radiance of the art of the capital in Macedonia during the first half of the fifteenth century.

During the second period, which lasted from the capture of Thessalonike (1430) to the beginning of the sixteenth century, it is clear that the historical conjunctures, so far unknown, favoured the creation of local artistic workshops in two urban centres of Macedonia, Veria and Kastoria. A third workshop may, perhaps, be noted in Servia near Kozani, which followed the anti-classical trends of the workshops of Veria.

The most important feature of this period, however, is the emergence and activity, in the second twenty years of the fifteenth century of a very important workshop, centred on Kastoria. This workshop produced wall paintings and icons with equal success, and, in some cases, of a high artistic quality. It was distinguished by the trend to renewal in Macedonian painting; its activities extended throughout the entire Balkan peninsula, and its emergence was the most important artistic phenomenon in Macedonia and the Balkan peninsula in the fifteenth century.

Although the Kastoria workshop did not create an artistic tradition comparable with that of the Cretan School, the influence it exercised on the artistic workshops of Western Macedonia and Epirus can be recognized in monuments of the sixteenth century and later.

EUTHYMIOS N. TSIGARIDAS
Ephor of Byzantine Antiquities

WORKING DRAWINGS
OF PAINTERS IN GREECE
AFTER THE FALL OF CONSTANTINOPLE

Icons and frescoes after 1453 belong to the last phase of a painting tradition which can be traced back into antiquity. The technological background of this painting is accessible, to some extent, to modern scholars, mainly through the Painter's Manual by Dionysius of Fourna, which was written on Mount Athos, roughly between 1730 and 1734. Dionysius's Manual provides detailed information concerning the production of drawings on tracing paper, and also of a specific type of imprinted cartoon, the so-called *anthivolon,* which was drawn from an existing work, whether a drawing, panel or wall painting: '... put some black colour into a scallop-shell with some garlic juice ... and mix them; then go over the forms of the whole figure of the saint that you are copying ... Then you mix red colour with garlic juice and go over the highlights of the face and clothes ... then wet a sheet of paper the same size as the prototype ... place it on the archetype and press it down carefully with your hand... You will thus have made a printed copy in every way identical to the prototype'.

The description by Dionysius refers to a familiar method of making working drawings, usually in red and black, and sometimes accompanied by abbreviated verbal indications of the colours to be used; it was possible from these to obtain further copies by means of pricking (*poncif*). Such pricked copies were often employed by panel painters in order to produce a pounced drawing over the gesso ground preparation of the panel. This in its turn was incised and the painters proceeded by adding the gold leaf and successive layers of egg tempera.

A considerable number of painters' working drawings has survived. The two most important (though largely unpublished) collections are found at the Byzantine Museum of Athens, which owns more than 3,000 drawings, and at the Benaki Museum of Athens, which has two painters' portfolios. A third, smaller collection of some 150 drawings owned by S. Mihalarias, is in London. The Benaki Museum portfolios are particularly important because they appear to have been accumulated over three centuries by successive generations of painters, and consist of two distinctly different types of working drawings, either freedrawn sketches or pricked cartoons. The first portfolio consists of 188 sketches, on most of which numbers have been written. The earliest of these sketches may date from *c.* 1600, and there are several indications that they were intended for use in the making of wall paintings. The numbers on the upper part of these drawings suggest that they were arranged by subject, roughly following the iconographical layout of the Manual by Dionysius of Fourna. This first portfolio must therefore be an iconographical inventory, and this explains why it includes a limited number of engravings, models for capital letters and recipes taken from the Manual of Dionysius. Among the most remarkable drawings are nine scenes of an Apocalypse cycle dating from *c.* 1600 and most probably derived from the illustrated Bibles of Cranach and Holbein. Another rare cycle, of the Sunday Prayer, is copied from the illustrated Bible of the Viennese engraver Christoph Weigel (1654-1725), which served as a painter's model book in Serbia. The drawings appear to have been bound into a volume, possibly in the course of the eighteenth century. The latest part of this portfolio contains large, unnumbered drawings, often signed by members of a workshop from Galatista, near Thessalonike. The painters from this workshop are known to have been active on Mount Athos in the first half of the nineteenth century. This and several other indications imply that the portfolio must have come from Mount Athos which, after 1453, was of course a major centre of art, particularly of monumental painting.

The second Benaki Museum portfolio was a gift of the Byzantine scholar A. Xyngopoulos. He related some of the drawings to icons by the Cretan painter Theodoros Poulakis (1622-1692). The portfolio contains some 308 sheets, onto which are pinned cartoons of different sizes for use in icon painting. The cartoons are in the form of either drawings or pricked copies, mostly folded into four. A number of the cartoons are on 'standard' paper measuring 31×42 cm and showing watermarks with the initials VG (Van Gangelt). This paper seems to have come from Amsterdam.

The cartoons are arranged by subject; for instance, scenes from the Old Testament, Prophets, Evangelists, portraits of Christ and the Virgin, Dodekaorton scenes, and scenes from the life of various saints. There are also three cartoons for church embroidery. The earliest of these drawings, such as, for example, a pricked copy with the Nativity of the Virgin, are connected with sixteenth-century icons. Four pricked cartoons have scenes from the life of St. George copied from an icon in Kerkyra (Corfu) by the Cretan master Michael Damaskinos (active 1555-1591) and Theodoros Poulakis, who is known systematically to have exploited Flemish engravings by J. Sadeler and J. Wierix. It therefore seems that the core of this second Benaki Museum portfolio represents the equipment of some well-organized workshop of icon painting of the seventeenth century in the Ionian Islands, most probably Kerkyra. This island developed into a major centre for icon painting after the fall of Crete to the Turks in 1669. Two of the most interesting aspects of this portfolio are the complicated permutation of scenes from the life of various saints (presumably to be explained by the rising demand for icons with such cycles in the course of the seventeenth century), and the growing infiltration of Western iconography, possibly due to the availability of engravings and printed books.

Additional information about the working drawings of icon painters is found in the Venetian Archives of Crete. The earliest reference is in the will of the outstanding Cretan master Angelos Akotantos (cat. nos. 43, 44), dating from 1436. Angelos wrote it on the eve of his departure on a trip to Constantinople, anticipating the dangers of travelling by sea. In his will the painter recorded a collection of drawings, his *teseniasmata* (disegni) or *skiasmata*. These were to be given to his unborn child which his wife was expecting at the time, provided it was a boy and providing it wished to become a painter. Otherwise the drawings were to be given to Angelos's brother John, also an icon painter. It transpires from later documents in the same archives that Angelos's only child was a girl, and so the drawings presumably ended in his brother's hands. In 1477, when he was elderly and sick, the brother, John Akotantos, is known to have sold 54 drawings of various saints (*exemplorum figurarum diversorum sanctorum, grece dicta sqiasmata*) to another major icon painter, Andreas Ritzos, for the considerable sum of three gold ducats. The transaction took place on the condition that the drawings were to be exclusively used by Ritzos himself and were not to be sold to other painters.

Angelos was a major figure in the formation of the Cretan School, and at least 16 works by him are known today. He appears to have established several iconographic formulas based on late Byzantine traditions, and also on a limited number of features deriving from Italian paintings of the International Gothic style, for instance, the dragon-slaying saints mounted on rearing horses. The fear of John Akotantos that his drawings might fall into the hands of lesser artists suggests that he was fully aware of their importance. Unfortunately, we know nothing about their precise nature – whether, for example, they were freehand drawings or pricked cartoons. Among the signed works of Angelos there is only one, the Christ Enthroned on Zakynthos (cat. no. 43) of which an exact copy is found in the Byzantine Museum of Athens. The existence of the two panels suggests that pricked cartoons may already have been in use in the first half of the fifteenth century. In any case, art historians have repeatedly observed certain formal iconographic similarities in the works of Angelos and Ritzos (such as those between the Christ Enthroned of Zakynthos and that by Ritzos on Patmos). Perhaps such relations between icons are better understood in the light of these recorded cases of the transmission of drawings.

The systematic use of pricked cartoons most probably began in the fifteenth century, when there was a substantial production of icons, resulting in the division of labour in painters' workshops. These developments coincide with the standardization of iconography that may be observed around the year 1500. It should be noted, however, that Cretan panel painters were not alone in this widespread use of pricked cartoons. Recent laboratory research has demonstrated that their use was common amongst European painters of the fifteenth and sixteenth centuries, including Van der Weyden, Memlinc, David, Joos van Cleve and Paris Bordone.

Apprentices' contracts in the Venetian Archives of Crete suggest that design retained an important role in the training of Cretan painters, but the systematic use of pricked cartoons and the accessibility of engravings may have adversely affected their ability in freehand drawing. However, exceptionally gifted masters such as Domenikos Theotokopoulos appear to have preferred freehand drawing to the use of cartoons. This is the case with two of his early works, the Dormition of the Virgin on Syros and the Adoration of the Magi in the Benaki Museum, Athens (cat. no. 72). Considerable evidence proves that working drawings were transmitted from hand to hand to be used by successive generations of icon painters. This process may account for the eclectic character of post-Byzantine art, and justifies the claim that its iconography was the outcome of a 'collective' process.

LASKARINA BOURAS
Benaki Museum, Athens

THE ICON AND CULTURAL IDENTITY
AFTER 1453

As the God-inspired Basil, who was learned in things divine, says,
'The honour [shown] to the image is conveyed to its prototype'.

St. John Damascenos (*c.* 730)

As mediators between heaven and earth, icons have provided for many centuries direct access to the Divine. Personal belief in the icon as protector, friend, and intercessor, shared by men and women, in both private and public life, existed in the Byzantine Empire from the sixth century, and by the twelfth century had spread to neighbouring lands, such as the Serbian and Bulgarian Kingdoms, and to more distant Russia. It was the high regard accorded to icons and their active presence in private and public life that visibly identified these cultures as Orthodox and differentiated them from the Catholic West. In short, icons became significant carriers of a tradition which, in parts of Eastern Europe, continued uninterrupted into the twentieth century.

The fall of Constantinople to the Turks in 1453 did not reduce the importance of sacred images in private devotion and in the Church liturgy, and there continued to be a demand for icons. However, as the social and financial structure of the Empire broke down, the market for these objects of devotion in what had been the centres of the Empire declined. This trend, which started in the fourteenth century and accelerated in the fifteenth, forced painters to move to foreign and provincial centres in search of work. Crete with its substantial Greek Orthodox population drew the largest number of these refugee artists. The large island was especially attractive because, under Venetian rule since 1204, it had by the fourteenth century come to provide a prosperous and open environment where painters could freely practice their trade. By the mid-fifteenth century a large colony of painters, some of whom were also teachers of painting, had established themselves in the main city, Candia (modern Iraklion) and the city became a training ground for those wishing to learn to paint in a Byzantine style.

Recent research in the notarial registries of Candia, in the Venice State Archives, has revealed that the colony of painters grew rapidly, as did the market for devotional images painted in the *maniera greca* (i.e., the Greek manner or Byzantine style) not only in Crete, but also in Venice, Dalmatia and elsewhere. A large proportion of the new clientele was Catholic and wanted panels in a Gothic style (*a la latina*), which the Cretan painters were able to successfully emulate. The recently discovered documents also shed light on the large size and number of commissions received and on the role of merchants in this flourishing enterprise.

The expanding Italian market for devotional images in a Byzantine style was stimulated by the continued and increasing presence of Greeks in Venice and elsewhere in Italy. These Greeks regarded Venice not merely as a place of refuge, but as 'another Byzantium', as Bessarion, Archbishop of Nicaea, phrased it in 1468, in a letter to the Doge of Venice in which he bequeathed his private library to the city. (Bessarion's collection, containing 500 Greek manuscripts, was the largest collection of its kind in the West). Bessarion had come to the West in 1438/39 in the retinue of the Byzantine Emperor John VIII Palaeologos who, together with the Patriarch of Constantinople and some 700 Greek clerics and laymen, attended the Ecumenical Council, in Ferrara and Florence, for the Union of the Churches. This large group of Greeks stayed in Italy for eighteen months and participated in what was probably one of the most elaborate and sumptuous ecclesiastical and political spectacles of the century.

Even more important than the presence of the emperor and 700 Greeks in Italy, was the permanent presence of the Greek colony in Venice, which grew rapidly in the fifteenth century and soon became one of the largest and most significant contingents of foreigners in the city. In 1514 it was granted permission by the Council of Ten to erect an Orthodox church and cemetery, the (still extant) Church of San Giorgio dei Greci. In the early sixteenth century Venice also became the principal European centre for Greek studies, and in this revival of classical scholarship Cretan men of letters played an important role.

By mid-sixteenth century the demand for devotional panel paintings in a Byzantine or Late Gothic style had, however, subsided. No large scale commissions like those of the late-fifteenth century are recorded in the notarial acts. This probably reflects a shift of taste in Italy, even among more conservative patrons. Other markets for Byzantine icons in Venice, Crete, the Balkans, and elsewhere in the Near East held up, however. Major clients were the large monastic foundations in Central and Northern Greece, and private individuals, who continued to commission icons. Wills and lists of inventories of portable property in Candia show that by the second half of the sixteenth and early seventeenth century most citizens owned at least one icon and that the more wealthy Candiotes owned as many as twenty or thirty. Icons were frequently included in dowry agreements, were listed in payments of debts, and were willed to relatives or churches.

An especially impressive icon of the Virgin and Child Exalted by the Prophets was given as a gift to the Church of San Giorgio dei Greci, in Venice, by John Mourmouris, c. 1560. Mourmouris himself is represented among the row of prophets below the Enthroned Virgin and Christ Child, and in the background are inscribed two prayers, one above his own portrait and the other above the figure of John the Baptist. The first is addressed by Mourmouris to the Baptist (his namesake) and implores him to intercede on his behalf to the Virgin. In the second, St. John is asking the Virgin to intercede on behalf of Mourmouris to Christ. These elaborate prayers for a double intercession show that in the mid-sixteenth century the religious function of the icon within a more secular society had not changed. Mourmouris was an educated man, a copyist from Nauplion, who resided in Venice between 1550 and 1563.

Not all such icons were commissioned by Greeks. In 1661 John Mengano Kydonio, a Venetian nobleman of Candia, ordered an icon of The Virgin Kardiotissa from one of the most important seventeenth-century Cretan painters, Emmanuel Tzanes Bounialis, active in Crete and Venice (1655-1690). The icon is signed and dated and bears both a dedicatory inscription, asking for the Virgin's protection in this life, and the donor's coat of arms. Mengano, who asked Tzanes to paint a characteristically Cretan type, the Kardiotissa, in a Byzantine style and with a Greek dedicatory inscription, belongs to the group of noble Venetians who absorbed the customs of the Greek population of Crete.

The war of Crete (1645-1669) and the subsequent Turkish occupation severed the ties between Venice and Crete and destroyed the financial and cultural life of the island. It also ended the movement of painters between Crete and Venice. Large numbers of Cretan artists fled to Venice and to the Ionian islands (still under Venetian rule), especially Kerkyra (Corfu), and there carried on the tradition of icon painting. These painters had to rely on their own ability to maintain a connection with the Byzantine past. Some were able to hold on to the severe Cretan style of the mid-sixteenth century. Others resorted to an increasing eclecticism and worked in several styles with various degrees of admixture of Western elements.

The eighteenth century was a turning point for the Greeks under Turkish domination. The conquest of the Peloponnese by the Turks in 1715 and the relative peace in the Balkans allowed Western commerce to penetrate into the East. This fostered the emergence of a Greek merchant class, since local commerce throughout the Balkans was almost exclusively in the hands of Greeks, and created a new clientele for icons. The greater wealth and the formation of commercial companies of craftsmen and farmers organized on the principle of collaborative capital in the villages of Chalkidiki, Epirus, the Peloponnese, and the islands resulted in a middle class which participated directly in the economic and administrative system. As a result, purely local centres acquired greater importance. A parallel phenomenon was that of itinerant painters, especially from Macedonia and Epirus, who became increasingly more important during the second half of the eighteenth century. These groups of painters, related by family ties or place of origin, organized into travelling companies that moved to villages, towns, and monasteries painting frescoes and icons for churches and private donors and decorating the houses of the new merchant class. Their activity spread from Epirus and Macedonia to Mount Athos and Thessaly, and to the Peloponnese and the islands. Their work acquired more of a folk-art character. The stylistic elements of folk art and its spontaneous realism gave the Byzantine style a new breath of life. Many painters active during this period are known by name (some 750 are recorded) and their productivity as well as their mobility are very impressive.

Within this more diversified milieu the Orthodox Church, centred since 1453 around the Patriarch in Constantinople, remained a strong unifying force and continued to be the major sustaining religious and cultural institution. The fact that Greek was the official language of the Church also helped to preserve the group consciousness of the Greeks. How vital the Church and religious beliefs still were in the eighteenth century is illustrated by the account of the activities of the monk Auxentius recorded by the historian Kaisarios Dapontes, an eyewitness. Auxentius, a popular preacher in the villages of Nicomedia (c. 1750), drew crowds of thousands who came to hear him from every part of the country. Dapontes tells us that this audience was composed not only of 'common people but high class people too and teachers and priests and bishops'. He also reports that among the religious objects owned by Auxentius the most important was an icon of the Virgin. Dapontes describes this icon in reverential terms and states that it helped immensely to enhance Auxentius's reputation because 'the people were striken by the love of the icon'.

This characteristically Orthodox reaction to an icon as to a living human being was also expressed in seventeenth- and eighteenth-century descriptions of icons in letters and *proskynetaria* (devotional books for pilgrims) in which they are referred to as 'empsychos' (having a soul) and 'holozontanos' (completely alive). It is, in fact, clear that the central Iconophile concept of the icon as sacred because 'The honour [shown] to the image is conveyed to its prototype', survived into the eighteenth century, as illustrated by Dionysius of Fourna who quotes it in his Hermeneia or Painter's Manual, written between 1728 and 1734. Dionysius, a monk and painter of icons and frescoes active on Mount Athos (1711-1734), also urged the student of painting to emulate the great examples of early Byzantine painters.

The return to earlier prototypes advocated by Dionysius is characteristic of much eighteenth-century work. It was part of the struggle of a cultural and religious minority under foreign domination to retain its ties to their past. But this conservatism did not prevent indigenous elements of folk art from being absorbed into the Byzantine context. This is illustrated by a lively and colourful icon by Konstantinos Kontarinis, in the Gennadeios Library, in Athens. Kontarinis, a native of Crete active in Kerkyra (1715-1732), painted in both a Byzantine and Western style. In a most interesting autobiographical icon of The Miracle of St. Luke and St. Eleutherios, of 1718, he combined these styles and also introduced elements of folk art. As stated in a lengthy dedicatory inscription, the icon represents an event that occurred on October 18, 1718, the feast day of St. Luke, when the painter's son Nicholas was miraculously saved from drowning in a well, near the Church of Ayios Eleutherios, in Kerkyra. Kontarinis, believing St. Luke and St. Eleutherios to have been responsible for his son's salvation, painted the icon as a sign of gratitude and dedicated it to the church. He represented himself, dressed in the contemporary attire of a gentleman and wearing a sword, kneeling in front of St. Eleutherios, under whose feet he has placed his signature. The story of the drowning is shown immediately below, in front of the church. In this lively and original icon, Kontarinis painted the heavenly apparition of St. Luke in a Western manner, St. Eleutherios in a Byzantine manner, and the church and human figures in a folk art style. These stylistic differentiations, which are well integrated and add to the vitality of the painting, also correspond to the hierarchical importance of the figures. Kontarinis here used stylistic modes as a means of symbolic differentiation in a manner reminiscent of early Byzantine painting.The very vital influence of folk art survived the Greek revolution of 1821 and continued throughout the nineteenth century. It was used, in conjunction with Byzantine stylistic elements, in icons painted in the early twentieth century.

Thus the icon as a cultural institution survived the vicissitudes of time to span a period of four hundred years, from the fall of Constantinople to the emergence of modern Greece. What is so remarkable is that throughout these centuries, in spite of stylistic variety, icons remained essentially Byzantine in form and content and in function and meaning. They continued to be holy images and recognizable portraits of protectors to whom prayers would be addressed and through whom these prayers would be conveyed to the prototype.

THALIA GOUMA-PETERSON
Professor at The College of Wooster, Wooster, Ohio

THE CONSERVATION OF WALL PAINTINGS AND ICONS IN GREECE

Endurance, resistance to time, is one of the most important aspects of a work of art. The artist-creator encloses in his work the irrepressible desire to transcend deterioration and decay.

Form, if it could be conceived of as existing independently, might claim the ability to do this. In the so-called musical arts, it does have this ability, up to a point. In the figurative arts, however, form is inseparable from material: the material by which it is expressed (painting) or given form (sculpture). And the material, of course, is subject to changes as a result of a variety of factors, which manifest themselves as deterioration.

Man has attempted to limit this deterioration, using different techniques at different periods, ranging from simple cleaning (washing etc.) to comprehensive repainting. In this way the conservation of works of art was born almost unconsciously, starting as part of artistic activity and today reaching the level of scientific research, with highly technical applications.

Within the post-Byzantine tradition there are a few statements in the literature, and some rudimentary guides as to the protection and preservation of painting. The most important of these are classified in the well-known manual by the monk and painter Dionysius of Fourna, Hermeneia, perhaps written at the beginning of the eighteenth century. Dionysius offers guidance to '(anyone) wishing to learn the art of painting' on 'how to wash old icons' (§35); he also notes the dangers attendant on this task, since someone who did not carry out the work properly, 'ended with the panel bare'. He later advises 'how to restore an old, rotted icon' (§71), now turning his concern to the conservation of the wood.

The earliest conservation of a Byzantine work of art in Greece was carried out in 1892-94 by the Italian mosaic artist F. Novo, who worked on the Daphni mosaics. The tradition of artists conserving Byzantine paintings was continued, or more accurately, was revived in the twentieth century by artists who began to paint in the traditional Byzantine style.

Dimitris Pelekasis (1881-1973), the son of a painter, studied art in Greece and Italy. A self-taught exponent of the Byzantine style, and of conservation, he worked as a conserver, mainly of icons in Greek and foreign collections. His method was acquired by experience, and he did not hesitate to fill in missing areas of paintings, imitating the style. The revival of the Byzantine style in modern Greece was mainly the work of Photis Kontoglou (1895-1965), a creative artist and distinctive writer, who continued in roughly the same direction. His knowledge of conservation was derived from his experience and from the study of old manuscripts on the subject. Having worked on icons in Greece (Byzantine Museum, Kerkyra 1930, etc.) and Egypt (Coptic Museum 1934), he went on to work on the conservation, or rather the cleaning of a very important ensemble of wall paintings, in the Peribleptos (fourteenth century) at Mistra (1936-39).

After the war, the painter Photis Zachariou (1909) devoted himself systematically to the work of conservation, though he, too, had not studied the art, except for his apprenticeship with the Hungarian conserver Kovacs. During the course of the thirty years or so that Zachariou worked with the Archaeological Service in Greece, he conserved more than 80 monuments and a large number of icons. He also carried out conservation in Cyprus. The monuments on which he worked included the most important buildings of Mistra (the Peribleptos, Metropolis and Aphentikon), of Thessalonike (the Rotonda, Ayios Nikolaos Orphanos, etc.), on Mount Athos (the Protaton, Stavronikita) and elsewhere, and involved strengthening, cleaning, detaching wall paintings, separating different layers of painting, and so forth.

A new period begins for conservation work in Greece about 1960. Initially it began to be carried out by artists who had specially studied the subject outside Greece (at the Instituto Centrale del Restauro in Rome), and subsequently by conservationists who had studied the art at university level. There are now schools of conservation in Greece at intermediate and advanced levels of education.

Conservation was organized at this time under the central guidance of the Byzantine Museum and led by its director Manolis Chatzidakis. The teams involved in the work were led by Photis Zachariou and the first of the conservers to have studied abroad, Anastasios Margaritoff (1925), Stavros Baltoyannis (1929), and Yannis Kolefas (1928-1986), who died prematurely; the last devoted himself to the conservation of mosaics, which he had specially studied in Italy.

In the years that followed there was extensive conservation work in Greece, and even abroad (Cyprus, Sinai, Jerusalem). Literally thousands of square metres of wall paintings were strengthened, and cleaned of grime, hard minerals and overpaintings. Earlier layers of wall paintings were revealed by the removal and – most importantly – the preservation of the more recent layers. When dire neccessity dictated (danger of collapse, etc.) wall paintings were detached from the walls.

When, for example, it became clear that the middle-Byzantine church at Episkopi in Evrytania was about to be inundated by a reservoir for a hydro-electric station, it was decided to detach the wall paintings that would probably be found (1965-67). The investigation (Ph. Zachariou) brought to light three layers of painting, dating from the ninth to the thirteenth centuries. Some of the wall paintings from Episkopi are included in this exhibition.

The wall paintings of the iconostasis and the sanctuary of a church at Veria in Lakonia (conserver: S. Papageorgiou) are a good example of the detaching of a more recent layer; it retains the shape of the architectural members it adorned, having the curving surfaces of the conch.

One of the most important tasks of conservation undertaken was at Protothroni on the Aegean island of Naxos (1971). The large painted dome of the church presented a number of problems. Since it could be seen, however, that there was another layer of paintings underneath this one, it was decided to detach it. A hemispherical painted surface with a radius of 1.90 m. was removed and brought down from the height of the dome entirely intact, without being cut into sections and without the least change in shape. This achievement was due to a system of strengthening devised and implemented by the Supervisor of conservation S.

Baltoyannis, who carried out the entire work with teams of workmen from the Archaeological Service. Since the earlier layer was not in a very good state of preservation, it was removed and reassembled on a model of the dome, constructed and prepared for exhibition in a Museum. The later layer (also dating from the eleventh century) was conserved, cleaned and reinforced, before being replaced in its original position on the dome of the church.

Examples can also be cited of work of equal importance in the field of icons. The Supervisor of conservation A. Margaritoff undertook an exceptionally interesting task (1959-1984) of conservation on the icon of the Three Church Fathers presented in the exhibition (cat. no. 17). The front of this had a representation of the Three Church Fathers (end of the seventeenth century) and on the back there was a thin encrustation of lime. The conserver suspected that beneath the painting there was an earlier representation, which was confirmed experimentally. For the work to be carried out more safely, however, the icon had to be X-rayed, and the lime was removed for this purpose. It then became clear that on the back there was an icon of the Virgin, and moreover an icon from Byzantine period. He detached this painting from the wood and transferred it to another surface. The X-ray of the other side revealed that the earlier layer was preserved in good condition. Using a method perfected by himself, the conserver removed the later painted surface, revealing another icon with the same subject, though dating from the fourteenth century. The later representation was transferred to another panel. In this way, a single seventeenth-century icon yielded three icons, two of which are Byzantine!

The conservation of Byzantine paintings in Greece (which is now under the guidance of a special Directorate of the Ministry of Culture) is based both on the traditional methods and on the achievements of modern science and research. In many instances, the Greek conservationists have significantly improved methods and materials borrowed from international practice. The general principle applied is that the products of modern technology are adopted, but are tested and adapted to Greek conditions so as to produce better and safer results.

Another rule of conservation in Greece is that the work should be preserved as it has survived, and that its history and different phases and periods should be respected. On no account is the restoration of lost areas of painting, or over-painting permitted.

The work of conservation, and discovery, has not only enriched our knowledge of Byzantine painting, but has for certain periods of history led to its revision, to the extent that the history of Byzantine painting needs to be rewritten to take these discoveries into account.

From this point of view, too, the contribution made by conservation to scholarship, and to the enrichment of our cultural heritage is of great importance, and all who love art, as a distillation of life and the soul, feel a special debt of gratitude.

NIKOS ZIAS
Director of Byzantine and Post-Byzantine Monuments
Director of the Conservation of Antiquities

PLATES

1

Carved wooden doors. 1296 or 1305.

1

Carved wooden doors. Details.

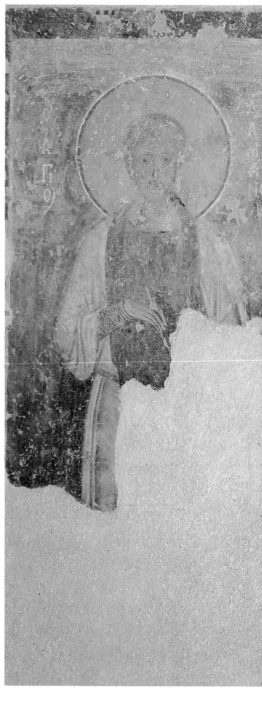

2

The Prophet Elijah. 10th-11th century.

3

SS Cosmas and Damian, and their mother, St. Theodote. Second quarter of the 13th century.

4
Angel. Second quarter of the 13th century.

5

St. Orestes. Second quarter of the 13th century.

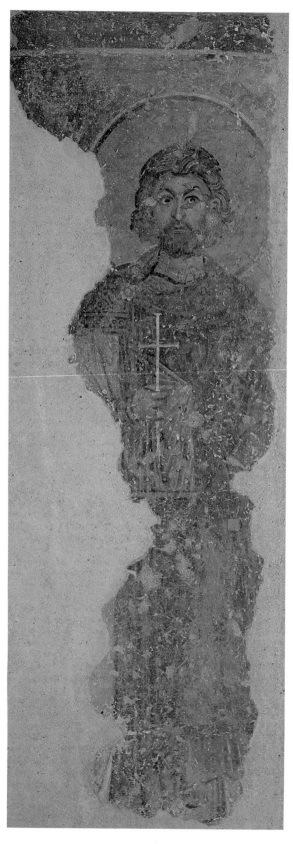

6
Unnamed martyr. Second quarter of the 13th century.

7

Wall paintings from the Church of Ayios Nikolaos in Veria, Lakonia. 1597.

8

The Raising of Lazarus. First half of the 12th century.

9

Double-sided Icon. A. The Virgin Hodegetria.
Second half of the 12th century.

9
Double-sided Icon. B. The Akra Tapeinosis.
Second half of the 12th century.

10
St. Spyridon. 12th century.

11
Archangel Gabriel. First half of the 12th century.

12
The Dormition. First half of the 13th century.

13

St. Peter. Last quarter of the 13th century.

14
St. John the Baptist. 13th-14th century.

15
Christ Pantocrator. Late 13th-Early 14th century.

16
Double-sided Icon. B. The Virgin Hodegetria.
Third quarter of the 16th century.

16
Double-sided Icon. A. The Virgin Hodegetria.
Beginning of the 14th century.

17

b. The Three Church Fathers. 17th century.

20
Virgin Intercessor. First half of the 14th century.

ОАΓΟ   ΜΑΤ
            ΘΑΙ
            Ọ

21
St. Matthew. First half of the 14th century.

22
St. Mark. First half of the 14th century.

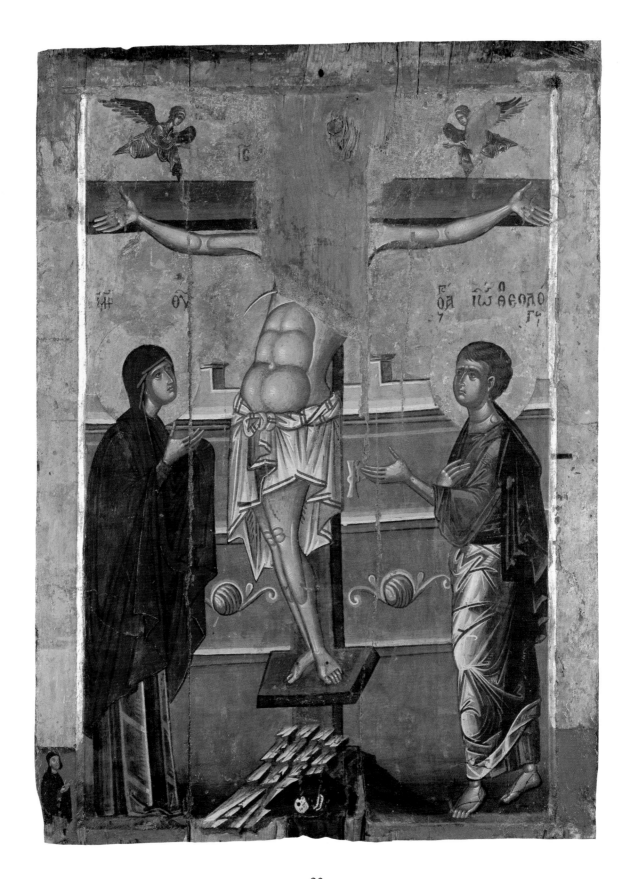

23
Double-sided Icon. B. The Crucifixion. 15th century.

23
Double-sided Icon with smaller Icon inlaid.
A. Christ with Angels, Apostles and Saints. 14th and 15th centuries.

24

The Virgin Hodegetria. Second half of the 14th century.

25
Six scenes from the Passion. Third quarter of the 14th century.

26
The Resurrection. Detail.

26
The Resurrection. Third quarter of the 14th century.

27
The Last Judgment. Middle of the 14th century.

28
St. Nicholas. Last quarter of the 14th century.

29

Christ Pantocrator. *c.* 1400.

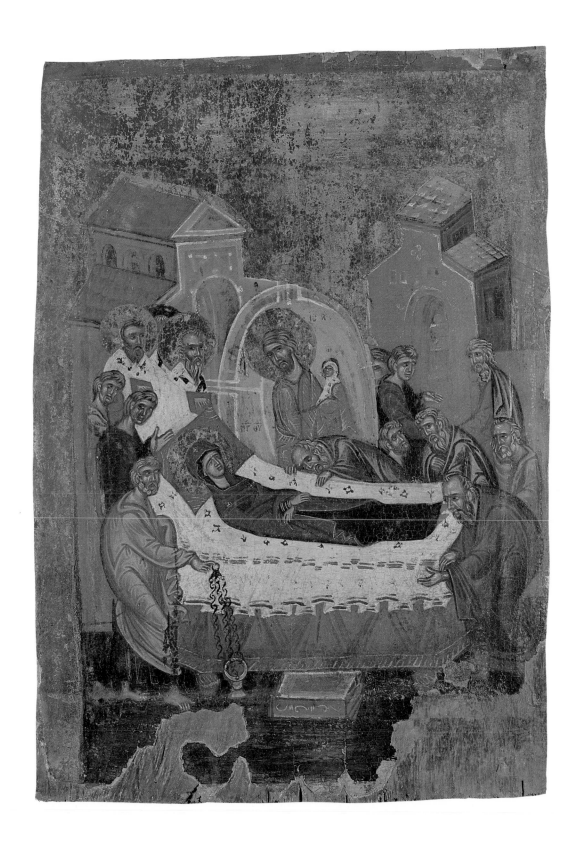

36

The Dormition. *c.* 1400.

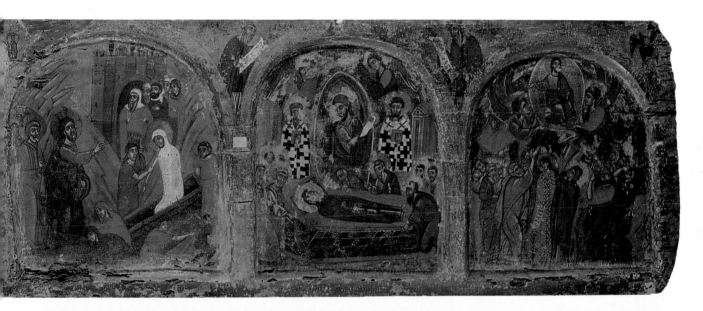

37

Epistyle of an Iconostasis, and details. 15th century.

38
Double-sided Icon.
A. St. Nicholas, 'Thermos Prostatis',
with scenes from his life. Detail.

38
Double-sided Icon.
B. The Dormition of St. Nicholas. 15th century.

38
Double-sided Icon.
A. St. Nicholas, 'Thermos Prostatis', with scenes from his life. 15th century.

39

Dormition of the Virgin and the Akathistos Hymn. First half of the 15th century.

40

St. Charalambos. End of the 15th century.

ΜΑΡ   ΝΑ

41
St. Marina. First half of the 15th century.

42

The Dormition. Beginning of the 15th century.

43

Angelos: Christ Enthroned. Second half of the 15th century.

44

Angelos: The Virgin Kardiotissa. Middle of the 15th century.

45

St. Demetrius. *c.* 1500.

46

St. Anne Enthroned with the Virgin and Christ. 15th century.

47

Sanctuary Doors. SS George and Demetrius. Second half of the 15th century.

48

Sanctuary Doors. The Annunciation, SS Peter and John the Theologian.
Second half of the 15th century.

49
The Virgin Hodegetria. 15th century.

50

Nikolaos Lamboudis: The Virgin Eleousa. 15th century.

51
Sanctuary Doors, right leaf.
Virgin of the Annunciation, SS Basil and Nicholas.
Second half of the 15th century.

51
Sanctuary Doors, right leaf. Detail.

52

Nikolaos Tzafouris: Christ Carrying the Cross. Detail.

52

Nikolaos Tzafouris: Christ Carrying the Cross. Second half of the 15th century.

53

Nikolaos Tzafouris: Virgin and Child. 15th century.

54

Madre della Consolazione with St. Francis. Second half of the 15th century.

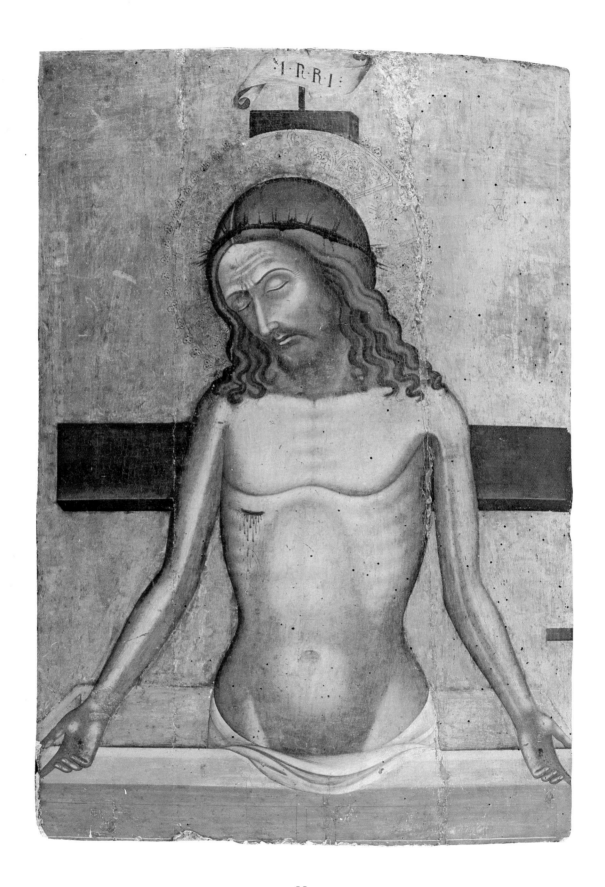

55

Nikolaos Tzafouris (?): The Akra Tapeinosis. Second half of the 15th century.

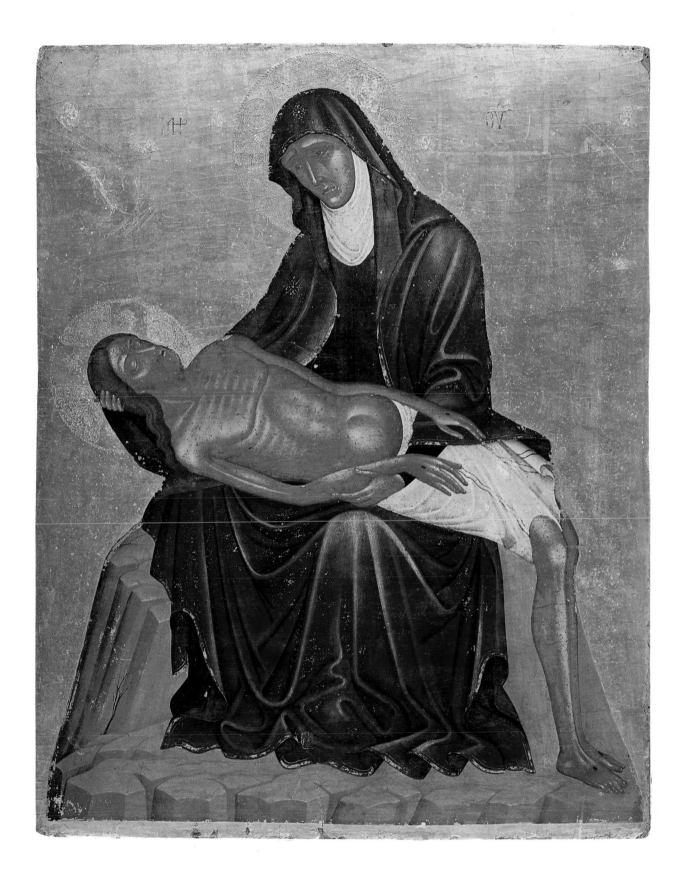

56

Pietà. Second half of the 15th century.

57

Christ and the Samaritan Woman. Last quarter of the 15th century.

62
The Holy Trinity. *c.* 1500.

63

Sanctuary Doors. b. Annunciation and Prophets. Second half of the 18th century.

63
Sanctuary Doors. a. Annunciation and Saints. 15th century.

64
The Hospitality of Abraham. Detail.

64

The Hospitality of Abraham. 15th century.

65
St. Nicholas. *c.* 1500.

66

St. Nicholas with scenes of his miracles. *c.* 1500.

67
Deesis. Early 16th century.

68
St. Demetrius. 16th century.

69

Georgios Klontzas: Triptych with the Last Judgment.
Second half of the 16th century.

69
Georgios Klontzas: Triptych with the Last Judgment.
Second half of the 16th century.

69

Georgios Klontzas: Triptych with the Last Judgment.

69

Georgios Klontzas: Triptych with the Last Judgment.

70

Georgios Klontzas (?): Triptych, central and left panels.
Second half of the 16th century.

70

Georgios Klontzas (?): Triptych.

71
Domenikos Theotokopoulos: St. Luke the Evangelist. Between 1560 and 1567.

72

Domenikos Theotokopoulos: The Adoration of the Magi. 1567-1570.

73
Emmanuel Lambardos: St. Onoufrios.
End of the 16th - Beginning of the 17th century.

74

Emmanuel Lambardos: The Adoration of the Magi. 16th century.

75
Michael Damaskinos: St. John the Baptist.
Second half of the 16th century.

76
St. John the Baptist. 16th century.

77
Symeon Theodochos. 16th century.

78
Triptych. End of the 16th century.

79

Triptych, with the Virgin Portaitissa, St. Paul Xiropotaminos and St. Eleutherios. 17th century.

80
Triptych with topographical view of Mount Sinai. First half of the 17th century.

CATALOGUE

1

Carved wooden doors
1296 or 1305
244×144 cm
Elasson, Larissa. Monastery of the
Olympiotissa, Sacristy

One of the rarest and most representative examples of Byzantine wood-carving from Greece, this door illustrates the importance of this art from the Early Christian period onwards and also its relationship to Islamic wood-carving, to which it had a similar development. Both leaves are divided into three differently decorated parts; the decoration consists of geometric motifs enclosed within borders, each of a different design. The inlaid ivory decoration is preserved at a number of points. The work as a whole is delicate and refined. There are inscriptions carved on the top, outer corners of each leaf: Left: [AN]EKAI/[NIC]ΘHCAN / [AI ΠI]ΛΕ. Right: ETOYC/5ΩΔΙ / EN (or Y) NΓ.

Provenance. Monastery of the Olympiotissa. Formerly incorporated into the main, west entrance of the katholikon.
Bibliography. Sotiriou 1927, pp. 327ff. Byzantine Art 1964, no. 127, p. 203. Skouvaras 1967, pp. 23ff. Byzantine Art 1986, no. 20, pp. 32-35. Affreschi e icone 1986, no. 1, pp. 40-41. From Byzantium to El Greco 1987, no. 1, pp. 59-61, 146.

E. M. Ch.

WALL PAINTINGS FROM EPISKOPI IN EVRYTANIA

The few fragments of wall paintings from Episkopi, Evrytania, included in the exhibition are only a small part of the group of wall paintings which formed three phases of decoration in a large domed cross-in-square church dating from the 9th century that is now submerged beneath the waters of the reservoir at Kremasta, Evrytania. Before the church was inundated, three layers of wall paintings were uncovered, separated and removed from the walls by the Archaeological Service (autumn 1965). The pieces were then cleaned, restored and framed in the Byzantine Museum laboratories (1965-67 and 1973-76) and the group was displayed in the exhibition Byzantine Frescoes and Icons, in Athens in 1976. The earliest layer, only a few fragments of which survived on the vaults, consisted mainly of a non-figurative decoration that served as a border for what appear to have been only a few scenes. It was probably contemporary with the church. The second layer which will have covered the lower part of certain walls only, is represented here by the prophet Elijah (cat. no. 2) and the remains of SS Cosmas and Damian and their mother Theodote and of St. Nicholas, preserved in the western arm of the cross. The lines and planes with which the figures are rendered, the vivid splashes of colour, the stiff stylized drapery, and the pearl-studded haloes suggest a date towards the end of the 10th or beginning of the 11th centuries for this particularly expressive art. It is also to be found in part in the Church of Ayios Stephanos in Kastoria and the earliest layer in the Church of the Ayioi Anargyroi in the same city (Pelekanidis-Chatzidakis 1984, pp. 23 and 28, figs. pp. 27 and 29).

The bulk of the wall paintings from Episkopi are from the third layer. This is executed in painting of a high quality dating from the first half of the 13th century, and is probably to be connected with the Despotate of Epirus, with its capital at Arta. The high quality of it, however, is such that it may be related to works from Thessalonike of this period, and therefore dated after 1224, when Arta was united with Thessalonike (cf. cat. nos. 3, 4, 5, 6).

Conservation. Ph. Zachariou and colleagues.
Bibliography. Chatzidakis 1966 (1), pp. 28ff., pls. 29-34. Chatzidakis 1967, pp. 62ff., figs. 4-6. Byzantine Frescoes 1976, pp. 27-37, nos. 3-43, colour plates I-XVI, monochrome plates 2-18. Affreschi e icone 1986, nos. 2 and 4-7, pp. 42-47.

2

The Prophet Elijah
10th-11th century
204×94 cm
Athens. Byzantine Museum

The prophet is portrayed full-length against a deep blue and red ground. The painting was in the sanctuary apse, which is an archaic feature. From the second layer.

3

SS Cosmas and Damian,
and their mother, St. Theodote
Second quarter of the 13th century
225×335 cm
Athens. Byzantine Museum

This large scale composition, with full-length portraits of the Saints Anargyroi and the bust of the aristocratic figure of their mother between them, belongs to the third and final layer of the wall paintings at Episkopi in Evrytania. The striking figure of Theodote clearly recalls the classical tradition, both in the portraiture (she is depicted here in the form of the *imago clipeata* of the ancients), and in the treatment of the border of the round frame of the Italian tondo. This monumental composition of the three saints, which also occurs elsewhere in this church, is by the best of the artists that worked on this phase, as is clear from the ethos of the young saints, with their noble figures, simple modelling and tranquil colour harmonies. This scene overlay the same scene in the second layer.

4

Angel
Second quarter of the 13th century
170×246 cm
Athens. Byzantine Museum

This piece is part of the large scene of the Ascension on the vault of the sanctuary. It shows the head of one of the four (?) angels — only three are preserved — who are supporting the gloria of the Lord as he ascends to heaven. Only part of the gloria is preserved, together with the right hand of Christ. This angel is perhaps by the same artist that painted Orestes (cat. no. 5): the rather careless execution, the liveliness of expression and the personal quality of the portraiture are appropriate to both these figures.

5

St. Orestes
Second quarter of the 13th century
266×246 cm
Athens. Byzantine Museum

Part of a composition with three of the five martyrs of Sebasteia, a three figural composition like cat. no. 3. Orestes, the youngest of the group, is portrayed as a soldier of the mountains, of tall, slender, though rather unstable, stature and with unruly hair. It has an unrefined, restless character, and it too belongs to the third layer, though it was probably not by the same painter as cat. no. 3.

6

Unnamed martyr
Second quarter of the 13th century
203×73 cm
Athens. Byzantine Museum

Also from the third layer, and probably by the same painter as Orestes (cat. no. 5).

M. Ch.

7

Wall paintings from the Church of Ayios Nikolaos in Veria, Lakonia
1597
343×217 cm
Yeraki, Lakonia. Laboratory of the 5th Ephorate of Byzantine Antiquities (temporary location)

The iconography of the wall paintings removed from the walls of the small domed Church of Ayios Nikolaos in Veria follows the familiar repertoire of the period for churches of this type. The Virgin, in the type of Platytera, is represented on the vault of the sanctuary apse, with the Melismos and the Officiating Bishops on the wall beneath; the Annunciation is depicted on the piers, and the Descent from the Cross is painted in the prothesis. The sanctuary walls have representations of bishops. Above the sanctuary door of the iconostasis is the inscription recording the decoration of the church:
+’Ανιστορήθη ὁ θεῖος κ(αὶ) πάνσεπτος ναός οὗτος τοῦ ἐν ἁγίοις πατρός ἡμῶν Νικολάου ἀρχιεπισκόπου Μύρων τῆς Λυκίας τοῦ θαυματουργοῦ Θεοφιλεστ(άτου) ἐπισκόπου Βρεστ(έ)ν(ης) Κυ(ρ)οῦ Νεοφήτου ἐν ἔτει ἀπό στάσ(εως) κόσμου ζ^ω ρ^ω ε^ω ἀπό δέ τῆς ἐνσάρκ(ου) οἰκονομί(ας) τοῦ κυ(ρίου) α^ω φ^{ω}Ν^ω ζ^ω...
To the right and left are Christ and the Virgin enthroned; on the north wall is the portrait of St. Nicholas af-

ter whom the church is named; and on the lunettes the apostles Peter and Paul. The prominent features of the dark, melancholy faces are emphasized by delicate parallel white lines, but these do not succeed in lighting up their countenances. The drapery, which is sometimes flowing in its treatment, is stiff, with angular edges and harsh lighting. An unsuccessful attempt is made to make the figures stand out from the flat background by dividing it into bands of different colour. There is no great variety in the colours used, though different tones of the same colour have been juxtaposed in a generally sensitive and careful fashion. This is a conservative style, which reflects the Palaeologan art of the surrounding area (notably Yeraki) and was clearly influenced by portable icons.

Provenance. The Church of Ayios Nikolaos in Veria, Lakonia. From the later (second) layer of wall paintings.
Conservation. S. Papageorgiou, G. Zitsas, A. Mitris, K. Zitsa, P. and H. Bougadis, Th. Vachaviolos, Th. Papageorgiou (1983-85).
Bibliography. Byzantine Art 1986, no. 67, pp. 64-66. Affreschi e icone 1986, no. 25, pp. 61-62. From Byzantium to El Greco 1987, no. 6, pp. 66, 149.

Ai. B.

8

The Raising of Lazarus
First half of the 12th century
21.5×24 cm
Athens. Private Collection

The rather compact, though well modelled figures, from an imposing composition, despite the small size of the icon. The figure of Christ in the centre dominates the scene because of its more imposing scale and larger head, and by virtue of its isolation and intensity. Elements defining the setting and landscape are reduced to a minimum, though the sombre colours used for the figures, in shades of blue, purplish red and ochre, stand out strongly against the vermillion background. This same, rather rare background is to be found in a small icon of the Transfiguration now in the Hermitage Museum, which comes from the same Dodekaorton as this icon. In addition to the similar red backgrounds and small size, however, these icons have in common certain stylistic features and an individualistic manner that enables them to be attributed to the same painter. The Leningrad icon has been assigned to the 12th century by Wulff, Lazarev and Bank, and the monumental quality of both icons is certainly typical of this century. Further evidence is furnished by the treatment of the faces: the features are clearly drawn, the brownish flesh tones are built up rather freely with gradations of colour tones, and the white highlights on the prominent features contrast with the red brush-strokes applied to the cheeks and forehead. This same kind of modelling is to be found in the Nerezi fresco of 1164 and in the Christ in manuscript 2645 of the National Library, Athens, which was painted before 1206. These features, together with a certain stiffness in the drapery, and the peculiar proportions of the figures suggest that both icons should be dated to the 12th century. These two icons, the Raising of Lazarus and the Transfiguration, now so far apart, thus seem originally to have belonged to a single series of icons of a Dodekaorton. The implication is that in the 12th and 13th centuries, such series celebrating the twelve major feast days of the Church were to be found above the iconostasis as a unified group of related pictures.

Provenance. Mount Athos.
Conservation. Ph. Zachariou (1958).
Bibliography. Chatzidakis 1964-65, p. 386, pl. 87α (= Studies chap. XVIII). Chatzidakis 1965 (2), pp. XXIV, LXXXIII, no. 37. Chatzidakis 1979 (1), p. 347, pl. XL. Chatzidakis-Babić 1983 (both French and English editions), p. 154. Byzantine Art 1986, no. 74, pp. 72, 74. Affreschi e icone 1986, no. 26, p. 63. From Byzantium to El Greco 1987, no. 7, pp. 69, 149.

M. Ch.

9

Double-sided Icon
A. The Virgin Hodegetria
B. The Akra Tapeinosis
Second half of the 12th century
115×77.5 cm
Kastoria. Archaeological Collection

This icon is one of the masterpieces of Byzantine painting, not only for its subleme artistic quality, but also for the originality in the subject, the Akra Tapeinosis (or Man of Sorrows), which appears here for the first time. It is clear from the notches at the bottom of the panel that this was a processional icon.

A. A feature of the icon of the Hodegetria is the contrast between the frightened expression and sidelong glance of the Virgin and the serenity of Christ, whose wrinkled forehead gives him a mature appearance. The emphasis on the emotions, and the linear nature of the composition are both features of the art of the second half of the 12th century.

This interpretation of the Virgin's highly emotional expression has been disputed. The view has been advanced that this is a reference to the scene on the other side of the icon, which is interpreted as a vision seen by the Virgin. It is suggested here that this manner was a 'common-place' of the emotional climate associated with the artistic expression of the painting of this period.

B. The portrayal of Christ on the type of the Akra Tapeinosis on the other side is contemporary with the Virgin. Here the ground is blue, whereas in the case of the Virgin it is ochre. The rougher modelling and the decidedly linear treatment of the face have close affinities with works from the end of the 12th century at Kurbinovo and in the Church of the Ayioi Anargyroi at Kastoria. This is one of the earliest known scenes of the Akra Tapeinosis.

The two sides were not painted at different dates; it is simply that two different styles were used in the same icon for two subjects having different contents.

Conservation. Ph. Zachariou.
Bibliography. Chatzidakis 1976, pp. 184ff., pl. XXXVII, 20-22. Byzantine Frescoes 1976, no. 106, p. 77. Chatzidakis 1979 (1), I, pp. 358ff., pl. XLV, 20-21. Belting 1980-81, p. 4, figs. 2-3. Belting 1981, pp. 143ff., figs. 49-50. Byzantine Art 1986, no. 75, pp. 72-73. Affreschi e icone 1986, no. 27, pp. 64-65. From Byzantium to El Greco 1987, no. 8, pp. 70, 150.

M. Ch.

10

St. Spyridon
12th century
60×44 cm
USA. Private Collection

Spyridon, 14th-century bishop of Tremithus, and one of the most famous fathers of the Cypriot Church, began his career as a shepherd; he was famous for his many miracles, including the transformation of a snake into gold, so that poor Cypriots could buy seed. Here, as is typical, he is portrayed as an old man with white hair and beard, simultaneously wearing the basket cap of a shepherd and the sticharion and cross-inscribed omophorion of a bishop. The saint is shown half-lenght and frontally, with a gem-incrusted book in his covered left hand, and his right hand raised in blessing – a pose nearly identical to that of Christ Pantocrator.

The composition is dominated by a few simple, striking shapes, and by rigorous bilateral symmetry. The bishop's large, round head is centred against a double-ring halo filled with punched decoration. It is covered by a tight, round cap formed of a simple grid, and tapers to sunken cheeks, from which descends a thich beard divided into highly stylized, matching curls. Spyridon's large eyes are broad and almond-like, his nose long and straight, and his nostrils almost box-like in their angularity. His blessing hand is large and simple, as is his white omophorion, with its four black crosses. The colour of the sticharion is subdued, but its highlights – especially over the right shoulder – are angular and lively. The cumulative effect of this fine provincial icon is one of solidity and sterness, although the panel is impressive as well for the sheer visual delight of its many purely abstract forms. The body and face of the figure are well preserved, but the background, especially on the left, has been damaged.

The punched decoration in the halo, the silver background, and the iconography all point to Cyprus. More specifically, the stylization of facial features and hair evoke comparisons with the large (and equally stern) icon of St. Nicholas tis Steyis, Kakopetria (Papageorgiou 1969, p. 35. Byzantine Icons 1976, no. 15) – which in turn recalls the St. Nicholas *vita* icon at Mount Sinai, which Kurt Weitzmann has assigned to the early 13th century (Weitzmann 1982 (1), p. 67). However, the softer facial modelling of the present panel, coupled with its more angular drapery highlights, suggests a Comnenian dating – though not as early as the St. Spyridon fresco at Monagri, which has been placed near the beginning of the 12th century (Boyd 1974, p. 287, fig. 10).

An icon of this size would likely have been set in the lower, 'despotic' tier of an iconostasis.

Bibliography. Unpublished.

G. V.

11

Archangel Gabriel
First half of the 12th century
61.7×39.5 cm
USA. Private Collection

Gabriel is portrayed half-length, turning slightly toward his right; in one hand is a staff and in the other a cross-inscribed globe, both customary attributes reflecting his authority in the heavenly court of Christ. The figure's oval head, enveloped by a thick braid and enframed by the oval void of his gilded wings, is slightly inclined and turned – but his large, almond-shaped eyes are fixed on the beholder. The archangel wears a salmon-pink tunic overlaid with a dense pattern of angular highlights and ornamented with an intricate gold collar; a dark mantle bearing V-shaped gold motifs is clasped near the right shoulder. The figure is very well preserved, although the panel's silver background is substantially worn.

The simple but subtle modelling of face and neck, the long, graceful lines defining eyebrows, nose, and chin, the unusually large, alert eyes, and the brightly coloured, energetically highlighted garments combine to create an icon of extaordinary visual and psychological impact – one in the finest tradition of mature Comnenian painting. Indeed, Gabriel's reserved dignity and subtle pathos anticipate, by more than a century, the art of Duccio.

This panel falls near the beginning of an impressive tradition of large

Archangel icons from Great Deesis friezes – the tradition to which, for example, the well-known Palaeologan St. Michael in the Byzantine Museum belongs (Weitzmann 1968, pp. XXXIff., pl. 65). Among those archangels closest in date to this one are examples in St. Catherine's Monastery on Mount Sinai, and the Monastery of Ayios Chrysostomos on Cyprus (Weitzmann 1982 (1), p. 66. Papageorgiou 1969, p. 14), both of which are usually dated around 1200.

That this panel is to be assigned to Cyprus is suggested by its silver background, and, more specifically, by its close stylistic parallels with 12th-century panels from that island, including the Virgin and Child from the Church of the Virgin Chrysaliniotissa, Nicosia (Papageorgiou 1969, p. 25. Byzantine Icons 1976, no. 3). But closer still is the earlier John the Baptist icon from the Church of the Virgin at Asinou (Papageorgiou 1969, p. 18. Byzantine Icons 1976, no. 2). Besides the silver background, the two icons show closely comparable hands (delicate though simple, with a double line across the thumb), eyes (extended upper lash, with a prominent line descending from the tear duct), and noses (long, continuous arch, with angular nostril). Moreover, the two panels are virtually the same size (at *c.* 62 cm high), are structurally the same (a single board hollowed out to form a relatively narrow frame), and both bear a pattern of geometrically incised circles on their frames. The John the Baptist is known to have come from the Church of the Virgin at Asinou, and has generally been dated to the very early 12th century on the basis of stylistic similarities to the dated (AD 1105/6) frescoes there (Winfield 1972. Byzantine Icons 1976, no. 2). A similar dating and localization is suggested for Gabriel, which may once even have formed part of the same Great Deesis.

Bibliography. Unpublished.

G. V.

12

The Dormition
First half of the 13th century
94×75 cm
Kastoria. Archaeological Collection

The body of the Virgin lies on a bier spread with a richly decorated cloth. The apostles stand in two groups at the ends of the bier, their faces contorted with pain and grief. A number of bishops and deacons stand behind the bier, and Christ, in the centre of the composition, is holding the soul of the Virgin in his hands An interesting feature is the uncertain attempt at the perspective of the buildings at the sides.

The painting in this icon is a good illustration of the tendency to abandon the idealistic values of the Comnenian style and establish the principles of a new conception of art, that attached importance to human qualities. This conception is very clear in the details of the faces, with their realistic rendering of human nature and emotions. The insistence on the human, and the wonderful colours – strong use was made of pink and blue – produce a work of great aesthetic originality. The trend in painting represented by this icon reached its culmination in works of unrivalled beauty, like the wall paintings in Sopočani in Yugoslavia

Provenance. From a church at Kastoria.
Bibliography. Byzantine Frescoes 1976, no. 109, p. 78. Affreschi e icone 1986, no. 29, pp. 67-68. From Byzantium to El Greco 1987, no. 10, pp. 73, 151.

Th. P.

13

St. Peter
Last quarter of the 13th century
93.1×61.3 cm
Washington, DC. The Dumbarton Oaks Collection (acc. no. 82.2)

This imposing, nearly life-size portrait is a masterful characterization of the Apostle Peter: His physical strength as a fisherman is suggested by the short, thich neck and massive torso, while his role as Apostle and Founder of the Church of Rome is evoked by his calm, yet intensely spiritual expression, his gaze looking past the beholder. Silhouetted against a gold ground and turning slightly to the right, the half-length figure has all three attributes associated with this saint: in his fleshy left hand, he holds rather awkwardly a long, cross-topped staff and a scroll tied with red string. With his right, he points toward the scroll, alluding to the writing of his Epistles. In an unusual departure from standard Byzantine iconography, the gold keys to Paradise, which are traditionally held in his right hand, are suspended from a thin gold cord around his neck. He wears a dark blue tunic with a red clavus and an olive green pallium, the latter highlighted in gold. The black outline of his halo and the (illegible) traces of an inscription to the left of his head are later additions.

The powerful realism of this icon is quite rare in Byzantine art, but it reflects a realistic current which comes to be fore in the region of Macedonia toward the end of the 13th century. The vigorous, expressive modelling of the facial features, which imparts an extraordinary vitality to the figure, also points to a Macedonian origin. While Weitzmann prefers a date in the third quarter of the 13th century, on the basis of stylistic comparisons with the frescoes of Sopočani, the darker, rather somber colours and the more sculptural (rather than linear) quality of the modelling of the face tend to indicate a date nearer the close of the century. The almost sculptural sense of mass and weight achieved through the manipulation of light and shadow, especially in the skilful treatment of the soft folds of drapery, are also consistent with the later date (cf. frescoes of the Protaton, Mount Athos and Ayios Euthymios, Thessaloniki). However, there are no wholly convincing stylistic parallels to this highly individualistic icon that would allow a more precise date or localization.

Its large size suggest that it was originally placed on an iconostasis screen between the columns supporting the architrave; because St. Peter turns to the right, it must have been balanced by another icon with the figure turning to the left. The logical pendant would have been St. Paul, who together with St. Peter embodied the foundation of the Christian Church. Most likely the two icons flanked the central, or Royal Doors, leading into the sanctuary.

The icon has been unevenly trimmed along the left edge of the engaged frame (*c.* 5 cm), but otherwise is in remarkably good condition. Small areas of loss occur over the mantle and more extensively over the tunic, and much of the gilding is abraded or lost; there is a major loss over and below the saint's right hand. It is painted in tempera on a prepared gesso base, and the gilding is applied over bole. Like many icons from this region, the wood panel was diagonally scored before the gesso was applied. Incised lines were used sparingly to define the head and the cross of the staff.

Provenance. Unknown.
Conservation. Technical and Conservation Laboratory, The Fogg Art Museum, Cambridge, MA. When acquired, the icon had been previously cleaned of a layer of overpaint and areas of loss had been filled extensively with wax.
Bibliography. Icons 1980, pp. 168ff. (M. Chatzidakis) and pls. 62-63. Weitzmann 1983 (1).

S. A. B.

14

St. John the Baptist
13th-14th century
38×23.5-24 cm
Athens. City of Athens Museum

St. John the Baptist is depicted half-length and frontally, holding in his left hand a long staff topped by a cross, and a closed scroll. He is blessing with his right hand. The facial features are simply drawn with quick brush-strokes, unequally distributed so as to emphasize the anxiety in the expression. The square face is framed by thick hair and an unkempt beard, underlining his character as the hermit of the wilderness. He is wearing a himation that leaves his right shoulder uncovered. The bare flesh is covered with what seems to be bodily hair, as is often the case in representations of this saint, rather than the melote, the short-sleeved chiton of sheepskin that he usually wears next to the skin. He is portrayed against a red background, with a halo of a deep ochre. The wood is not particularly well worked and has a slightly raised frame. The inscription, in white letters, reads O A - O Π ΔP M PO OC (St. John the Forerunner); the syllable PO is out of position.

The iconographic type of the saint derives from the full-length representation of him in icons from the 6th century (the encaustic icon of Kiev, which originated in Sinai, Weitzmann 1976, pp. 32-35, pl. XIV) and later from the 11th century (mosaic icon in the Patriarchate in Constantinople; Sotiriou 1937, pls. 10-11, pp. 24ff.), to mention only the two best known. In these representations, the hand with which the Baptist is blessing is raised up, instead of held in front of his breast, and the scroll is unrolled, showing a text; and a chiton covers his body beneath the himation-melote. However, scenes in which part of his body is uncovered are known in 11th-century manuscripts (Dionysiou 587; Weitzmann 1976, fig. 16). In the

famous 13th-century icon on Sinai, he is also shown standing, with the right part of the torso uncovered, and with a very emaciated body and thin arms; these are usual features of the figure of the Baptist when he is portrayed as the hermit of the wilderness.

The intense anxiety in the expression is also to be found in some of the icons of the Crusader group of the second half of the 13th century, such as the small icon with a bust of St. Nicholas, which has the same asymmetrical facial features as the present icon, and which is attributed by Weitzmann to a workshop of Acre (Weitzmann 1963, p. 195, fig. 20. Sotiriou 1956, p. 93, fig. 81). Amongst the icons of another Crusader group, attributed to Apulia or Cyprus, there is an interesting icon of St. John the Baptist with several features in common with the present work, though he is depicted standing and holding the Lamb in a medallion, an element drawn from Western iconography (Weitzmann 1966, p. 70, fig. 44): in this icon St. John is portrayed against a red background, a feature also found, however, in purely Byzantine icons, such as the Raising of Lazarus (cat. no. 8). He is shown frontally, and wearing the melote, which leaves uncovered the right side of his body, covered with hair; despite the fact that it is the work of a good artist, the face resembles the present icon in the arrangement of the hair and beard and the anxious expression.

No icons of St. John the Baptist shown half-length and in the type of the present icon are known before the 14th century; this does not mean that they did not exist, however since figures, of saints depicted frontally and half-length were amongst the most popular subjects in icon painting. The resemblance between this icon and three famous 14th-century works, all of them examples of very high quality Palaeologan art (icon in the British Museum, cf. From Byzantium to El

Greco 1987, no. 11, and two icons in private collections, Splendeur de Byzance 1982, p. 45, Icons 1980, figs. 72-73) is confined to the iconography. The naive style and pronounced expressionistic character here give rise to a few minor differences from the type of the emaciated hermit, such as the disproportionately large head, supported on the roughly drawn body of the saint, with no neck.

The painter's clumsiness is also apparent in the incorrect order of the inscription with the name of the saint, and in the use of rough, undressed wood. All these elements make it difficult to assign the work to a particular workshop or style, and also prevent us from dating it more precisely. The representation was covered by a later layer of painting with the figure of St. Nicholas, full-length, wearing a phelonion decorated with crosses. This is an example of late 18th-century painting.

The metal, silvered revetment is also an example of later popular metalware, which was very widespread at this period.

Conservation. A. Margaritoff.
Bibliography. Byzantine Art 1986, no. 77, p. 75. Affreschi e icone 1986, no. 30, p. 68.

N. Ch.

15

Christ Pantocrator
Late 13th - Early 14th century
88×55 cm
Kastoria. Archaeological Collection

The icon of Christ is painted on a panel with a raised frame, the edges of which are emphasized by a red border. Gesso on canvas.

Christ is portrayed half-length on a silver ground. In his left hand he holds a richly bound Gospel book, and his right hand is extended in blessing. He is wearing a light brown chiton and a dark blue himation. The drapery hangs in broad, sweeping lines, in deep folds; it is broken by very few angular features and consists of a series of flowing planes that give the figure a feeling of volume. The face is particularly lively and expressive, an effect achieved by the light lines stressing the wrinkles on the forehead; by the delicate red lines defining the eyelids, ears and the base of the nose; by the olive green underpaint on which much use is made of the brown skin-colour; by the linear highlights on the forehead and around the eyes; and by the diffused areas of red on the cheeks. The physical type of Christ, with the oval face, long fleshy nose, arched eyebrows and deeply shadowed eyes, derives from 12th-century models (Byzantine Icons 1976, p. 36, fig. 7), which were revived in the art of the second half of the 13th and the beginning of the 14th century (Ioannou 1959, fig. 15. Naumann-Belting 1966, pl. 37a. Mouriki 1978, p. 76, fig. 51). The basic features of technique and style are also related to artistic trends of the same period: the realistic portrayal of the figure, which is anti-classical in character, the metallic gleam in the chiton, the drapery with its deep, wide folds, and the almost sculptural sense of volume, can all be detected in the art of the second half of the 13th century (Chatzidakis 1977-79, p. 160, pls. 47, 60). Some of the technical features of the icon of St. Demetrius in the Monastery of Vatopedi (Chatzidakis 1967, fig. 60), the wall paintings of Ayios Dimitrios in Makrychori, Euboea (1302/3, Ioannou 1959, fig. 15. Mouriki 1978, p. 76), and the wall paintings in the Church of the Panayia at Kalamoti, on Chios (between 1295 and 1320, Mouriki 1978, p. 78, fig. 51). The silver ground and halo are related to certain technical features of Byzantine painting that can be detected from the 12th century onwards in icons from Cyprus, Veria, Kastoria and Macedonia in general. In Kastoria this technique continued without interruption until the 15th century. Another icon in the Kastoria Archaeological Collection is attributed to the painter of the icon of Christ. This is an icon of the Ayioi Anargy-

roi (Chatzidakis 1966 (1), pl. 40α-β), which has certain technical and stylistic features in common with the icon of Christ Pantocrator.

Provenance. Church of Ayios Nikolaos in the parish of Ayios Loukas, Kastoria.
Conservation. Ph. Zachariou (1972).
Bibliography. Affreschi e icone 1986, no. 31, pp. 68-69. From Byzantium to El Greco 1987, no. 14, pp. 77, 155.

E. N. T.

16

Double-sided Icon
A. The Virgin Hodegetria
Beginning of the 14th century
B. The Virgin Hodegetria
Third quarter of the 16th century
115×85 cm
Veria. Archaeological Museum, 117

A. The Virgin is shown half-length, in the most common type of the Hodegetria. She holds herself upright and looks directly towards the viewer. She supports the Christ Child with her left arm and raises her right hand to point at him. She is wearing a purple maphorion with a yellow-brown edging. There is a little blue in her head-dress and right sleeve. Christ, seated as though on a throne, extends his hand in benediction, and holds a closed scroll. The drapery of the yellow-brown chiton and himation is relieved by the use of ochre to suggest gold webbing. The delicate physical features of the faces, with their firm lines and bright surfaces, attest to the artistic maturity of the painter and his deep knowledge of human nature. The fact that the icon is dated to the beginning of the 14th century and that it comes from the Church of Christos in Veria, and a comparison of the painting with the wall paintings of this church both suggest that it is to be assigned to the oeuvre of Georgios Kalliergis, the 'best painter in all Thessaly' (as he describes himself in a painting in the church).

B. The Virgin is shown in much the same form as the one on the other side, and has the inscription H ΠΑ-ΜΑΚΑΡΗCΤΟC. Despite a certain roughness in the handling of the drapery, the work is impressive for the exceptionally careful treatment of the faces, with their contrasts between light and shade. The anonymous painter of this icon is thought to be responsible for some of the best 16th-century icons and wall paintings in Veria. Any resemblance to the Cretan painting of this period is merely superficial; the roots of the painting represented by the icon are to be sought in northern Greece.

Provenance. The Church of Christos in Veria.
Conservation. A. Margaritoff.
Bibliography. Byzantine Art 1964, no. 221, p. 264. Chatzidakis 1965 (1), p. 13, pl. 11α-β. Xyngopoulos 1967, p. 77, fig. 3. Talbot Rice 1968, p. 115, pl. 101. Byzantine Frescoes 1976, no. 102, p. 47. Papazotos 1980, pp. 167ff. Byzantine Art 1986, no. 79, pp. 76-77. Affreschi e icone 1986, no. 32, pp. 70, 71. From Byzantium to El Greco 1987, no. 15, pp. 78-79, 156.

Th. P.

21

St. Matthew
First half of the 14th century
c. **62×46 cm**
USA. Private Collection

Matthew, inscribed Ο ΑΓΙΟC-ΜΑΤ-ΘΑΙΟC, is portrayed half-length, turning slightly toward his left. Dressed in a full burgundy himation, with soft, angular highlights, over a bluish-green chiton with a gilded clavus, the Evangelist inclines his head downward, as if he were lost in thought. With his right hand he grasps a large manuscript (his Gospel) bound in an elaborate gilt cover, to whose upper corner he gently touches his open left hand. Matthew's grey beard falls in a few thick corkscrew curls; his head, set atop a thick, short neck, is distinguished by its sculptural three-dimensionality. Noteworthy also is the elaborate punched decoration in the halo and frame.

This panel is one of a set of at least six icons interrelated through figure style, punched background decoration, dimensions, and provenance (cf. cat. nos. 20 and 22; and Temple 1982, no. 31). Within that group, which in turn breaks down into at least two subsets, this panel is most closely linked to the icon of St. Mark (cat. no. 22), now in the same private collection; the two are virtually mirror images of one another.

That this panel – with the others – belongs to the 14th century is clear from the dramatic inflation of neck, shoulders, and drapery, and from the sculptural modelling of the facial features; together they create a sense of tension and restrained power that characterizes much of the best in Palaeologan art. More specifically, there is much to connect this Evangelist with its counterpart in the Great Deesis of the Chilandari Monastery on Mount Athos, which is usually dated around mid-century (Weitzmann 1982 (1), p. 188). Yet at the same time, the greater tension and volume in the face, upper torso, and right hand of this Matthew recall the earlier, more forceful style of the Kariye Djami murals (*c.* 1320), and therefore suggest a dating in the first half of the century – in contrast to the more fleeting highlights and the softer drapery, hair, and flesh modelling characteristic of the later Chilandari panels (cf. Weitzmann 1983 (1), pp. 16ff.).

As for localization, the punchwork suggests Cyprus (cf. Papageorgiou 1969, pp. 40, 65), although specific parallels for figure style from the early part of the 14th century have not appeared from the island. Instead, a case might be made that these panels are the early Palaeologan counterparts to the later Great Deesis icons (Gabriel, Peter, and John the Baptist) from the Church of the Virgin Chrysaliniotissa in Nicosia, usually dated toward the end of the century (Papageorgiou 1969, pp. 31, 33, 40. Byzantine Icons 1976, nos. 23-25).

St. Matthew and its related panels were likely set into an iconostasis, where, like their Chilandari and Nicosia counterparts, they would have formed part of a Great Deesis.

Bibliography. Roozemund 1981, pp. 18ff. Temple 1982, p. 85.

G. V.

22

St. Mark
First half of the 14th century
63.5×47.5 cm
USA. Private Collection

Mark, inscribed O AΓIOC-MAPKOC, is portrayed half-length, turning slightly toward his right. He wears a voluminous green himation over a burgundy chiton with a black (formerly gilded?) clavus. In his left hand he clutches a large manuscript (his Gospel) with elaborate binding, whereas his right hand is raised toward his chin, two fingers and thumb extended (very tentatively) to support a large reed pen. Noteworthy is the tense musculature of the face, which is emphasized by a schematic pattern of linear highlights, and the elaborate punched decoration of halo and boarder. The panel is generally well preserved, although surface wear over time has robbed the drapery of nearly all its highlighting.

This panel is one of a set of at least six icons interrelated through figure style, punched background decoration, dimensions, and provenance (cf. cat. nos. 20 and 21; and Temple 1982, no. 31). Within that group, which itself breaks down into two or more subsets, it is most closely linked to the icon cat. no. 21 – a St. Matthew panel in the same private collection, which is virtually its mirror image.

For the dating, localization, and original function of this icon, see cat. no. 21.

Bibliography. Byzantine Icons 1979, no. 32. Temple 1982, no. 32.

G. V.

23

Double-sided Icon
with smaller icon inlaid
A. Christ with Angels, Apostles
and Saints
B. The Crucifixion
Middle of the 14th
and end of the 15th centuries
98×71 cm
Thessalonike. Monastery of Vlatadon,
Sacristy.

The double-sided icon has a small icon inlaid on the front, which has decoration in two registers. In the upper register, beneath a slightly raised arch, is a portrayal of Christ Pantocrator flanked by the venerating archangels Michael and Gabriel. There are long inscriptions elucidating the dogmatic significance of the representation. In the top left corner of the frame: AΓIOC AΓIOC AΓIOC KYPIOC CABA/OΘ ΠΛHPHC [O OY-PANOC KAI H] / ΓH T(HC) / ΔO-ΞI[C] / COY / ΩCANA EN T(OIC)/ YΨICTIC and the top right of the frame: EYΛOΓHMENOC O EPXO/-MEN(OC) EN ONO[M]ATI / KYPIOY. Ω]CA[NNA O EN] THC [YΨICTOIC] (Holy, holy, holy, Lord of Sabaoth, Heaven and Earth are full of thy Glory, Hosanna in the highest; Blessed is he that cometh in the name of the Lord, Hosanna in the highest). The text is from the Epinikios hymn, sung during the Liturgy at the moment of the communion. In the top right corner of the icon is the inscription [O BACIΛEYC TΩN OY]PANΩN (The King of Heaven), and at either side of Christ's head: I(HCOY)C X(PICTO)C - O I/Ω/ME/N(OC) / [ΠA]/CAN / NO/-CON (Jesus Christ, who healeth all thy diseases), an extract from Psalm 103.3, sung during the Morning Liturgy. The portrayal of Christ between the two archangels is a reproduction of the composition that used to adorn the sanctuary apse in some churches; the scene has an apocalyptic content and is inspired by the prayer recited secretly by the priest during the Liturgy, before the Epinikios hymn. It is the majestic portrayal of Christ in his heavenly glory, being worshipped by the angels: Christ the king of Heaven, as the half-preserved inscriptions inform us.

The lower register of the small icon has a depiction of the Virgin Hodegetria, flanked by the archangel Michael, who is represented in an attitude of prayer, and St. John the Baptist, who has his right hand raised in a gesture of speech and holds in his left an open scroll with the inscription ΙΔΕ Ο Α/Μ[Ν]Ο(C) ΤΟΥ / Θ(ΕΟ)Υ Ο ΑΙ/Ρ[ΩΝ] (Behold the Lamb of God, which taketh away) (John 1.29). This composition is an allegorical representation of the Service of the Proskomide – which refers to the Incarnation and the Passion of Christ – for, according to the Byzantine liturgical texts, the bread of the oblation for the Eucharist symbolizes the Virgin, who bears in her womb the Son of God. The presence of St. John the Baptist may be interpreted as a symbol of the priest conducting the Service of the Proskomide who, during the preparation of the Holy Gifts reads the passage from the Gospel written here on the scroll; the archangel Michael represents the deacon who assists in the celebration. This interpretation is consistent with the ideas of some of the leading Byzantine theologian (Pseudo-Germanos, Symeon of Thessalonike).

This connection between the two compositions, and the doctrinal interpretation of them indicates that they were an allegorical reference to the Incarnation, the Passion of Christ, and his heavenly Glory, which is consonant with the range of subjects preferred by 14th-century painting. The painterly modelling of the figures, with soft chiaroscuro and a few highlights is also characteristic of a group of works from the middle of this century.

The large icon, in which this small one is inlaid, has a scene of the Crucifixion on the reverse; the front side is divided, into three registers containing Christ Pantocrator between the archangels Michael and Gabriel, the Apostles Peter and Paul, and the military saints George, Theodore the Tiro and Demetrius. The representations on both sides are closely related, in terms of their iconography and doctrinal significance, with those in the small icon. The portrayal of the Pantocrator accompanied by the archangels, the leading apostles and the military saints-defenders of the Faith on the front of the icon repeats in greater detail the ideas expressed in the upper register of the small icon; and the Crucifixion translates into visual terms the Incarnation and the Passion of Christ to which symbolic reference is made in the lower register of the small icon. The subjects of both icons, with their related iconography and doctrinal significance, form an indivisible whole referring to the Passion and Glory of Christ.

A number of features suggest that the large icon may be dated to the end of the 15th century: the modelling of the figures, with the strong contrasts between light and dark surfaces and white highlights applied in a standard system of lines; the severe character of the figures; the linear treatment of the drapery and the restricted number of colours, of a metallic texture.

The complex range of subjects illustrated in the icon, with their high theological meaning, was the product of educated religious circles. This is supported by the portrayal on the reverse of the monk who dedicated it. The subject matter and the fact that it was a processional icon suggest that it was probably the main devotional icon of the Monastery of Vlatadon, which was dedicated to Christ Pantocrator.

Conservation. Ph. Zachariou.
Bibliography. Xyngopoulos 1948, pp. 114ff. Byzantine Art 1964, no. 199, p. 253. Tourta 1977, pp. 133ff. Byzantine Art 1986, no. 83, pp. 82-83. Affreschi e icone 1986, no. 36, p. 75. From Byzantium to El Greco 1987, no. 21, pp. 86-87, 160.

A. T.

24

The Virgin Hodegetria
Second half of the 14th century
90×71 cm
Thessalonike. Monastery of Vlatadon, Sacristy

A work of high quality executed in the spirit of Constantinopolitan painting. From a stylistic point of view, the icon has very close affinities with the wall paintings recently uncovered in the nave and the south chapel of the katholikon of the Monastery of Vla-tadon. It was probably produced by the same workshop and, like the wall paintings, must have been painted in the period 1360-1380, not in the 15th century, as was previously thought to be the case.

Conservation. Byzantine Museum laboratories (N. Nomikos) (1985).
Bibliography. Stoyoglou 1971, pp. 132ff. Byzantine Art 1986, no. 84, p. 83. Affreschi e icone 1986, no. 37, p. 76. From Byzantium to El Greco 1987, no. 24, pp. 90, 162.

Ch. M.-T.

25

Six scenes from the Passion
Third quarter of the 14th century
51×41 cm
Thessalonike. Monastery of Vlatadon. Sacristy

The icon is divided into three registers, in which are depicted six scenes from the Passion, in chronological order. The original painting on some of these (The Agony in the Garden, the Flagellation and the Procession to Calvary) was damaged and clumsily repaired at a later period.

In the scene of the Last Supper, Christ sits at the left end of the table. He is blessing with his right hand and the other rests on the back of John, who has fallen into his arms at the announcement of the coming betrayal. The other disciples are discussing the event, calmly talking in pairs. In the centre of the table, Judas is trying to reach a plate, with a clumsy movement. In the Washing of the Feet, Christ is wiping the feet of Peter, who is sitting on a high bench with four other disciples. The others are standing behind it, with the exception of one who is kneeling in front of it, untying his sandal. In the Agony in the Garden, there are two representations of Christ. At the left, he is kneeling in prayer, with the angel who came to strengthen in his agony (Luke 22.43) flying above him. At the right, he is depicted standing, with the sleeping disciples; he is rebuking Peter, who has woken and is shown at the left of the closed group, for their unconcern. The core of the Betrayal is the kissing of Christ and Judas. All around them are soldiers with raised clubs. At the extreme right, a group of Jews holding torches are following events. In the Flagellation, Christ is tied to a column, while the two torturers are circling round him with powerful movements. This type of the Flagellation, the main feature of which is the column to which Christ is bound, makes its appearance in Byzantine painting in the 14th century. It seems to have been created under the influence of Constantinople, where the column and rods of the Flagellation were worshipped; they were kept in the Church of SS Apostles in Constantinople. The Procession to Calvary is organized around the central figure of Christ, who is bound and is being dragged along by a soldier. The figures behind the soldier are possibly the women who followed Christ to Golgotha. At the end of the procession is Simon of Cyrene carrying the cross.

The characteristic features of the

modelling of the figures are the lack of any outlines and the rendering of the flesh by means of light and dark tones. Lit areas of a brown-pink colour are used on the brown-green of the underpaint, and white lines, of different lengths and thicknesses, are applied with free brush-strokes to highlight the prominent parts of the flesh. The flowing drapery is rendered by means of different tones of the same colour, or by colour contrasts. The cobalt blue that is the main determinant of the colour harmonies, together with the gold of the background, creates a transcendental atmosphere, enlivened by the vermillion red.

The iconographical features of the scenes are the avoidance of prolix narrative, the economical use of the elements defining the space, and the restriction of the figures to those entirely essential; these, and the tranquil, restrained air of the figures betray the hand of a painter who was reluctant to make use of the innovations introduced into early Palaeologan art, and adhered closely to earlier models. The academic quality of the work is consistent with the predominant trends of middle of the 14th-century painting.

The icon has close similarities with relatively securely dated works, such as the Incredulity of Thomas in the Monastery of the Metamorphosis at Meteora, with the portraits of Maria Palaeologina and Thomas Preliubović, the Serbian Despot of Ioannina from 1361-1384 (Xyngopoulos 1964-65, pp. 53ff.); and the miniature of the Transfiguration in the manuscript Par. gr. 1242, which contains theological writings by John Cantacouzenos, and which was decorated between 1372 and 1375 (Talbot Rice 1959, pl. XXXIX); these similarities suggest a dating to the third quarter of the 14th century. This is supported by the close relationship between the icon and the wall paintings recently discovered in the katholikon of the Monastery of Vlatadon; these have been dated to between 1360 and 1380,

on the basis of the depiction in them of Gregorios Palamas, who died in 1359 and was sanctified in 1368 (Mavropoulou-Tsioumi 1985, pp. 231ff.). The source of inspiration for the painter of this icon was very probably an earlier illustrated manuscript, as is clear from the choice and arrangement of the scenes, the outmoded iconography, and the treatment of them, which recalls that of miniature painting.

Provenance. The Monastery of Vlatadon, Thessalonike.

Conservation. Ph. Zachariou (1977).

Bibliography. Tourta 1982, pp. 154-179. Byzantine Art 1986, no. 85, pp. 80-81, 83. Affreschi e icone 1986, no. 38, pp. 76-77. From Byzantium to El Greco 1987, no. 22, pp. 88, 160.

A. T.

26

The Ressurection
Third quarter of the 14th century
36×26.5 cm
Baltimore. The Walters Art Gallery, 37.751

Christ, highlighted with a dense grid of gold striations and surrounded by a radiating mandorla, descends into Hades to free the righteous of the Old Testament. With his right hand he lifts the kneeling Adam from a sarcophagus; just behind are John the Baptist, and Kings Solomon and David, as well as an undifferentiated group of the righteous. As counterpart to Adam on the right, Eve kneels in supplication just above her own tomb; in the dense crowd behind her only the youthful Abel (pointing) and Moses (with the Tablets of the Law) are clearly identifiable.

In the lower portion of the panel two sequential narrative scenes appear. On the left, Mary Magdalene and the other Mary, on the evening of the Crucifixion, look mournfully at the tomb in which Christ has been buried; 'and they were sitting opposite the grave' (Matthew 27.61) is inscribed beside them. On the right they reappear, two days later, confronted by the angel at the empty grave with the news that Christ has risen from the dead; 'Mary Magdalene and the other Mary came to see where he was buried' (Matthew 28.2) is inscribed between angel and women. Clearly the sequence was carefully chosen, since it culminates in the Resurrection (Anastasis), above, which is taking place more or less as the angel speaks. And although highly unusual for this scene, such narrative elaboration and symbolic complexity is characteristic of Palaeologan art generally.

This type of Resurrection, in which Christ grasps the kneeling Adam, developed after the 11th century (Kartsonis 1986, pp. 204ff.). By the early 14th century, such innovations as Eve's placement opposite Adam (as opposed to behind him) emphas-

ized her individual plea for salvation. A comparison between the angular outline of Adam's drapery in the Walters panel and (for example) Eve's in the Resurrection of the Kariye Djami (of *c.* 1320; Underwood 1967, no. 201, pls. 343, 359) leaves no doubt that the Baltimore icon should be placed in the 14th century. Its facial types also bear considerable resemblance to their counterparts in the Kariye Djami murals (e.g. the righteous at the right of the Resurrection fresco). A more specific date is suggested by the icon's composition. An increase in the number of figures, a tendency toward 'anecdotal' narrative, an elaboration of setting, and a decrease in both absolute panel size and the proportion between figures and setting all suggest that the Walters Resurrection should be dated after the Resurrection icon from the Church of St. Clement at Ochrid (Gouma-Peterson 1984-85, fig. 5: 'beginning of the 14th c.'), which maintains the more 'heroic' narrative mode and the clearer spatial relationships characteristic of early Palaeologan painting. An Incredulity of St. Thomas icon from Meteora (dated between 1359 and 1384 due to the inclusion of the portrait of a Byzantine princess; Gouma-Peterson 1984-85, pp. 52ff., fig. 11) offers parallels in composition, setting, and figural proportion to suggest that the Walters Resurrection should be placed in the third quarter of the 14th century.

Technical research has revealed evidence of an early restoration of this panel, probably within a hundred years of its original manufacture (M. Sebera in Gouma-Peterson 1984-85, pp. 57ff.). Repainting followed the compositional lines of the original painting, and in some cases covered an original ultramarine glaze. Christ's bright blue tunic, the intense red in Eve's garments (and in those of the kings), as well as the purple and orange in the background are all part of that restoration. Thalia Gouma-Peterson has suggested that this renovation was completed in Russia around 1470, where the icon could have travelled after its production in Greece but reuse could also have occured in Crete or Venice at the time. This small icon was probably origi-nally one of the series of Great Feast (Dodekaorton) icons that would have lined the epistyle beam of an iconostasis.

Bibliography. Gouma-Peterson 1984-85, pp. 48-61.

G. K.

27

The Last Judgment
Middle of the 14th century
64×66 cm
Athens. Kanellopoulos Museum

Egg tempera on wood. The icon has a scene of the Last Judgment, a composition that draws iconographical elements both from the Scriptures (the Vision of Daniel, Psalms of David, Gospels according to St. Mark and St. Luke and the Revelation of St. John) and from the Patristic Texts (St. Basil, Discourse on the Coming Judgment). The upper register has a representation of the Deesis with Christ in a mandorla, the Virgin and St. John the Baptist to the right and left of him, the twelve apostles, and angels. The rest of the composition is divided by the river of fire in the middle into two roughly vertical sections. At the left are two bands containing groups of the righteous at the top, with Paradise and the Preparation of the Throne below them. At the right is the Weighing of the Souls, with the Earth (in the form of a woman wearing a conical head-dress of leaves) and the Sea (in the form of a half-naked woman seated on a sea-monster, carrying a model of a boat), who are giving up their dead, and the sinners being led into the 'Gehenna of fire' to be judged. At the bottom, between the Preparation of the Throne and the river of fire, the two donors of the icon pray for their souls. The inscription reads: Δέησις τοῦ δούλου τοῦ Θεοῦ Ἰωάννου (Prayer of the servant of the Lord, John).

The representation follows the basic arrangement of the subject as arleady formulated in the first depictions of it, both in monumental painting (fresco in the Panayia ton Chalkeon in Thessalonike, 1028) and in miniature art (miniatures, fol. 51^v and 93^v in the Paris manuscript gr. 74, ivory plaque in the Victoria and Albert Museum, London, 11th century), and in icons (wing of a polyptych from Sinai, 11th century). The eschatological content of the composition still retained its immediacy in the Palaeologan period (1261-1543), and was painted in a large number of churches (the Metropolis at Mistra, Gračanica, Dečani etc.). The present icon of the Last Judgment contains a number of iconographic and stylistic elements recognizably from this period (the Palaeologan), to which it should be dated.

Provenance. Georgiadis Collection, Thessalonike.
Bibliography. Byzantine Art 1964, no. 264, pp. 283ff. Brenk 1966, pp. 79ff. Lexicon 1972, col. 513ff. Splendeur de Byzance 1982, no. 6, p. 41. Brouskari 1985, fig. p. 115, pp. 113ff. Affreschi e icone 1986, no. 39, p. 78.

M. V.

St. Nicholas
Last quarter of the 14th century
129×78 cm
Kastoria. Archaeological Collection

The saint is depicted frontally at half length, wearing bishop's robes. He makes a benediction and holds a closed book.

Although large areas of colour have been lost, the size of the saint and the warmth of the colouring still make this an impressive work. The design is vigorous, but the saint's face has a translucent quality, as though lit by an inner light, and evokes in the believer a feeling of tranquility and security. The firmness of line and the calculated use of thinly applied layers of colour, without any sudden, abrupt transitions, emphasize the saint's human quality. This work has many affinities with the monumental painting of the early Palaeologan period, at the end of the 13th century. The revival of the values and achievements of the painting of that period

at a time after the middle of the 14th century is an indication of the general concern to underpin religious values at a historical period of crisis and political instability in Byzantium. The suggestion that the icon of St. Nicholas should be dated to the final quarter of the 14th century is supported by a comparison with more accurately dated works of art from the second half of the 14th century, such as the wall paintings in the Monastery of the Pantocrator on Mount Athos (1360-70), of the Church of Prophet Elias in Thessalonike, and of the Church of St. Andrew near Skopje (1388/9).

Provenance. From a church in Kastoria.
Conservation. Ph. Zachariou.
Bibliography. Byzantine Frescoes 1976, no. 110, p. 78. Affreschi e icone 1986, no. 41, pp. 80, 82. From Byzantium to El Greco 1987, no. 25, pp. 91, 162.

Th. P.

Christ Pantocrator
c. **1400**
27×20 cm
Athens. Byzantine Museum, T. 185

The painting is damaged. Christ, in the type of the Pantocrator, has the title O CΩ-THP (The Saviour). The austere figure, with its dark colours, illuminated by the gold light of the ground, has all the force of its monumental model.

A work of artistic quality with the hallmarks of the painting of the turn of the 14th century, it has certain stylistic features in common with an icon of the Virgin in the Sinai Monastery, where similar small-scale icons of Christ and the Virgin are to be found (Sotiriou 1956, 1958, no. 226, pp. 198ff., and nos. 227-229, pp. 199ff.).

Provenance. Acquired in 1985.
Conservation. Byzantine Museum laboratories (Th. Papageorgiou) (1985).
Bibliography. Byzantine Art 1986, no. 87, p. 85. Affreschi e icone 1986, no. 43, pp. 82, 83. From Byzantium to El Greco 1987, no. 26, pp. 92, 163.

M. A.-P.

Christ the Wisdom of God
End of the 14th century
156×100 cm
Athens. Byzantine Museum, T. 185

A bust of Christ in the type of the Pantocrator. He is blessing with his left hand, and in his right holds an open Gospel book with a text.

The imposing figure of Christ is treated in terms of contrasting light and dark surfaces, with white highlights on the prominent cheek-bones, and on the forehead, over the eyebrows. The beard and the hair are worked with fine parallel lines. The volumes of the face seem to stand out almost as though in relief, drawing attention to an unattractiveness that is complemented by the anxious expression of the face.

These features are known in a series of Palaeologan paintings of a strongly anti-classical character which are found at the end of the 14th century in various parts of the Empire, alongside the more classical painting of the period represented in the Peribleptos at Mistra (Chatzidakis 1974 (4). A characteristic of works in this style is the halo, painted as though in relief, as in the Akra Tapeinosis (From Byzantium to El Greco 1987, no. 27),

to render the true relief haloes in 14th-century Macedonian icons like the icon of Christ in the Byzantine Museum.

Christ's anxious expression and prominent features are similar to those in a group of icons depicting the same subject dated to the last quarter of the 14th century, which includes the icon of Christ in the National Museum of Stockholm (Byzantine Art 1964, no. 202) and especially the icon of Christ Zoodotis (Life-giver) in Skopje painted by the archbishop John (1393/4) (Miljković-Pepek 1972, pp. 247-248, fig. 8; cf. also Chatzidakis-Babić 1983, fig. p. 192).

The large size of this icon and its artistic quality made it a fitting decoration of the iconostasis of the Church of Ayia Sophia in Thessalonike, from which it comes.

Provenance. The Church of Ayia Sophia, Thessalonike.
Conservation. Ph. Kontoglou (1930), A. Margaritoff (1959).
Bibliography. Sotiriou 1931, p. 80. Sotiriou 1956, p. 17, pl. XX. Chatzidakis 1960, p. 11, pls. 6-7. Chatzidakis 1969, p. 8. Chatzidakis 1974 (3), p. 336, fig. 14. Chatzidakis 1974 (4), p. 184, fig. 18. Chatzidakis 1977 (1), pp. 83-84. Chatzidakis-Babić 1983, p. 192. From Byzantium to El Greco 1987, no. 20, pp. 85, 159-160.
N. Ch.

31

The Nativity
c. 1400
58.5×49.5 cm
Kastoria. Archaeological Collection, 50

The icon of the Nativity comes from the Dodekaorton on the iconostasis of the Church of the Ayioi Treis (1401) in Kastoria. The Dodekaorton consisted of a group of icons depicting scenes from the life of Christ in chronological order; five other icons survive from it, and are presented in this exhibition: the Presentation in

the Temple (cat. no. 32), Raising of Lazarus (cat. no. 33), Entry into Jerusalem (cat. no. 34), Transfiguration (cat. no. 35), and the Dormition of the Virgin (cat. no. 36). Another icon from this group, with a scene of the Ascension, has only a few surviving fragments of the representation.

The icon of the Nativity, like all the other icons from the Dodekaorton in the Church of the Ayioi Treis, is painted on a panel hollowed out to form a raised frame, on which is painted a red border. Another feature common to the icons from the Kastoria Dodekaorton is the use of silver paint instead of gold for the backgrounds of the icons and the haloes. This is a feature local to icons of Veria, Kastoria, Ochrid and also of Cyprus, from the 12th century onwards.

The scene is dominated by the cave, within which the Virgin is portrayed lying diagonally on a pallet; next to her is the crib with the Christ Child and the animals keeping him warm with their breath. Over the crib is the star which, according to the Gospel and the ecclesiastical literature led the Magi to Bethlehem. The Magi are depicted worshipping the child to the right, inside the cave. The secondary scenes that accompany and complete the representation of the Nativity are disposed around the main scene. At the bottom left is Joseph, reflective and isolated from the other figures in the scene. To Joseph's left is a depiction of the Bathing of the Child, which is a visual symbol of Christ's human nature, whereas the isolated position occupied by the reflective figure of Joseph derives from the tendency to emphasize the mystery of the divine incarnation. At the top left, three angels are glorifying, in the heavens, the Nativity of Christ, while, to the right the seated shepherd who is receiving the glad tidings from the angel is the human witness of the incarnation of the Son of God.

The basic conception of the subject, and the types of the individual figures are borrowed from the iconography of the Nativity in the Church of Ayios Athanasios tou Mouzaki in Kastoria (1383/4) (Pelekanidis 1953, pl. 146), which had a decisive influence on the artistic production of Kastoria and the wider area of Macedonia at the turn of the 14th-15th centuries.

For the technical and stylistic features of the icon, see the icon of the Dormition of the Virgin (cat. no. 36).

Provenance. Kastoria, Church of the Ayioi Treis.
Conservation. Ph. Zachariou (1973).
Bibliography. Unpublished.

E. N. T.

32

The Presentation in the Temple
c. 1400
57.5×49 cm
Kastoria. Archaeological Collection, 46

The scene unfolds before an imposing, complex building, symbolizing the Temple in Jerusalem to which the Virgin went with Joseph to dedicate Christ to God and make a sacrifice, to fulfil the requirements of the Mosaic law.

The Virgin is portrayed holding Christ in her arms and moving towards the aged Symeon, who is standing on a stepped plinth, ready to receive Christ in his outstretched arms. The Virgin is accompanied by Joseph, who is holding two doves, for the sacrifice to God. Behind Symeon, the prophetess Anna with a movement of her arm confirms the reality of the incarnation of the Word of God.

From an iconographic point of view, the artist follows the very widespread iconographic type of the subject, in which the Virgin, and not Symeon, is holding the Infant. This feature, along with the painting of Symeon on a high plinth, and the fact that the scene is framed by a complex building, indicates that the iconography of this icon had its origins in early 14th-century works, such as the wall painting of the Presentation in the Temple in the Church of Christos at Veria (1315) (Pelekanidis 1973, pl. 17). This iconographic type was local to monuments from the second half of the 14th century in Kastoria (Ayios

Athanasios tou Mouzaki, 1383/4, Djurić 1975, fig. 42) and the surrounding area (Prespa, Mali Grad, 1368/9, Djurić 1975, fig. 43), which came under the influence of the artistic output of the Kastoria workshops. For the technical and stylistic features of the icon, see the icon of the Dormition of the Virgin (cat. no. 36).

Provenance. Kastoria, Church of the Ayioi Treis.
Conservation. Ph. Zachariou (1973).
Bibliography. Unpublished.

E. N. T.

33

The Raising of Lazarus
c. 1400
56×48 cm
Kastoria. Archaeological Collection, 45

The composition consists of two carefully balanced groups, linked by the gestures of Christ and the Jews and by the pose and gestures of Mary and Martha, who are shown in the foreground.

Christ is portrayed moving to the right at the head of a group of apostles who accompany him, with the apostle Peter in the foreground. Lazarus is depicted on the right, in a tomb with a pediment, the covering slab of which has fallen away to the right; he is wrapped in a winding-sheet, the end of which is held by a young servant. Behind the servant, and next to Lazarus, is a group of Jews, one of whom makes a gesture, another touches his beard, and a third holds his hand to his nose against the smell of the open tomb. The sisters of Lazarus are shown kneeling in worship before Christ. Two rocks rise in stages in the background and lean outwards, revealing the city of Bethany in the distance.

This simple iconographic scheme is a revival in the 14th century of late Comnenian types (Hadermann-Misguich 1975, figs. 57-58), and is close to the spirit of the scenes of the Four gospels from the Monastery of Iviron (Millet 1916, fig. 212), in the Church of Christos at Veria (Pelekanidis 1973, fig. 20), in Cretan monuments from the end of the 14th century (Kalokyris 1973, figs. 28-29), and in St. Sophia in Trebizond (Millet 1916, fig. 231). The present icon differs from icons of the so-called Macedonian School, such as the paintings at Arilje (Zivcović 1970, fig. 19), in the Church of St. Clement at Ochrid (Millet - Frolow 1962, pl. 3,3), and in that of Ayios Nikolaos Orphanos in Thessalonike (Xyngopoulos 1964, pl. 20), in that Lazarus is not shown rising from a sarcophagus placed horizontally on the ground, but follows an earlier model and stands upright in a tomb built in the form of a temple within the rock.

For the technical and stylistic features of the icon, see the icon of the Dormition of the Virgin (cat. no. 36).

Provenance. Kastoria, Church of the Ayioi Treis.
Conservation. Ph. Zachariou (1973).
Bibliography. Tsigaridas 1972, p. 572, pl. 512α. Affreschi e icone 1986, no. 44, pp. 84-85. From Byzantium to El Greco 1987, no. 28, pp. 94, 164.

E. N. T.

34

The Entry into Jerusalem
c. 1400
57×49 cm
Kastoria. Archaeological Collection, 51

Christ is depicted sitting on an ass, moving to the right. He holds a closed scroll in his left hand, and his right hand is extended in a gesture of blessing. His head is turned to the group of apostles following him, and he is talking to Peter, who gesticulates vigorously. Christ and the apostles stand out against the mass of the Mount of Olives that rises abruptly in the background. On the right, in front of the gate in the wall of Jerusalem, a crowd of Jews, both men and women, has come out of the city to meet Christ. In front of this group of Jews, a child is holding a palm branch, and a second child is shown in the branches of a tree. The circular building that can be seen in the city of Jerusalem is the Church of the Anastasis.

The composition involves only a limited number of figures, symmetrically balanced around the central figure of Christ, and follows a simple iconographic scheme, the successor in the 14th century to the iconography tradition of the late Comnenian period (Hadermann-Misguich 1975, fig. 61). A similar iconographic scheme in the 14th century is found in the Church of Ayios Nikolaos Orphanos in Thessalonike (Xyngopoulos 1964, fig. 23), the Church of Christos at Veria (Pelekanidis 1973, pl. 21), in the monastery at Marko (Millet-Velmans 1969, fig. 166), and in 15th-century monuments in Prespa and Ochrid (Subotić 1980, figs. 18, 43 and 111, pl. 46).

For the technical and stylistic features of the icon, see the icon of the Dormition of the Virgin (cat. no. 36).

Provenance. Kastoria, Church of the Ayioi Treis.

Conservation. Ph. Zachariou (1973).

Bibliography. Affreschi e icone 1986, no. 45, pp. 86-87. From Byzantium to El Greco 1987, no. 29, pp. 95, 165.

E. N. T.

35

The Transfiguration
c. 1400
57×49 cm
Kastoria. Archaeological Collection, 49

Christ is portrayed at the summit of mount Thabor, within a gloria that can be made out with some difficulty. He is dressed in white, in accordance with the Gospel (Mark 9.2-13). He is blessing with his right hand, and holds a closed scroll in his left. On high, steep rocks either side of Christ are depicted the venerating prophets Elijah and Moses, to the left and right respectively, the latter holding the Tablets of the Law.

At the bottom of the icon the three apostles Peter, John and James are shown in dramatic postures, revealing their fear at the revelation of the 'unapproachable glory', according to the Gospel story (Matthew 17.1-8).

From the point of view of iconography, the icon follows the traditional iconography of the subject, though the violent, dramatic postures and gestures of the apostles are especially associated with the art of the 13th and early 14th centuries (see the Protaton on Mount Athos, the katholikon of the Monastery of Chelandari, the Church of Christos at Veria, etc.), which aspired to emphasize the dramatic and realistic elements in the scene.

For the technical and stylistic features of the icon, see the icon of the Dormition of the Virgin (cat. no. 36).

Provenance. Kastoria, Church of the Ayioi Treis.

Conservation. Ph. Zachariou (1973).

Bibliography. Unpublished.

E. N. T.

36

The Dormition
c. 1400
56.5×40.5 cm
Kastoria. Archaeological Collection, 48

The Virgin is portrayed in death on a luxurious bed covered with a white, embroidered sheet. Christ is painted standing behind the bed, within a radiant mandorla, holding in his hands the soul of the Virgin in the form of a baby wrapped in swaddling clothes. The Dormition of the Virgin is attended by the apostles, who are distributed in two groups within the scene, led by Paul on the right, and Peter, who holds a censer, on the left. The apostle John is portrayed behind the bed in a pose of reverent veneration. The group to the left includes three Church Fathers, two of whom are St. Dionysius the Areopagite and St. James the brother of the Lord. The scene is framed by two buildings, set obliquely in the background.

Iconographically, the scene follows a simple iconographic scheme, the basic elements of which are drawn by the artist from the iconographical tradition of the 14th century (the Church of Christos at Veria, Pelekanidis 1973, pl. 40; of Ayios Nikolaos Orphanos in Thessalonike, Tsitouridou 1986, pl. 30). This simplified version of the scene adopted in the Kastoria icon is to be found in monuments of the second half of the 14th century, such as the Church of the Panayia Phaneromeni in Kastoria (unpublished) and that of Ayioi Konstantinos and Eleni in Ochrid (*c.* 1400) (Grozdanov 1980, fig. 203). Some of the iconographic details and types are local to monuments of Kastoria from the second half of the 14th century (cf. the Church of Ayios Georgios tou Vounou, Tsigaridas 1985, pp. 386-389).

To summarize what has been said about the icons of the Dodekaorton of Kastoria, we may note that, in iconographic terms, almost all the icons follow a simple scheme, with its origins in the tradition of the late Comnenian period, which was revived in the 14th century (the churches of Ayios Nikolaos in Thessalonike, and that of Christos in Veria), which in their turn influenced the iconography of monuments of the second half of the 14th century. In developing the subjects, it is worth noting that the artist does not hesitate to go beyond the borders of the background and make use of the frames of the icons.

The compositions are simple and compact in their organization, and usually aspire to a symmetrical balance of the individual volumes in the scene. The figures included in the scenes are slender, almost fleshless, with regular proportions, and, if exception is made of the apostles in the Transfiguration, are rendered in tranquil, almost conventional poses. Nevertheless, one of the main characteristics of the figures is their unattractiveness; there is a pronounced tendency towards realistic portraiture, and a certain intensity in their gaze. The faces are modelled in a soft, painterly manner, the predominant colours being the olive green of the underpaint and the red used liberally on the ochre of the cheeks. The drapery is generally developed rather simply, the artist showing no particular interest in rendering the volumes of the body. In some cases, indeed, the drapery is executed in a completely linear manner on the monochrome background. The impressive feature of the treatment of the garments, however, is the use of strong, vivid colours, particularly light red, light green, dark blue and orange. Strong colours are also used for the conventional rocky landscape and the buildings, with a preference for light green, olive green and blue-green.

The technical and stylistic features noted, which are common to all six icons from the Kastoria Dodekaorton, assign these pieces to the production of a local workshop, to which other icons from the Kastoria Archaeological Collection are attributed (Tsigaridas 1980-81, p. 286, pl. 76β). This workshop appears to have been involved in the decoration of the Church of the Ayioi Treis in Kastoria (1401) (Tsigaridas 1985-86, p. 384), for which the Dodekaorton icons in this exhibition were painted, and also in the decoration of the Church of the Panayia Phaneromeni (Tsigaridas 1985-86, p. 384). On the other hand, the expressionistic character of the unattractive figures, and the use of vivid, conflicting colours, assign this workshop to an anti-classical artistic current dating approximately from the late Comnenian period, the expressions of which can be recognized in monuments in Kastoria, and also the wider area of Macedonia at the end of the 14th and beginning of the 15th centuries. Finally, the frugality and austere character of the compositions, in which all narrative elements are removed, make the icons of the Kastoria Dodekaorton statements of the doctrinal truth of the Orthodox Church.

Provenance. Kastoria, Church of the Ayioi Treis.
Conservation. Ph. Zachariou (1973).
Bibliography. Unpublished.

E. N. T.

37

Epistyle of an Iconostasis
15th century
35×183 cm
Veria. Museum

The epistyle is a long, narrow piece of wood with an arcade carved in relief, beneath which are six scenes: the Annunciation, Nativity, Presentation in the Temple, Raising of Lazarus, Dormition of the Virgin and Ascension. Between the arches are small figures of prophets. The iconography has some local features in a few of the scenes: the bath at the left and the figure of Joseph at the right in the Nativity, and the figure of Lazarus arising from inside a sarcophagus. The prototype for both scenes may have been Ayios Athanasios tou Mouzaki in Kastoria (1355) (cf. Pelekanidis 1953, pls. 146 and 147). The Dormition has an arrangement similar to that of the Taxiarch and Ayios Georgios tou Kyritzi in Kastoria (Pelekanidis 1953, pls. 159 and 127). The heavy, inelegant figures fill the background, though some of them have certain reminiscences of Palaeologan charm (the Nativity). The choice of scenes does not betray any subtle theological thought, and the roughness of the working of the wood is typical of the local workshops of the area and period.

Conservation. Ph. Zachariou.
Bibliography. Byzantine Frescoes 1976, no. 90, p. 46.

M. Ch.

38

Double-sided Icon
A. St. Nicholas, 'Thermos Prostatis',
with scenes from his life
B. The Dormition of St. Nicholas
15th century
107×61 cm
Kastoria. Archaeological Collection

A. On this side of the icon the wood has been hollowed out so as to form slightly raised frames, within which are depicted scenes from the life of St. Nicholas, set in a broad band around all four sides. The panel in the centre has a full-length representation of the saint, wearing priestly vestments, blessing and holding a closed book. The scenes do not follow the chronological order of the narrative in the synaxarion. Although the story seems to begin in the top left corner and proceed to the right, two of the scenes on the top, the dream of Constantine the Great and the dream of the eparch, belong historically after the three scenes down the right side. Here too the narrative is out of sequence: the three generals offering gifts to the saint (top corner) in the narrative follows the saint rescuing them from imprisonment (St. Nicholas is seen stretching to snatch the executioner's sword), and their imprisonment. There follows a rare motif, involving a miracle 'of drought' after which comes one of the saint's miracles connected with the sea. The narrative continues from the top of the left side, and ends in the Dormition of the saint at the bottom.

The neutral background of the central panel (in which the figure of St. Nicholas is given prominence) and the subdued colours of his vestments are designed to draw attention to the face; here, the sure brush-strokes and control of colour have been deployed to create a portrait of a tranquil, reflective saint. This contrasts with the scenes of his life, in which the colours are clearer and more vivid, while the uncertainty of the drawing in general and the stylized representation of the clothes form a contrast with the sure lines of the figure of the saint in the centre. Although the characters in the scenes, executed in the manner of miniature painting, are portrayed with a certain skill and liveliness, this is not enough to offset this contrast. The eclecticism in the choice of painting styles reflects the fragmentation of ecumenical Byzantine art observable in the 15th century, which accounts for the independent activity of painters in the provincial urban centres. During this period, Kastoria was the home of one of the most important workshops in the Balkans.

B. Of the scene that originally covered the entire surface of the icon, only the central part now survives. It contains the relic of the saint on the death-bed, the figure of a chanter and part of the body of a figure clad in white.

Provenance. From the Church of Ayios Nikolaos tou Magaleiou (1485/6) in Kastoria.
Conservation. Ph. Zachariou.
Bibliography. Chatzidakis 1966-69, pp. 303ff. Zias 1966-69, pp. 277ff. Byzantine Frescoes 1976, no. 198, p. 77. Affreschi e icone 1986, no. 51, pp. 92-93.

Th. P.

39

**Dormition of the Virgin
and the Akathistos Hymn
First half of the 15th century
75×47.5 cm
Skopelos. Church of Zoodochos Pigi
in Livadi**

Gesso without canvas. The wood has been hollowed out to form eight arched panels in the centre and twenty two rectangular panels around the border, each with a raised frame. In these are miniature paintings of the Dormition of the Virgin, and the Assumption, and the twenty four stanzas of the Akathistos Hymn. The gold background of these miniature icons extends into the frame and to some extent illuminates the rather heavy, dark composition. The general articulation of the icon, with the distinctly arched, hollowed-out panels in the centre, is suggestive of Western influence. The Dormition is painted on a larger scale in the centre; above it is the Assumption, flanked by four small icons, each with three Apostles, coming 'from the ends of the earth' on clouds to attend the funeral. The compressed, balanced representation of the Dormition has some striking typological similarities with 15th-century Cretan icons (Chatzidakis 1962, no. 15, pp. 33ff., pl. 14, no. 16, pp. 35ff., pl. 15. Chatzidakis 1974 (1), p. 182, pl. IΓ´, 1): these can be seen in the main figures, and the form and decoration of the death-bed and candlesticks in the foreground. The Assumption, unusually, is an independent scene, set in a separate panel, with the open tomb at the bottom in a rocky landscape. The stanzas of the Akathistos Hymn encircle the border of the icon in regular order, starting at the top left, and culminate in the last two stanzas, in praise of the Virgin, which are given a prominent position below the Dormition. The choice and treatment of the iconographic types in these attest to a good model with interesting details, which

the anonymous painter has interpreted conscientiously, in a lively, expressive style. The stylistic features of the icon point to the late Palaeologan period and probably to a workshop in mainland Greece.

The Skopelos icon is one of the few surviving late Byzantine icons to handle the theme of the Akathistos Hymn. Its combination here with the Dormition, otherwise unknown, suggests that the icon was used in a church dedicated to the Dormition of the Virgin. It may not be completely wide of the mark to suppose that it was one of the treasures brought to Skopelos by the monks of the Pantocrator Monastery, when they fled there in the face of the Turkish invasion of Mount Athos in 1822 (Smyrnakis 1903, p. 182. Tsigaridas 1978, p. 188). The chapel on the north side of the katholikon of this monastery, dating at the latest from the 15th century, honours the Dormition of the Virgin (Tsigaridas 1978, p. 184).

Conservation. Byzantine Museum laboratories (E. Anapliotou) (1985).
Bibliography. Lazaridis 1964, p. 285, pl. 317. Makris 1982, fig. 128. Lafontaine-Dosogne 1984, p. 658. Byzantine Art 1986, no. 99, pp. 99-100. Affreschi e icone 1986, no. 50, pp. 90-91.
                                                                                M. A.-P.

40

St. Charalambos
End of the 15th century
22.5×17.5 cm
Athens. Kanellopoulos Museum

St. Charalambos is portrayed half-length with a long white beard and a pale pink sticharion. His aged appearance is consistent with his advanced years – in his 'Life' he is said to have been 113 years old (Vassilaki 1985-86, p. 254) and he is so described in the Painter's Manual of Dionysius of Fourna (Papadopoulos-Kerameus 1909, p. 199). This small icon is one of the earliest known icons of this saint, who is depicted in two other icons of the same scale in the Ekonomopoulos

Collection (Baltoyanni 1986 (2), p. 44, nos. 46, 47). The technique in the facial features, the clothing, and the small-scale embossed decoration of the halo suggest that this icon may be assigned to a group probably made in a north Greek workshop, possibly in Thessalonike; these features are to be found in icons on Mount Athos and in two icons of similar size in the Kanellopoulos Museum (St. Matrona and St. Sabbas). The style of this icon was associated in earlier studies with that of Theophanes the Greek.

Bibliography. Byzantine Art 1964, no. 249, p. 276. Splendeur de Byzance 1982, p. 47. Byzantine Art 1986, no. 121, pp. 121-122.

N. Ch.

41

St. Marina
First half of the 15th century
114.5×78 cm
Athens. Byzantine Museum, T. 85

Frontal, half-length portrait of St. Marina on a gold ground, with her left hand in a gesture of prayer. She is holding a small gold cross in her right hand. Both the bearing and the austere, noble face of the saint are reminiscent of the figure of the Virgin. The dark underpaint has a few white highlights on the nose and cheeks, in the manner of Palaeologan icons, like the icon of Christ in Leningrad (Weitzmann 1983, pp. 82, 83). Her dress, however, points to a later date. The red maphorion is traced in straight folds of a darker tone and has no sense of volume; it is like that of St. Anne in the 15th-century icon of the Benaki Museum (From Byzantium to El Greco 1987, no. 34). The luxurious dress emphasizes the aristocratic origins of the saint. The red maphorion has a decorative gold band with a fringe at the top, and three pieces of gold embroidery, one

on the forehead and one on each shoulder. Her headband has pseudo-kufic decoration embroidered in gold, of the type found mainly in Italo-Cretan icons of the 15th century (Chatzidakis 1974 (1), p. 180). Beneath the dress, can be seen a chemise worked in gold, covering her breast, fastened in the centre by four small buttons. Each sleeve is adorned with two gold-embroidered bands. These features of her dress are to be found in 15th-century Venetian costume, also worn in Crete (Maltezou 1986, pl. IX), and suggest that the icon was the work of a Cretan painter of the first half of the 15th century. This large icon was probably intended to decorate the iconostasis of a church dedicated to St. Marina.

Provenance. Presented to the Christian Archaeological Society.
Conservation. A. Margaritoff (1960).
Bibliography. Sotiriou 1931, p. 75. Sotiriou 1962, no. 85. Chatzidakis 1965 (2), no. 83. Babić-Chatzidakis 1983, p. 329. Affreschi e icone 1986, no. 49, p. 89. From Byzantium to El Greco 1987, no. 31, pp. 99, 167.

N. Ch.

42

The Dormition
Beginning of the 15th century
54.5×39.5 cm
Athens. Kanellopoulos Museum

The central scene of the icon depicts the Dormition of the Virgin. On the broad, slightly raised frame are representations of four hymnographers who wrote hymns on the theme of the Dormition, alternating with four scenes from the Virgin's childhood. The four panels at the corners depict the Meeting of Joachim and Anne, the Birth of the Virgin, the Virgin Blessed by the Priests, and Presentation of the Virgin in the Temple. The verticals of the frame have the figures of Cosmas Maiouma|on the left, and John Damaskinos on the right, turned to face the central scene; Damaskinos is wearing the characteristic turban. Busts of Joseph and Theophanes are set above and below the central scene. They are wearing monk's habits and holding open scrolls with texts.

The main scene follows the iconography of the Monastery of Chora (Underwood 1966, pl. 320). The main axes of the composition are formed by the tall slender figure of Christ in a bright mandorla and the body of the Virgin on the bed. At either side is a compact group of apostles giving restrained expression to their grief. Angels are worked in grisaille on the mandorla. Further emphasis is lent to the vertical axis by the inclusion of a six-winged seraph in the mandorla, hovering above Christ's head. The icon differs from its model in the form of the buildings in the background, and in the addition here of the angels high in the sky. The arrangement is similar to that of an icon from Patmos dated to the first half of the 15th century (Chatzidakis 1977 (1), no. 7, pl. 7), though there are important differences in the buildings in the background; it is also to be found in the 15th-century wall paintings in the Church of Ayios Fanou-

rios at Valsamonero, Crete (Kalokyris 1973, fig. BW 55).

Both the composition and the tall buildings in the background, with their small decorative balconies and large numbers of openings, bring this work even closer to 15th-century Cretan icons like the one by Andreas Ritzos in Turin (Babić-Chatzidakis 1983, p. 317), icons in Venice (Chatzidakis 1962, nos. 15, 16, pp. 35ff., pls. 14, 15), and especially a scene on the frame of an icon by Nikolaos Ritzos in Sarajevo (Babić-Chatzidakis 1983, p. 321), which even has the small trees that can be seen behind the wall in the background.

A further point of similarity is the treatment of the bed, with the typical decorated band around the edge. Finally the precision of the drawing of the figures, and the linear, geometrical handling of the drapery can also be found in the above mentioned works by Cretan painters.

There seems, however, to be a closer connection with Palaeologan models. The small scenes on the frame, such as the Birth and the Presentation of the Virgin (cf. Chatzidakis (N.) 1983, no. 3) seem to be unaware of the iconography that was formulated in Crete in the second half of the 15th century; in its place we find the iconography associated with the capital in the 14th century (cf. Lafontaine-Dosogne 1965, pp. 172-181). The flawless technique in the painting of the faces recalls miniatures in manuscript illuminations from the end of the 14th century, like the Cantacuzen manuscript (Par. gr. 1242, Talbot Rice 1959, pl. 190), and the richness of the buildings, the relatively large number of classicizing figures painted in monochrome in the background, like the angels in Christ's mandorla, and the decorative masks on the architecture recall the painting of Constantinople (Monastery of Chora) or of Mistra (Church of the Peribleptos and Church of the Pantanassa). Finally, the extensive texts relating to the Dormition of the Virgin on the scrolls held by the hymnographers reveal that the painter was a man of learning. The icon may be considered to be one of the best examples of early 15th-century Palaeologan art, fore-shadowing many of the characteristic features of Cretan painting.

Bibliography. Byzantine Art 1964, no. 197, p. 252. Affreschi e icone 1986, no. 40, pp. 80, 81. From Byzantium to El Greco 1987, no. 23, pp. 89, 161-162.

N. Ch.

43

Angelos: Christ Enthroned
Second half of the 15th century
105.5×59 cm
Zakynthos. Museum

Christ enthroned is to be found, with the same details in the drapery, in the works of other painters of the period, such as Andreas Ritzos and the anonymous painter of Patmos no. 34 (Chatzidakis 1977 (1), pp. 84ff.). The icon by Angelos has the same slender figure and fine face. The green marble throne is an original departure; it is clearly of Venetian type, and is a typical feature of a number of 15th-century Cretan icons. Another feature of this icon is the different relationship in size between the figure of Christ and the throne. This new type must have been successful in its time, since it was used as a model for later works: cf. the Virgin by Andreas Ritzos in the Monastery of Patmos (Chatzidakis 1977 (1), pp. 61ff.) and especially an icon by Emmanuel Tzanes in the Byzantine Museum, Athens, dating from 1666. The signature ΧΕΙΡ ΑΓΓΕΛΟΥ (hand of Angelos) is in the bottom right-hand corner. Icons bearing this signature (cf. cat. no. 44) are all of a high artistic quality, use a harmonious range of colours, and have noble figures and well-balanced compositions.

Provenance. The Church of Ayios Spyridon Flambouriaris on Zakynthos (retrieved in 1953).
Conservation. Zakynthos Museum laboratories.

Bibliography. Drandakis 1962, pl. 38β. For the date of the painter, cf. Vassilakes-Mavrakakes 1981, pp. 290ff. Babić-Chatzidakis 1983, p. 314, colour plate on p. 360. Byzantine Art 1986, no. 100, pp. 99, 101. Affreschi e icone 1986, no. 53, pp. 94, 95. From Byzantium to El Greco 1987, no. 33, pp. 101, 168.

M. Ch.

44

Angelos:
The Virgin Kardiotissa
Middle of the 15th century
121×96.5 cm
Athens. Byzantine Museum, T. 1582

Half-length portrait of the Virgin, in the type of the Glykophilousa, wearing a dark maphorion. She is holding the child in her right arm and her left is raised in an attitude of prayer. The child is very lively; he has his back turned towards the viewer and is stretching both arms around the face of the Virgin, with his head thrown back, so that it is at right angles to that of his mother. He is wearing a white chiton embroidered with gold fleur-de-lis and a sash of red material tied at the waist and passed over his shoulders like a pair of braces. His himation is richly decorated with gold webbing; it has slipped down and covers only the lower part of his body, leaving his right leg bare. Similar features of the dress, recalling Christ 'Anapeson', are found in the earliest variations of the type of the Glykophilousa, such as that in a 12th-century icon in the Byzantine Museum (Chatzidakis 1976, I, pl. XLVI, fig. 22).

The sandal on his left foot is tied in the same way as in icons of the Virgin of the Passion. At the top of the panel are two small angels praying. At the bottom, on the slightly raised border, the signature of the artist is painted in white letters on a red band: XEIP AΓΓΕΛOY, as in the icon of the Presentation of the Virgin (Chatzidakis (N.) 1983, no. 3).

The scene is accompanied by the incorrectly spelt inscription H KAPΔIOTHCA, which points to Crete, where there are still many monasteries dedicated to the Virgin Kardiotissa (on the etymology of the word, cf. G. Chatzidakis, Aθηνά KΓ΄, p. 496. Mastoropoulos 1983, pp. 129-131). The earliest is perhaps the monastery in the village of Kera Pediados, Lasithi, which has some 14th-century wall paintings (Borboudakis 1973, pp. 483ff.).

The iconographic type occurs in two unpublished Byzantine works: an icon on Sinai dating from the period of the Crusades, and one in the Byzantine Museum (T. 2322), dated on stylistic grounds to the beginning of the 15th century; it is also found in a number of icons from the second half of the 15th century, on Naxos (Zias 1971, pl. 501), Siphnos and Paros (unpublished), and in the Loverdos Collection (Λ. 285-Σ.Λ. 247); much later, in the 17th century, it was painted by Emmanuel Tzanes in the icon of Ioannis Menganos (Maltezou 1973, pl. 1) and an icon in the Loverdos Collection (Λ. 150-Σ.Λ. 149). It is a variation of the well-known type of the Glykophilousa (From Byzantium to El Greco 1987, no. 40) which incorporates features more usually associated with the Passion and with the type of the Virgin with the Playing Child (Hadermann-Misguich 1983).

This is one of the most important large icons by Angelos, and probably decorated the same iconostasis as the icon of St. John the Baptist in the Chatzidakis Collection and the Presentation of the Virgin in the Temple of the Byzantine Museum, Athens (Chatzidakis (N.) 1983, nos. 2, 3, pp. 18-19).

None of the known Italian influences on the work of Angelos (cat. no. 43 and From Byzantium to El Greco 1987, no. 32) can be detected in this icon. The quality of the art and the grandeur of the pose of the figure of the Virgin make this a work to be compared with the art of Constantinople just before 1453.

Conservation. Byzantine Museum laboratories (1951). Th. Papageorgiou (1976).

Bibliography. Sotiriou 1956, p. 32, pl. XXα. Xyngopoulos 1957, p. 170. Embiricos 1967, fig. 88. Chatzidakis 1979 (2), pp. 223-224, pl. 88. Chatzidakis (N.) 1983, no. 1, pl. 17. Hadermann-Misguich 1983, fig. 6. From Byzantium to El Greco 1987, no. 35, pp. 103, 170.

N. Ch.

45

St. Demetrius
c. 1500
92×46 cm
Athens. R. Andreadis Collection

The saint is depicted standing full-face in military dress. He holds a lance in his right hand and a sword in his left. His shield can be seen behind his left shoulder. He wears a red and green cloak, whose outer surface is painted so as to give the impression of heavy fabric. The thongs binding his legs, the sleeves, and the whole of the lower part of his costume are treated with similar realism. The concern for accurate detail is clear in the gold webbing with which the breast-plate is decorated, and the drapery in the lower part of his costume; this has the two attached embroidered panels with the pseudo-kufic decoration usually found on this kind of costume in the 15th century (Chatzidakis 1977 (1), p. 118, pl. 27. Chatzidakis (N.) 1983, no. 6, p. 22). The halo has an incised floral decoration. Gold ground with a brown area at the bottom. Slightly raised frame. The facial features and dress of the saint have affinities with an icon depicting St. Fanourios which is attributed to the painter Angelos (Chatzidakis (N.) 1983, no. 12, pp. 26ff.). This is the only one of the icons with warrior saints (icons on Patmos, in the Benaki Museum, and in other collections; cf. Xyngopoulos 1936, no. 5, pl. 7β. Chatzidakis 1977 (1), pls. 26, 27, 204γ. Vassilakes-Mavrakakes 1981, pls. 52α-β, 57α-β, 58, 59) that has so many points of similarity with the present work. The stylistic details, such as the soft straps binding the legs of the saint, which are so similar to those of St. Theodore by Angelos (From Byzantium to El Greco 1987, no. 32) suggest that this icon was also by him. We may note that St. Demetrius's hair falls in small curls behind his ears, just like that of

St. Fanourios. It may be conjectured from a number of traces on the gold ground, near the lance and the lettering in the inscription, that this was originally a representation of St. Fanourios holding the cross, but that it was later adapted as a portrait icon of St. Demetrius.

Bibliography. Chatzidakis (Th.) 1982, no. 3. Chatzidakis (N.) 1983, no. 13, p. 27. Affreschi e icone 1986, no. 58, pp. 100-101. From Byzantium to El Greco 1987, no. 37, pp. 105, 172.

N. Ch.

46

St. Anne Enthroned
with the Virgin and Christ
15th century
87×61 cm
Zakynthos. Museum

St. Anne sits on a marble throne, the back of which is decorated with fleurs-de-lis. She wears a bright red maphorion, and holds the Virgin on her lap, her right hand resting on the Virgin's arm, and the left on her knee. The Virgin is holding the baby Christ in a similar posture. The way in which the composition is symmetrically balanced about the vertical axis recalls the treatment of the Holy Trinity in Byzantine miniatures, as in the wall painting in the Church of the Koumbelidiki in Kastoria (Papadopoulos 1968, pp. 133ff., figs. 9-10); in terms of its symbolism, it has affinities with the icon of St. Anne with the Virgin in the Benaki Museum (From Byzantium to El Greco 1987, no. 34). Certain characteristic features of the art of the painter Angelos can be recognized here: the modelling of the flesh, with large surfaces of a dark brown underpaint on the faces of the three figures, the firm white highlights, and the treatment of the drapery as a series of strongly drawn geometrical surfaces. Further points of similarity with the Benaki Museum icon can be detected in the colours

used in the garments of St. Anne and the Virgin. There are also some similarities with the signed icon of the Virgin and St. Catherine by Angelos on Patmos (Chatzidakis 1977 (1), no. 68, pls. 49, 127). They can be seen in the proportion of the figure of the Virgin to that of Christ, in the treatment of the drapery of the brick-red maphorion and the deep blue dress worn by the Virgin, and also in the delicate gold webbing on Christ's himation. An icon signed by Angelos depicting the Embracing of Peter and Paul was retrieved from the same church in Zakynthos in 1952; it was destroyed in a fire in 1953.

The form of the marble throne has affinities with two well-known icons painted by major 15th-century artists: the lower part of it resembles that on an icon of Christ by Angelos (cat. no. 43), and the upper part, with the fleurs-de-lis recalls an icon of the Virgin Enthroned by Andreas Ritzos on Patmos (Chatzidakis 1977 (1), pp. 59-61, pls. 12, 13, 15). St. Anne's posture, however, differs from that of the Virgin in this latter icon. The figure deviates slightly from a strictly frontal position, the lower part of the body is turned to her left, and the strong projection of the right leg is revealed by the clinging drapery.

A similar enthroned figure in this posture is to be found in a Palaeologan icon of the Virgin from Mount Sinai (Sotiriou 1956, 1958, no. 222) and in a slighty later icon in the Nikolenko Collection (Icônes 1975, no. 2). A 16th-century icon, now in Korcula, Yugoslavia (Karaman 1932, p. 374, fig. 136), has the three figures, organized in the same composition, as its main subject.

Provenance. The Church of Ayios Nikolaos Molos on Zakynthos (retrieved by M. Chatzidakis, 1953).
Conservation. Zakynthos Museum laboratories.
Bibliography. Byzantine Art 1986, no. 103, pp. 103, 104-105. Affreschi e icone 1986, no. 57, pp. 99-100. From Byzantium to El Greco 1987, no. 36, pp. 104, 171.

N. Ch.

47

Sanctuary Doors
SS George and Demetrius
Second half of the 15th century
127.5×65.7 cm
Tinos. Evangelistria Museum

The sanctuary doors form a 'flamboyant' arch that divides the painted decoration from the carved wooden section at the top; this is decorated with foliage scrolls and multifoil palmettes, the leaves of which are reminiscent of Gothic art in texture. The top part of the vertical joint-cover is missing, and a strip at least three centimetres wide has been cut away from the bottom of the doors. The left door has a scene of St. George slaying the dragon, while on the right, St. Demetrius is portrayed crushing a scorpion, shown larger than life-size. The two saints, in symmetrically balanced contrapposto, are wearing elaborate military dress, which is based on Palaeologan models. They are dressed in a short chiton with leather maniples, and a breast-plate, which is supplemented by a double row of leather 'wings' in the area of the pelvis and on the upper arms. There is a double metallic strip with monochrome decoration around their chest and neck. The saints are wearing 'hose', and the lower part of the leg is wound around with leather bands. Those worn by St. Demetrius are of soft white leather, and have the characteristic red line that can be seen in the icon of St. Fanourios on Patmos. St. George's sword is also to be found in icons

by Angelos, and St. Demetrius has a sabre in a leather scabbard with gold ornamentation. The same type of sword and the same gestures occur in two icons of St. Fanourios and St. Demetrius attributed to Angelos (cat. no. 45).

At the top of the doors, the hand of God emerges from a painted blue arc and holds out a crown to each of the two martyrs. The haloes are bordered by a row of impressed roundels, as in three icons from Spilia, Kissamos (Byzantine Art 1986, nos. 105-107), which are thought to be the work of Andreas Ritzos.

The type of the standing, dragon-slayer saint occurs in late Palaeologan works, like that in the katholikon of the Monastery of Vlatadon in Thessalonike (Mavropoulou-Tsioumi 1985, pl. 3). A number of original variations of this theme are to be found in icons attributed to the painter Angelos (Chatzidakis 1977 (1), p. 76, no. 24). The type showing St. Demetrius and the scorpion is much rarer, and is clearly inspired by the miracle of the scorpion when the saint was in prison (cf. Xyngopoulos 1970, p. 21). The two prominent military saints are commonly found together, though not with the triumphant character they have here, thanks to the inclusion of the dragon and the scorpion.

It is possible to detect in both saints features typical of the art of Angelos, whose work has recently been dated to the first half of the 15th century (Vassilakes-Mavrakakes 1981, pp.

290-298). Although the drawing is fine, the figures here are heavier and lack the grace of authentic pieces by Angelos, such as the icon of St. Fanourios on Patmos. The light and shadow in the face of St. George, especially the long shadow cast by the nose, with its white border and the dense white highlights, are reminiscent of works by Andreas Ritzos (cf. Chatzidakis 1977 (1), p. 60). The same is true of the geometric treatment of the drapery, which extends to the hose of St. George. The sanctuary doors from Tinos should therefore be attributed to a very good Cretan workshop that continued to use the vocabulary of Angelos, and possibly to the workshop of Andreas Ritzos, which inherited Angelos's working drawings (Cattapan 1973, pp. 251, 262). If this is true, the Tinos doors, the Patmos doors (cat. no. 48), and the doors in the Ekonomopoulos Collection (Baltoyanni 1986 (2), pls. 10-11) are the earliest known sanctuary doors by the Cretan School.

Bibliography. Koutelakis 1981, p. 9. Byzantine Art 1986, no. 109, pp. 109-111. Affreschi e icone 1986, no. 61, pp. 105-107. From Byzantium to El Greco 1987, no. 38, pp. 106, 172-173.

L. B.

48

Sanctuary Doors
The Annunciation, SS Peter and John the Theologian
Second half of the 15th century
165×41 and 146×37 cm
Patmos. Monastery of St. John the Theologian. New Sacristy.

The flat surface of both doors is divided into two registers. The upper register has a representation of the Annunciation, and the lower depictions of St. Peter and St. John the Theologian. The poses of the archangel Gabriel and the Virgin in the Annunciation are those typically found in Cretan icons. Here, however, the background has been enlivened by the addition of a large number of quite complex buildings. The particular form given to the volumes of these buildings was probably dictated by the space available, and there is no logic to their articulation; the general idea seems to be that the figures are standing on a terrace, with the buildings below them. This idea, which is not a particularly Byzantine concept, is to be found in an icon of the Zoodochos Pigi from the Monastery of Sinai.

Peter is turned three-quarters to the centre of the door, with his hand emerging from his himation in a gesture of intercession. Opposite him, St. John the Theologian, also turned towards the centre of the doors, is holding upright a half-open book with both hands. In his right hand he holds the pen, and has the ink-pot secured under his left arm. It is interesting to note that only words and syllables, and not the more usual full text, can be read in the book, as though this were really what could be seen of the text: XH HN O ΛΟ/]ΑΝ/]ΟC/]ΟΝ/-]ΝΟΥ/]ΤΟ/]ΕΝ.

This more realistic – though not more scholarly – type is to be found in other icons of this period, such as the Bari icon, the Naxos icon, and others. The Annunciation is one of the most common iconographic motifs painted on sanctuary doors, and is found in this position from at least the 11th century. This phenomenon is to be explained in terms of the symbolical meaning of the scene, which alludes to the concept of the Virgin as Gate to be found in hymns (see cat. no. 63). Peter and Paul, the foundations of the Church, are also frequently painted here, though other saints may be found instead, more directly connected with the saint to whom the church was dedicated, or with its founders. The stylistic affinity with works by Andreas Ritzos is clear, both in the drapery and the architecture, and the painting may unhesitatingly be assigned to Ritzos or his workshop.

The doors are surmounted by Late Gothic wood-carved open-work decoration enlivened by young shoots and foliage, of a high quality. One extremely interesting feature is the small, but expressive bust of the prophet David, at the top of the vertical joint-cover: he is shown emerging from the cup of a flower, wearing a crown and holding an open scroll.

Tradition has it that the iconostasis of the Church of Ayios Georgios Aporthianon comes from the katholikon of the Monastery on Patmos. This tradition is confirmed by the icono-graphy of the sanctuary doors and its association with the art of Andreas Ritzos: this, one of the finest and largest of the Cretan sanctuary doors will have accompanied icons by Ritzos on the iconostasis.

Provenance. The Church of Ayios Georgios Aporthianon in Chora, Patmos.
Conservation. Byzantine Museum laboratories (Th. Papageorgiou) (1986-88).
Bibliography. Chatzidakis 1977 (1), no. 11, pp. 61ff., pls. 80 and 81. Byzantine Art 1986, no. 108, pp. 108, 109. Affreschi e icone 1986, no. 60, pp. 103-104. From Byzantium to El Greco 1987, no. 39, pp. 107, 174.

M. Ch.

49

The Virgin Hodegetria
15th century
47.5×37 cm
Athens. Private Collection

The Virgin is portrayed half-length holding the Child on her left side, in the type of the Hodegetria. Her head is turned slightly towards the child, and she holds her right hand in front of her breast. Christ is depicted almost frontally, his body slightly turned to the right and his face towards the spectator. He is blessing with his right hand, and holds an open scroll in his left with the inscription ΠΝ(ΕΥΜ)Α C(ΥΡΙΟ)Υ Ε/Π ΕΜΕ ΟΥ / ΕΝΕΚΕΝ (ΕΧΡΙCΕ ΜΕ) (The Spirit of the Lord God is upon me because the Lord hath anointed me) (Isaiah 61.1); this is a common feature of icons of the Virgin of the Passion and the Virgin Glykophilousa, as well as of the Hodegetria (Talbot Rice 1937, p. 213, no. 31. Martinelli 1982, p. 91, no. 18). The icon has a gold background. The purple-brown maphorion worn by the Virgin has a gold band around the fringe of the head-cover and an open triangle at the neck, allowing the dark brown inner garment to be seen. The light brown himation and dark green chi-ton worn by Christ are lavishly decorated with delicate gold-webbing.

The sad, serious gaze of the Virgin and her slight turn towards the child relate her to the iconographic type of the Virgin of the Passion, as formulated in a number of icons painted by 15th-century Cretan artists. Another feature characteristic of this type is the open triangle of the maphorion at the Virgin's neck (Chatzidakis 1974 (1), pp. 180-181. Baltoyanni 1985, p. 28). In contrast, the figure of Christ, who is portrayed almost frontally, blessing with his right hand held in front of his mother's breast, follows the standard features of the type of the Hodegetria. The open scroll in his left hand, however, clearly reveals Western influence; this iconographic element was not part of the Orthodox repertoire, but entered the compositions of the 15th- and 16th-century Cretan painters (Chatzidakis 1974 (1), pp. 201-202). The infant's slightly wavy hair is also due to Italian influence.

The icon is also connected with 15th-century Cretan painting by its style and technique. The shape of the Virgin's eyes, with the well-drawn brows, her broad cheeks and the care shown in the modelling of her hands, with their long fingers, are all to be found in the works of the Cretan painter Andreas Ritzos (Czerwenka-Papadopoulos 1984, pp. 203ff., pls. 1-8. Koshi 1973, pp. 37ff., pls. 6-8, 11). In the composition as a whole, the modelling of the face, the rendering of the features and the geometric treatment of the drapery all connect this icon with the art of Andreas Ritzos (cf. Cattapan 1973, pp. 238ff., pls. A´-H´).

Conservation. Byzantine Museum laboratories (N. Nomikos) (1985).
Bibliography. Byzantine Art 1986, no. 116, pp. 116, 119. Affreschi e icone 1986, no. 71, pp. 118-119.

K. Ph. K.

50

Nikolaos Lamboudis: The Virgin Eleousa 15th century
67×47.5 cm
Athens. Private Collection

The Virgin is portrayed in the type of the Hodegetria, holding Christ in her left arm and leaning gently towards the child, while he lifts his head towards his mother, in a composition of mutual tenderness and affection. There are miniature portraits of the archangels Michael and Gabriel in the top corners. Gold ground and fine gold decoration on the dress. A delicate pattern of floral tracery is stippled on the haloes. The icon is of the same iconographic type as the Virgin Eleousa in the Monastery of Gonia in Kissamos, Crete, which may be attributed to Andreas Ritzos (Borboudakis 1985, no. 17, pp. 126ff.), and other icons also by Ritzos and his circle (Czerwenka-Papadopoulos 1984, pp. 203ff., figs. 1, 3-4, 6-8): it has all the hallmarks of a Cretan masterpiece of the late 15th century, with strong roots in Palaeologan art and elements of Western sensitivity in the modelling. On the frame, at the bottom is the signature: ΧΕΙΡ ΝΙΚΟΛΑΟΥ ΤΟΥ ΛΑΜΠΟΥΔΗ ΣΠΑΡΤΙΑΤΟΥ. This is the only known work by this hitherto unknown painter from Sparta, who probably worked in Crete. The family is known from the 14th century under the name Lamboudios (Zakythinos 1975, pp. 98ff., 101, 114, 215), and the 15th-century scribe Ματθαῖος σεβαστός Λαμπού-δης ὁ Πελοποννήσιος (Matthaios Lamboudis the Peloponnesian) who worked in Florence and Ferrara in Italy (Lambros 1907, pp. 176ff. Zakythinos 1975, pp. 215 and 230) was probably also a member of it.

Provenance. Acquired at Sotheby's (1984).
Bibliography. Sotheby's 1984, no. 30, pp. 14-15. Byzantine Art 1986, no. 115, pp. 114, 116. Affreschi e icone 1986, no. 70, pp. 117-118. From Byzantium to El Greco 1987, no. 41, pp. 109, 175.

M. A.-P.

51

Sanctuary Doors, right leaf
Virgin of the Annunciation, SS Basil
and Nicholas
Second half of the 15th century
123×39 cm
Patmos. Monastery of St. John the Theolo-
gian. New Sacristy.

The top of this leaf has the shape of
half a trefoil arch, and together with
the lost left leaf, will have formed a
high, pointed, ogee arch of Late Gothic type; arches of this shape were
frequently used for the windows of
15th-century buildings in Venice and
in Crete under Venetian rule. At the
top of the door, a simple, narrow
raised border follows the elegant outer
curve. The raised parts of the lower
section of the door consist of a double
arch carried on a twisted colonnette
with a capital and a base, in the
middle, and two half colonnettes at
the sides. Each of the arches is surmounted by a pediment, with a relief
anthemium at the top, and the ground
between the pediments is filled with
Late Gothic floral decoration. This
work has all the hallmarks of Cretan
wood-carving, which was already
flourishing in the 15th century, and
did not shrink from using pure Venetian motifs and manners in works for
both Orthodox and the Catholic
churches.
These raised borders enclose scenes
commonly found on sanctuary doors:
at the top is a representation of the
Virgin of the Annunciation, with the
Hierarchs Basil and Nicholas in the
lower register. The Virgin is seated on
a wooden stool, with no back support, which is decorated with gold
striations. She is sitting on an embroidered cushion, with her right
hand held in a gesture of acceptance
and the other moving gently to her
left. Her dress is covered with tightly
packed striations, resembling the
'combs' in the painting of Paolo
Veneziano in the 14th century; the
stiff drapery is accurately rendered.

Her short maphorion of Frankish
brocade has a dense pattern of fleur-
de-lis. On the Byzantine lectern to her
right is a book open at a text from St.
Luke (1.38), painted in elegant black
letters:

ΗΔΟΥ   ΝΗΤΟ
Ι ΔΟΥΛ ΜΗ ΚΑΤΑ
Η ΚΥΡ   ΤΟ ΡΗ
ΙΟΥ ΓΕ ΜΑ ΣΟΥ

(Behold the handmaid of the Lord; be
it unto me according to thy word).
Behind the Virgin is a square, two-
storey building, with rather curious
pilasters-cum-buttresses, and arched
double windows with open-work pure
Gothic tracery. To the right, at a lower level, is a terrace garden carried on
an arcade. The fabrics, the buildings
and the pose of the Virgin all point to
the cycle of Italo-Cretan icons.
A rather different art is represented in
the two Hierarchs, who are portrayed
full-length and frontally. They are
blessing with their right hand and
hold a closed book in their covered
left hand. Basil is wearing a phelonion richly decorated with crosses and
an epitrachelion of a Venetian fabric,
while Nicholas wears a plain, monochrome phelonion. The modelling
and the drapery are drawn and
executed almost as meticulously as
miniature art; the effect is to repro-
duce the individual features of the
faces, which are asymmetrical, heavily
wrinkled, and have grim expressions.
All these characteristics suggest that
the sanctuary door should be assigned to the Cretan cycle of the last
decades of the 15th century.

Provenance. The Church of Christ Dimarchias
or Megalis Portas in Chora, Patmos.
Conservation. Ph. Zachariou (1977). Byzantine
Museum laboratories (F. Galakou) (1987).
Bibliography. Chatzidakis 1977 (1), no. 38, pp.
87ff., pls. A and 98-99. Byzantine Art 1986, no.
113, pp. 112, 114-115. Affreschi e icone 1986,
no. 68, pp. 115, 116. From Byzantium to El
Greco 1987, no. 48, pp. 117, 180.

M. Ch.

52

Nikolaos Tzafouris:
Christ Carrying the Cross
Second half of the 15th century
69.2×52.1 cm
New York. The Metropolitan Museum of
Art, Bashford Dean Memorial Fund, 1929:
The Bashford Dean Memorial Collection,
29.158.746

A Roman soldier with menacing glance drags Christ toward Golgotha with a rope. Bending his knees slightly under the strain of the cross, Christ inclines his head backwards, toward a group of soldiers following, the foremost of which places a hand on Christ's shoulder.
NICOLAUS ZAFURI PINXIT (Nikolaos Tzafouris painted (this) is written in large Latin characters across the lower edge of the panel. This work is one of just five signed icons by this famous 15th-century Cretan master, who was especially skilled at integrating Italian elements into the Byzantine tradition he learned on his native island. This integration is clear even in the juxtaposition of a Latin signature with a Greek inscription: ΕΛΚΟΜΕΝΟC ΕΠΙ CΤΑΥΡΟΥ.

Tzafouris, a master of many styles, here demonstrates his virtuosity. The 'flamboyant gothic' upper frame is supported by Italianate twisted columns. Christ, wearing the traditional eastern colobium, is set before mountain peaks that are purely Byzantine. The soldiers on the left are dressed as Greek warrior saints, whereas the one on the right is wearing heavy Western armor. Tzafouris is following the Italian *maniera greca* in giving a gentle, poignant expression to Christ's face, but uses his Greek heritage to characterize and differentiate the cluster of soldiers. Especially striking throughout is his attention to detail — most clearly displayed in such minor elements as the leather straps and decorative tooling of the armor.
This fine work should be placed within Tzafouris's documented career, from 1489 to 1500 (the year of his death), and is most comparable in handling of the facial types to his signed Akra Tapeinosis in Vienna (Chatzidakis 1974 (1), p. 184).

Bibliography. Wehle 1940, p. 1. Chatzidakis 1974 (1), p. 187.   G. K.

53

Nikolaos Tzafouris: Virgin and Child
15th century
56.5×45 cm; 106×85 cm (with frame)
Athens. P. Kanellopoulos Collection

The Virgin is portrayed in the familiar Western type of the Madre della Consolazione, as painted by the Cretan artists of the 15th century (Chatzidakis 1977 (1), p. 91). Characteristic features of this type include the placing of the child in a position that provides an element of contrapposto, the sphere in his left hand, his western-style shirt, the gold band with pseudo-kufic decoration along the edges of the Catholic maphorion worn by the Virgin, and above all, the Late

Gothic style in which the two figures are painted. A cross with leaves and the symbols of the Passion is painted on the reverse of the icon, on a ground prepared with gesso, and a Latin inscription in capital letters can be made out at the bottom, giving us the name of the famous 15th-century Cretan painter Nikolaos Tzafouris: M(AISTR)O NICOLO ZAFURI (..) ADI (..) OTUBRIO. The damaged area after the word ZAFURI, which has space for only two letters, presumably contained the year MD (1500) and the small space after ADI will have contained the date, since the name of the month October can be recognized in the word OTUBRIO.

According to documents preserved in the archives in Venice (Cattapan 1972, pp. 202ff. Chatzidakis 1974 (1), p. 183), Tzafouris lived and worked in the second half of the 15th century, and was no longer alive in 1501. He is known from four icons bearing his signature: an icon of the Akra Tapeinosis in Vienna (Kreidl-Papadopoulos 1970, p. 605, pl. 39. Chatzidakis 1974 (1), p. 184); the Betrayal in the Metropolitan Museum, New York (Wehle 1940, p. 1. Chatzidakis 1974 (1), p. 187); the Leningrad triptych (Chatzidakis 1974 (1), pp. 184ff.); and the icon of the Virgin and Child in Trieste (Bianco Fiorin 1983, p. 164, fig. 1). All four combine Italian features with the expressive means of 15th-century Cretan painting. Until recently, we had no information about the iconographic and stylistic features of the fifth icon by Tzafouris depicting the Virgin which, according to Bettini, was once sold in Venice (Bettini 1940, p. 72, no. 1. Chatzidakis

1974 (1), p. 184). On the back it had an inscription identical to the one on the present icon. In the space between ADI and OTUBRIO, Bettini read the number IV, which was still preserved at that date. The fact that the inscription is identical in wording makes it certain that the icon exhibited here is the Venice icon, which somehow came into the hands of the Athenian collector.

Stylistically, it belongs to the well-known school of Italo-Cretan paintings, and to a large group of icons portraying the Virgin and Child in the type of the Madre della Consolazione (Chatzidakis 1977 (1), p. 91) which have the same features. This icon now furnishes the definitive solution to the problem of the origins and date of this group.

Bibliography. Baltoyanni 1986 (1), no. 10. Affreschi e icone 1986, no. 62, pp. 107-108. From Byzantium to El Greco 1987, no. 42, pp. 110, 175-176.

Ch. B.

54

**Madre della Consolazione
with St. Francis
Second half of the 15th century
60×52 cm
Athens. Byzantine Museum, T. 233**

A few small pieces of the wood panel and some paint at the edges are missing. Gesso on canvas. Gold ground and haloes, the latter decorated in a pointillé technique with a stylized floral design.

The Virgin is depicted in the well-known Italian type of the Madre della Consolazione as rendered by the Cretan painters of the 15th century (cf. cat. no. 53), holding Christ in her right arm; the latter is making a benediction and holding the sphere of the world in his left hand. To his left is a full-length portrait of St. Francis of Assisi, with the stigmata, on a smaller scale. He is facing the Virgin and Child, and holds a cross in his left

hand and a closed bible in his right. The position of the saint, his gaze directed towards Christ, and the cross that he is holding, suggest with a subtle symbolism the miracle of the stigmata from the wounds of the crucified Christ that St. Francis received in a vision (the theme is found in Italo-Cretan icons of the 15th century, cf. Pavan 1979, no. 157, p. 95, Chatzidakis (N.) 1983, no. 37, p. 44) and anticipates the future suffering of Jesus.

The presence of the saint of Assisi, who does not appear in other Italo-Cretan icons of the Madre della Consolazione, and the established fact that the Byzantine Museum icon came from Crete, make it very probable that it either adorned a church of the Franciscans on the island, or was owned by a member of the Venetian or Cretan nobility.

The type of the Madre della Consolazione was particularly popular in Cretan painting and met the requirements of both Catholic and Orthodox Churches until the 17th century. This is attested by the archival sources, which refer to countless icons of the Virgin painted *a la italiana*, and by the large number of them that survives in Greece and elsewhere, amongst which are two signed icons by important 17th-century artists, Emmanuel Tzanes (in a private collection in Athens, unpublished) and Victor (in the Monastery of Ayioi Theodoroi on Kerkyra, unpublished). The Byzantine Museum icon, one of the finest and earliest, stands out from those contemporary with it for its spirituality and the severe character of the figures. Its typological features are akin to those of the Madre della Consolazione by Nikolaos Tzafouris, known from earlier written sources, which was recently discovered by Ch. Baltoyanni in the P. Kanellopoulos Collection in Athens (cf. cat. no. 53), and also to a similar icon of the Virgin signed by Nikolaos Tzafouris, recently discovered in a private collection in Trieste (Bianco Fiorin 1983, pp. 164ff., fig. 1).

Notable features of the icon include: the exceptionally fine technique and the mature use of colour; the figure of Christ with his red himation; the partial lighting of the flesh, similar to that of the Virgin in the two icons by Tzafouris; the soft, Late Gothic drapery, strongly lit at the peaks of the folds of the maphorion worn by the Virgin; the soft, stylized folds crowning her face, as in the Trieste Virgin and in another icon by Tzafouris in Vienna (Kreidl-Papadopoulos 1970, pp. 62ff. and 93ff., no. 2, fig. 39); and the special care taken in the fine gold decorative details on the child's shirt, the Virgin's maphorion, the haloes and St. Francis's leather-bound bible. Taken together, the stylistic and typological features of this icon suggest a date in the second half of the 15th century, and an attribution to the workshop of Nikolaos Tzafouris, though perhaps not to the hand of the artist himself (cf. Bianco Fiorin 1983, p. 167, fig. 8, who erroneously identifies the saint with St. Anthony of Padua).

Provenance. Crete. Donated by I. Frangoudis in 1897 to the Christian Archaeological Society (XAE 2338).

Conservation. Byzantine Museum laboratories (Th. Papageorgiou, 1974), (A. Simandoni, 1986).

Bibliography. Chatzidakis 1977 (2), p. 688, fig. 49. Bianco Fiorin 1983, p. 167, fig. 8. Affreschi e icone 1986, no. 67, pp. 113-115. From Byzantium to El Greco 1987, no. 46, pp. 114, 179-180.

M. A.-P.

55

Nikolaos Tzafouris (?):
The Akra Tapeinosis
Second half of the 15th century
77×56.5 cm
Patmos, Chora. Monastery of Zoodochos Pigi

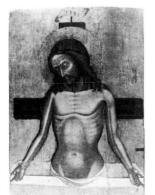

This Byzantine subject is here rendered in accordance with Western models, in the type that was formulated in Italy, and more specifically in Florence and Venice, during the 14th and 15th centuries (Belting 1981, pp. 118ff.). Its relationship to Italian painting is clear not only from the extended arms, and the perspective in the sarcophagus, a motif copied by Theophanes in the Monastery of Anapafsas (1527; cf. Chatzidakis 1974 (1), p. 201, pl. IΔ΄, 3), but also from the rendering of the scroll with Gothic capital letters at the top of the cross. Features of particular interest include the treatment of the torso, the rendering of the flesh in soft monochrome tones, the wonderful precision in the incised design of the halo, and the minute detail in the drawing of the hair and the crown of thorns; all these are characteristic of the miniature painting of the Cretan painter Nikolaos Tzafouris (attested 1489-

1500), to whom the icon is attributed. It has a particularly close affinity with the signed work by him in Vienna (Kreidl-Papadopoulos 1970, p. 30, fig. 39).

Conservation. S. Baltoyannis (1964).
Bibliography. Byzantine Art 1964, no. 213, p. 260. Chatzidakis 1977 (1), no. 40, pp. 89ff., pls. 33 and 101. Byzantine Art 1986, no. 111, pp. 111, 112. Affreschi e icone 1986, no. 63, pp. 108-109. From Byzantium to El Greco 1987, no. 44, pp. 112, 177-178.

M. Ch.

56

Pietà
Second half of the 15th century
71×58 cm
Athens. Benaki Museum, 3050

Egg tempera on wood. Gold background. The Virgin is sitting on a rock and holding the body of Christ on her knees. The subject of the Pietà is the Western parallel of the Byzantine Lamentation at the Tomb. It is thought to have been a creation of north European, and particularly German art which, through the travelling German artists (Wackernagel 1981, pp. 76-77) became known to the Siennese, Florentine and Venetian painters from the 14th century onwards (e.g. the Pietà by Taddeo Gaddi in Yale, 14th century, Meiss 1978; the Pietà by Giovanni da Milano, middle of the 14th century, formerly in a private collection in Paris, Antal 1947, pl. 47 and Belting 1981, fig. 46; and the Pietà by Giovanni Bellini in the Galleria dell'Accademia in Venice, Robertson 1968, pl. XCVII).
Identical versions of the Benaki Pietà are found in a group of Cretan icons dating from the second half of the 15th century (icon by Andreas Pavias in Rossano, Chatzidakis 1977 (2), fig. 53; icons in the Kanellopoulos collection, Baltoyanni 1986 (1), no. 8, and the Ekonomopoulos collection, Baltoyanni 1986 (2), pls. 16-17; icon formerly in the Church of Santa Maria della Misericordia in Venice, Rizzi 1972, pl. KA', 2; icon in the Nikolenko Gallery, Icônes 1975, fig. 9; in Split, Prijatelj 1974, fig. p. 55; and in the central panel of two triptychs, one in the Vatican, Muñoz 1928, pl. 22, 4 and Poglayen-Neuwall 1943-49, fig. 1,

and the other in the Ashmolean Museum in Oxford, unpublished, information supplied by M. Mango).
The Cretan artist of the Benaki Pietà has borrowed not only the overall composition but also a number of iconographic details from Italian painting of the 14th century (cf. the attitude of the Virgin's head, and the head-dress covering her hair and throat in a composition by Paolo Veneziano dedicated to the Doge Fr. Dandolo in 1339 (Muraro 1970, pl. 25. Muraro 1972, pl. Z', 11) and of the 15th century (cf. the bare rock in the Transfiguration by Giovanni Bellini in the Correr Museum in Venice, 1455-60, Robertson 1968, pl. XII, and in the Agony in the Garden by the same painter and by Andrea Mantegna in the National Gallery in London, Robertson 1968, pl. XV and Lightbown 1986, pl. II). The incised haloes of the Virgin and Christ, with rosettes and leaves, are a familiar element in Italian painting from as early as the 13th century (Frinta 1965. Frinta 1981).
The Benaki Museum icon of the Pietà has many iconographic and stylistic features in common with the Akra Tapeinosis (the Man of Sorrows) by the Cretan painter Nikolaos Tzafouris (second half of the 15th century) in Vienna (Weitzmann 1982 (1), pl. p. 322) and is probably to be attributed to the same painter.
The abbreviations MP ΘY, in Greek, leave open the question of the nationality of the customer for whom the icon was intended, since an icon is known with a subject taken from Italian painting, suitable for a Catholic customer, which has a Greek inscrip-

tion (cf. the icon of the Virgin Galaktotrophousa with angels, in the Benaki Museum, Affreschi e icone 1986, no. 75). It thus belonged either to a Catholic of Greek education, or to an Orthodox with Western tastes. The problem of the customers for whom icons *a la maniera greca* and *a la maniera latina* were intended is thus a complex one that needs to be considered in the light of a wide variety of evidence.

Conservation. Benaki Museum laboratories (K. Milanou) (1982).
Bibliography. Chatzidakis 1974 (2), pp. 108ff., fig. 81. Chatzidakis 1977 (2), pp. 688ff., figs. 52-53. Prijatelj 1974, pp. 55ff. Chatzidakis (N.) 1983, no. 45, p. 52. Affreschi e icone 1986, no. 65, pp. 110-111. From Byzantium to El Greco 1987, no. 45, pp. 113, 178.

M. V.

57

Christ and the Samaritan Woman
Last quarter of the 15th century
38.5×48 cm
Athens. Kanellopoulos Museum

Christ is seated before a well in the foreground, with the Samaritan woman standing opposite him. The landscape is filled with picturesque episodes set in different planes (for the iconography, cf. Millet 1916, pp. 602ff.). On the left two groups of apostles are walking towards Christ. On the right there is a group of people gathered before the gate of the city which has the inscription SAMATIE. There is a similar scene on the left depicting the city of Jerusalem, with the inscription JERUSALEM. The monks on the right and many of the other figures are painted on a small scale, with great attention to detail (such as the two figures in the middleground walking towards a small building on a hill, and the man dismounting from his horse behind the city on the right). Deer and other animals can be seen scattered amongst the trees and bushes.

The composition is influenced by 14th- and 15th-century Tuscan painting: the traditional gold background has been replaced by a landscape with blue sky and small clouds in the distance, as frequently found in the painting of Gentile da Fabriano; and the cities recall those in the wall paintings of Ambrogio Lorenzetti (Carli 1957, pls. 72, 83). The drawing of the faces indicates a knowledge of Palaeologan painting; but the combination of this with familiarity with Italian art suggests that the icon was painted in the mixed cultural environment of 15th-century Crete. This is a painting of the highest quality.

Bibliography. Chatzidakis 1974 (1), pl. XXXIV. Chatzidakis 1974 (2), p. 113, fig. 80. Chatzidakis (Th.) 1982, no. 19. Chatzidakis (N.) 1983, no. 48, p. 55. Byzantine Art 1986, no. 112, pp. 112, 113. Affreschi e icone, no. 66, pp. 112-113. From Byzantium to El Greco 1987, no. 49, pp. 118, 181.

N. Ch.

58

The Transfiguration
Second half of the 15th century
45×36 cm
Athens. Benaki Museum
(Stathatos Collection)

In the centre of the scene, the figure of Christ in a circular glory stands at the summit of the rocky triangle of Mount Thabor. The three apostles have fallen to the ground with tormented movements, their bodies following the slopes of the mountain. Two prophets, Elijah and Moses, stand on the top of two rocks at the sides, flanking the figure of Christ in the centre.

Two episodes from the narrative can be seen behind the slopes of the rock in the centre: Christ leads the apostles up Mount Thabor, and then leads them away (Millet 1916, p. 231, figs. 198, 200). The composition is skilfully balanced, with delicately designed figures. These are slender, with small heads, executed in the manner of miniature painting. The rich drapery is fragmented into smaller planes, with hanging folds deriving from Palaeologan art. The same refinement can be seen in the harmony of the palette. Ochre is used for the rock in the centre and blue-grey for the two at the sides, with deep red, deep blue and light olive green on the chitons and himatia worn by the apostles.

An icon with similar iconography and style is to be found in the Tsakiroglou collection (Karakatsani 1980, fig. 4). Two icons with the same subject on a larger scale, in Sifnos (Aliprantis 1979, pl. 1α), considerably overpainted, and the other in Zagreb (Djurić

1961, no. 66, p. 124 (16th-17th century), pl. LXXXVII), are connected by their style and iconography with the present icon.

The signature of Emmanuel Tzanfournaris is a forgery (cf. Chatzidakis 1962, p. 48, note 11, p. 93, note 2).

Conservation. Benaki Museum laboratories (1982).

Bibliography. Xyngopoulos 1951, p. 10, no. 7, pl. 7. Xyngopoulos 1957, p. 172, pl. 47, 1. Chatzidakis 1962, pp. 48 and 93. Embiricos 1967, fig. 89. Karakatsani 1980, p. 15.

N. Ch.

59

St. Nicholas with scenes from his life
c. 1500
41×36 cm
Athens. R. Andreadis Collection

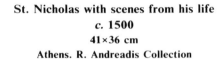

Egg tempera on wood. The central scene is a portrayal of St. Nicholas enthroned. In the border surrounding it there are twelve scenes from the life and miracles of the saint. Starting in the top left corner, and proceeding left to right, these are: the birth of the saint; his election as bishop; the saint rescuing the three daughters from prostitution; the saint rescuing the three innocents from the executioner; the saint destroying the idols in the temple; the miracle of the ship (the calming of the waves); the three generals in prison; the saint appearing in a dream to Constantine the Great; the saint appearing in a dream to the general; the three generals offering gifts to Constantine the Great; the Dormition of the saint; and the three generals offering gifts to St. Nicholas. These episodes from the life and miracles of the saint are not in the chronological order of the synaxaria (lives of the saints). This is also true of other icons of St. Nicholas roughly contemporary with this one (icon on Patmos from 1430-60, and a late 15th-century icon from Kastoria) and also of earlier icons (icon from Sinai,

from the end of the 12th century).

The icon has been attributed to a Cretan painter and is dated to *c.* 1500. Certain Palaeologan iconographic features may have been transmitted through the works of 15th-century Cretan painters such as Angelos Akotantos (cf. the type of the throne in the Deesis icons by this painter in the Monastery of Viannou and the Kanellopoulos Collection) and Andreas Ritzos (cf. the type of the throne in the icon of Christ on Patmos, and the architecture in the Christological scenes in the icon of the Virgin Enthroned in the Benaki Museum). However, the flowing drapery of the saint's garments, typical of Cretan icons in the Italian manner (e.g. cat. no. 56), demonstrate that Italian features could find their place even in an icon like this, which otherwise followed the Greek manner, in terms of both iconography and style.

Bibliography. Chatzidakis (Th.) 1982, no. 24. Chatzidakis (N.) 1983, no. 33, p. 41, fig. 33. Ševčenko 1983. Affreschi e icone 1986, no. 81, pp. 130-131. From Byzantium to El Greco, no. 57, pp. 126, 186-187.

M. V.

60

The Entry into Jerusalem
Last quarter of the 15th century
49.1×48.3 cm
Athens. P. Kanellopoulos Collection

The composition is divided into two equally balanced parts by a tall tree which rises outside the walls of Jerusalem. Christ, the main figure, is shown on the left, sitting on the ass and moving to the right, accompanied by the twelve apostles in a compact group. The background consists of a rocky landscape, in which is set a depiction of a smaller walled city; from it are departing a number of figures painted in miniature, one of them mounted on a white horse. On the right of the panel rise the walls of Jerusalem, with the different buildings precisely drawn. Before the walls of the city, two dense groups of Jews appear from two gates to meet Christ; other small figures are leaning out over the wall. Young children are scattered throughout the composition, engaged in lively activities: some are climbing trees to cut palm branches, others are spreading their clothes on the ground, and at the bottom others still are wrestling and playing on a hill in front of a fountain. The two cows in front of this fountain, and three more on a low plateau at the right add a bucolic element to the scene which is not part of the traditional iconography. The naturalistic manner in which they are painted recalls works from the quattrocento (Berenson 1968, II, fig. 657). Their 'arbitrary' inclusion in the scene may be compared with that of the various animals that 'inhabit' 15th-century Cretan icons influenced to different degrees by Italian painting (Chatzidakis 1974 (1), pp. 203-204). This iconographic type of the Entry into Jerusalem was popular in Cretan painting, as was the type found in a number of other icons (cf. Chatzidakis (N.) 1983, no. 28, Vocotopoulos 1977-79, pls. 116, 117, 121). It also occurs in the 15th-century wall paintings at Sklaverochori, and in an icon in the Monastery of Dionysios from the same period (Chatzidakis 1969-70, figs. 122, 130).

The iconographic model for the composition is to be sought in Mistra, in the wall paintings of the Church of the Peribleptos, and particularly that of the Pantanassa (1430) (Chatzidakis 1981, figs. 52, 67, 68). Close similarities can be detected in the narrative aspect of the composition, the very rocky landscape, and the graphic details of the episodes with children, amongst which is the *spinario* (the boy removing a thorn from his foot) (Mouriki 1970-72, pp. 58ff., pls. 23a-b). The similarities extend to other details, like the miniature figures of women leaning out from the walls of Jerusalem, and the form of the spring. Finally, the large number of classicizing mask-motifs executed in grisaille on the buildings is another feature of the painting of the Pantanassa (Mouriki 1980-81) that is also found in the Entry into Jerusalem. The obvious links between this icon and its model in the Pantanassa illustrate just how widespread was Constantinopolitan model amongst the leading painters working in different parts of Greece in the 15th century.

The composition of the icon is more strictly organized, and the groups of apostles are treated in a more compact way; the rendering of the details of the human figures and of the buildings reflects the academic character of Cretan icons produced in the second half of the 15th century.

Bibliography. Chatzidakis 1969-70, p. 325, fig. 129. Chatzidakis (Th.) 1982, no. 11. Chatzidakis (N.) 1983, no. 27. Affreschi e icone 1986, no. 82, pp. 132, 133. From Byzantium to El Greco 1987, no. 50, pp. 119, 181-182.

N. Ch.

61

The Seven Sleepers of Ephesos
c. 1500
42.5×34.5 cm
Athens. City of Athens Museum

The Seven Sleepers of Ephesos are depicted inside a cave that takes up the entire surface of the icon, leaving only a small area of gold background. Their postures recall those of the apostles in the traditional iconography of the Prayer in Gethsemane (Millet 1916, pp. 654ff., figs. 659-662), as for example in the Church of Ayios Ioannis Koudoumas in Crete (Bougrat 1982, fig. 27). The same subject, well-known in Byzantine painting (cf. the Vatican 'Menologion' of Basil II), is also found in 15th- and 16th-century Western engravings (Massignon 1961, pp. 12ff., 20ff., pls. VI, 1, VII, 1-5), and in 15th-century Cretan icons (cf. an icon from Sinai, Massignon 1961, pl. VII, 2). It also occurs in the wall paintings by Theophanes in the refectory of the Great Lavra (Millet 1927, pl. 147, 2) and in 17th- and 18th-century icons in the Benaki Museum and the Loverdos Collection.

The icon is the work of a major Cretan painter; the drawing is unusually precise and the painter has a rare sense of colour. Particularly striking is the translucent quality of the white and blue-grey tones, and the bold combinations of different hues of red. The small basket of olives hanging in the cave is well modelled, demonstrating that the artist was familiar with Italian painting. It may be suggested that the icon is to be dated to c. 1500. On the reverse is a cross standing on a stepped plinth, painted at a later date (1639).

Conservation. S. Stasinopoulos.
Bibliography. Chatzidakis (Th.) 1982, no. 13. Chatzidakis (N.) 1983, no. 35, p. 42. Byzantine Art 1986, no. 129, pp. 126-127. Affreschi e icone 1986, no. 85, pp. 134, 135. From Byzantium to El Greco, no. 52, pp. 121, 183.

N. Ch.

62

The Holy Trinity
c. 1500
100×71 cm
Athens. Benaki Museum

Christ and God, the Ancient of Days, are represented frontally, seated on the same throne. The former, on the left, is blessing and holds a Gospel book, the latter, on the right, a half-open scroll. The Ancient of Days has a distinctive white beard and white garments. A white dove, symbolizing the Holy Spirit, is depicted at top centre. In the background are two tall buildings from which two monks are emerging, holding two scrolls with long texts: St. Theodore the Studite and St. Athanasios of Sinai. The head of the figure of the donor at the bottom right has been completely destroyed; he is wearing a white robe with a cross on the breast (a Catholic prelate?).

The subject is found in 15th-century icons on Sinai and in the Historical Museum of Iraklion (Iraklion 1971, fig. p. 359), and occurs with greater frequency in 16th-century works (Xyngopoulos 1957, pl. 34, 2. Chatzidakis-Djurić 1968, no. 32. Borboudakis 1975, no. 32, pl. 63. Galavaris 1980-81, pl. 11a). The figure of Christ Enthroned in the present icon recalls representations of the Deesis belonging to the end of the 15th century (see Chatzidakis (N.) 1983, nos. 4-5). The type of the buildings, the delicate contours of the facial features, and the handling of the drapery permit us to assign the present icon to the same period. Finally, the naturalistic treatment of the dove and the form and perspective treatment of the scrolls reveal the adoption of Italian manners, similar to those found in other Cretan icons of this period. The icon is cut away at the bottom and has the forged signature of Michael Damaskinos (report by Ch. Baltoyanni to the Christian Archaeological Society 1977).

The overpainting resulting from previous conservation work was removed when the icon was fully restored in 1982 in the Benaki Museum laboratories.

Conservation. Benaki Museum laboratories (1982).
Bibliography. Guide to the Benaki Museum 1935, p. 30. Xyngopoulos 1936, nos. 8, 15-17, pl. 10. Felicetti-Liebenfels 1956, pls. 121, 135. Xyngopoulos 1957, pp. 114ff. Embiricos 1967, fig. 79. Delivorrias 1980, p. 67. Chatzidakis (Th.) 1982, no. 7.

N. Ch.

63

Sanctuary Doors
Annunciation and Saints
15th century and second half of the 18th century
142×78 cm
Athens. Byzantine Museum, T. 737

a. This is the original scene, revealed in 1980 in the laboratory of the Byzantine Museum by the removal of the more recent repainting. The Annunciation occupies most of the area of the two doors, and includes the figures of the prophets Isaiah and David, busts of whom are painted on a smaller scale. At the top of the doors there are two other saints, who have been identified as St. Nicholas and the apostle Andrew. At the bottom is the faded inscription ΔΕΗCΙC ΤΟΥ ΔΟΥΛΟΥ ΤΟΥ ΘΕΟΥ ΑΝΔΡΕΟΥ ΤΟΥ [ΛΙ]ΜΟΓΑΛΛ[ΟΥ], which explains the inclusion of the apostle Andrew: he was the patron saint of the man who dedicated this icon, who was also called Andrew. Iconographically it is related to the miniature by Plousiadinos in Cod. Sin. 1234, which is dated to 1469 (Weitzmann 1973, pp. 30-31, pl. XXXI); to the Annunciation in the margin of the icon by Nikolaos Ritzos in Sarajevo (Chatzidakis 1977 (1), pl. 202); to the same scene in the margin of the Benaki Museum icon of the Virgin (Xyngopoulos 1939, pl. 54); and to a series of icons and sanctuary doors (Baltoyanni 1984, p. 51) that follow a Palaeologan model, transformed and adapted to the principles of Cretan painting.

The stylistic relationship of the icon to the above works points to 15th-century Cretan painting, with its characteristic eclecticism, as do the few Western elements in the scene, for these are to be found in all the painting of this period in Crete. The detail with the column surmounted by a flower pot separating the two figures, which seems rather detached and unconnected with the composition, has been shown to be connected with the colonnade that was invariably included in scenes of the Annunciation painted by the Siennese artists of the 14th and 15th centuries (Baltoyanni 1984, p. 58). A number of stylistic features, such as the diaphanous, light-coloured eyes of the angel, the oversweet face of the Virgin and the realistic expression on the face of David, also have their origins in Western art. The Annunciation, the supreme symbol of the Incarnation, here gains in meaning by virtue of its being painted on the leaves of the sanctuary doors. The significance of the connection between the sanctuary doors and the Annunciation (Chatzidakis 1973, col. 343) is perhaps indicated by the fact that the evidence for the first use of the scene on such a door points to a date in the 12th century (Weitzmann 1964-65, pp. 17-18), when the doctrinal meaning of the Incarnation was widely disputed (Babić 1968, pp. 368-386). It is also known that one of the most frequent metaphors and similes used in Byzantine hymnography and homilies relating to the Virgin is the 'Gate' of Ezekiel ('This gate shall be closed') (Ezekiel XLV.2); at a very early date this came to be regarded as a prefiguration of the role of the Virgin in the Incarnation. One of the applications of this symbolism, which was difficult to render iconographically, was to paint a scene of the Annunciation on the sanctuary doors. This interpretation further accounts for the inclusion of Isaiah, who is also to be found in Western scenes of the Annunciation, influenced by the Latin 'Meditationes Vitae Christi' of Pseudobonaventura; according to this text, at the time of the Annunciation the Virgin was reading the prophecy of Isaiah (Robb 1936, p. 485): ΙΔΟΥ Η ΠΑΡΘΕΝΟC ΕΝ ΓΑCΤΡΙ ΕΞΕΙ ΚΑΙ ΤΕΞΕΤΑΙ ΥΙΟΝ ΚΑΙ ΚΑΛΕCΟΥCΙ ΤΟ ΟΝΟΜΑ ΑΥΤΟΥ ΕΜΜΑΝΟΥΗΛ; this is also the text on the scroll held by the prophet in the icon.

b. The painted surface of the two leaves is divided into two registers, with a scene of the Annunciation at the top and below, in the two large arched panels, the prophets Moses and Aaron. In the Annunciation, which follows the general scheme of the familiar iconographic type, the Virgin is not turning her head towards the angel, but is portrayed almost frontally, with only her face slightly turned to the left. The theatrical sweep of her left arm is consistent with this contrapposto pose.

The two prophets are portrayed standing and frontally, wearing the dress of the Jewish high-priest, with the long tunic, over-garment and cloak, clasped in front of the breast. On their heads, too, they wear the small conical cap of the Jewish high-priest. They are blessing with their right hands, and Moses is holding a scroll, and Aaron the 'flowering rod' in their left. The presence of the two prophets on the sanctuary doors, in association with the Annunciation, is connected with the prophesying by the two of the Incarnation. The flowering rod was explained in the Early Christian period as a prefiguration of the Virgin and her role in the mystery of the Divine Incarnation (Mouriki 1970, p. 218). The presence of Moses is further accounted for by the great probability that the sanctuary doors were painted by the monk from Sinai who painted the doors (Byzantine Museum, no. T. 738), which are signed: ΧΕΙΡ ΙΕΡΕΜΙΟΥ ΙΕΡΟΜΟΝΑΧΟΥ· ΣΙΝΑ·Ι·ΤΟΥ ΤΟΥ ΚΡΗΤΟC ΑΨΜΕ´ (hand of Jeremiah, the priest-monk from Sinai, the Cretan 1745). The present doors are similar to the sanctuary doors from Messene by Jeremiah, both in iconography and in style.

Finally, the date on the sanctuary doors signed by Jeremiah, 1745, also dates the present doors, which were probably painted at the same period.

Provenance. Messene, Italy.
Conservation. Byzantine Museum laboratories (S. Baltoyannis, S. Varotsis, A. Simandoni, G. Skaraki) (1981).
Bibliography. Baltoyanni 1984, pp. 43-72. Affreschi e icone 1986, no. 87, pp. 136-138. From Byzantium to El Greco, no. 53, pp. 122, 183-184.

Ch. B.

64

The Hospitality of Abraham
15th century
97×72 cm
Athens. Byzantine Museum, T. 90

The scene is an illustration of Genesis (18.1-15), describing the dinner given by Abraham to the three angels near the 'oak of Mamre'. It includes three angels seated around a square table loaded with dishes and food. Abraham and Sarah, two tall, narrow buildings at the sides, and two leafy trees leaning inwards, all arranged in a closed composition, developed vertically around the figure of the central angel. The two-line inscription on the gold ground between the two trees refers to the theological content of the scene: [Η ΕΝ ΤΗ C]ΚΗΝΗ ΤΟΥ ΑΒΡΑΑΜ [Τ]ΗC ΖΩ[ΑΡ]ΧΙΚΗC ΤΡΙΑΔΟC ΦΑΝΕΡΩCΙC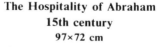. The frequent occurrence of this Old Testament scene from the Bible in the Byzantine and Post-Byzantine periods is accounted for by the fact that it symbolizes the Holy Trinity.

The iconography of the Hospitality of Abraham was established in Early Christian times, but the iconographic type in the Byzantine Museum panel was most probably formulated in Constantinople during the Palaeologan period, as may be inferred from a number of examples in manuscript miniatures, icons and wall paintings. The prevailing aesthetic preferences of the refined circles of artists and patrons in the capital at this period were centred on the revival of antiquity, and can be detected in this icon in a variety of ways. We may note, for example, the classical proportions, the elegant postures and the refined faces of the angels, the 'patriarchal' appearance of Abraham, again following ancient iconographic types, and also a number of details, such as the carafe covered by an upturned glass on the table, which can be seen in a wall painting from Herculaneum, the lion mask with foliage coming out of its mouth, executed in grisaille on the one facade of the building on the right, and the red cloth on the roof of the one on the left. The monumental size of the figures and the reduced scale of the architecture and trees in the background, the return to a flatter conception of space, and the dry modelling of the flesh and drapery are some of the features that provide arguments for dating this icon to the period after 1453. The Byzantine Museum icon panel has been dated variously to the 15th century (Sotiriou 1931, p. 74), to the first half of the 16th century, in relation to the early creations of the Cretan School (Chatzidakis 1961, no. 3, with colour plate. Charalampous-Mouriki 1962-63), or more precisely to the middle of the 16th century, while still being considered a Cretan work (Chatzidakis 1969, fig. p. 45). However, the view that this icon was the work of the Cretan School can be questioned after the publication of pertinent documents in the Venice archives by Cattapan, and the discovery of hitherto unknown pictorial material assigned to this school. The result is that the dates that have been suggested for the majority of icons from this circle have to be raised, by a century in some cases. Taking the recent discoveries into account, it may be suggested that the Byzantine Museum icon of the Hospitality of Abraham should be placed in the second half of the 15th century. Some reservation is also needed as to its precise relationship to the Cretan School, at least until the study of the dated 15th-century ensembles of wall paintings is completed, amongst which the decoration of the Pantanassa at Mistra is of special importance (c. 1428). The Byzantine Museum icon has close iconographic and stylistic affinities with two more icons depicting the same subject, in the Hermitage and the Narbonne Museum, which were probably painted earlier, though still in the 15th century. The same iconographical type, with minor variations, is frequently repeated in later paintings, mostly icons.

Provenance. Acquired on Zakynthos.
Conservation. A. Margaritoff.
Bibliography. Sotiriou 1931, p. 74. Chatzidakis 1961, no. 3, with colour plate. Charalampous-Mouriki 1962-63. Chatzidakis 1969, fig. p. 45. Affreschi e icone 1986, no. 88, pp. 138-140. From Byzantium to El Greco 1987, no. 54, pp. 123, 184-185.

D. M.

65

St. Nicholas
c. **1500**
90×56 cm
Ioannina. Chapel of the Bishop's Palace

The severe modelling, the drapery and the conservative iconography suggest that this icon belongs to the same group as the icons from the Monastery of the Eleousa on the Island in the Lake of Ioannina (cf. Affreschi e icone 1986, no. 73, p. 119).

Provenance. The Monastery of the Eleousa on the Island in the Lake of Ioannina.
Conservation. Ch. Archimandritis (1977).
Bibliography. Triantaphyllopoulos 1977, pp. 165ff. Byzantine Art 1986, no. 122, p. 122. Affreschi e icone 1986, no. 79, p. 129. From Byzantium to El Greco 1987, no. 55, pp. 124, 185.

D. D. T.

66

St. Nicholas with scenes of his miracles
c. **1500**
92×62 cm
Ioannina. Chapel of the Bishop's Palace

Gesso on canvas. Gold ground. Frame with mouldings. Bust of St. Nicholas, with Christ and the Virgin in miniature above him, offering him the gospel and omophorion. The narrow band below encloses three scenes of his miracles painted on a smaller scale in a continuous composition: the saint saving the three innocents from the sword of the executioner, providing dowries for the three daughters of the impoverished noble, and rescuing a ship in danger at sea. The haloes have rough pointillé decoration, and vivid colours are used. The dark underpaint of the faces contrasts with the flesh tones and white highlights. The scenes of the miracles contain many Western elements of Italian origin. The seascape in the miracle of the ship is particularly impressive for this period. The icon is painted in the manner of Cretan painting of the 15th-16th centuries, and the model for the saint is to be found in icons by

Andreas Ritzos (Chatzidakis 1977 (1), pl. 203α. Byzantine Art 1986, no. 107, p. 108). A number of elements, however, suggest that it should be attributed to a workshop in Ioannina. An icon of the Virgin in the Monastery of the Eleousa on the Island in the Lake of Ioannina may be attributed to the painter of St. Nicholas.

Provenance. The Monastery of the Eleousa on the Island in the Lake of Ioannina.
Consérvation. Ch. Archimandritis (1974).
Bibliography. Acheimastou-Potamianou 1973-74, p. 613. Byzantine Art 1986, no. 123, pp. 122-124. Affreschi e icone 1986, no. 80, pp. 129, 130. From Byzantium to El Greco 1987, no. 56, pp. 125, 186.

M. A.-P.

67
Deesis
Early 16th century
25.5×21. cm
Princeton. The Art Museum, Princeton
University, University Purchase, 51-4

The chipped edges, areas of gold missing from the background, and occasional flaking of paint on the figures are minor losses from the otherwise well-preserved surface of this icon. A dark yellow varnish makes it difficult to define the colours precisely.

The figure of Christ and the flanking figures of the Virgin and John the Baptist are depicted standing on a ground of light purple textured with white dots in imitation of flecked marble. Christ stands on a rectangular pink footstool that abuts the margin of the panel. He raises his right hand and holds a book decorated with pearls and jewels in his left. Flanking his cross-nimbus is the inscription IC XC. The Virgin and John the Baptist are depicted in attitudes of prayer with their heads inclined toward Christ. The Virgin wears a bright blue chiton and purple maphorion. MP ΘY is inscribed above and to the left of her nimbus. John the Baptist wears an ochre chiton and dark olive himation. Unlike the Virgin, he extends his hands in a cross-like gesture, the left hand raised and the right lowered. Inscribed above and to the right of his nimbus is IΩ Ο ΠΡΟΔΡΟΜΟC.

The hierarchic poses of the figures and the delicate modelling of faces, hands, and feet have led to an attribution to a Cretan school of painting for this icon and to a date in the first half of the 16th century (Mouriki 1968, pp. 13ff.). More specific parallels can be found in the icons of Nikolaos Ritzos (cf. the Deesis icon from Sarajevo, Mirković 1936, p. 134, fig. 66) and especially Angelos, who came to Crete from Constantinople in 1434, and there he continued to paint in the Constantinopolitan tradition. Two Deesis icons recently attributed to Angelos and dated in the mid-15th century exhibit almost identical composition of figures and modelling of faces and drapery (Chatzidakis (N.) 1983, nos. 4-5), suggesting that the Princeton icon should be attributed to the school of Angelos as well. The darker palette, however, suggests a slightly later date, perhaps at the end of the 15th or the early 16th century. Because of its small size and devotional iconography, this icon probably was a private commission for use in the home or in a private chapel.

Bibliography. Record of the Art Museum, Princeton University 10 (1951), p. 23. Mouriki 1968, pp. 13-28.

N. T.

68
St. Demetrius
16th century
108×82 cm
Kerkyra. Antivouniotissa Museum

The patron saint of Thessalonike is portrayed mounted on a horse, a type inspired by models from the Italian Renaissance. He is being blessed by the hand of God, while the city of Thessalonike (as we are informed by the inscription) rises in the background, protected by very high walls. This type of the saint on horseback, in which the horse is shown from the side, moving slowly forward, while the saint is turned towards the viewer, was probably created in Crete in the 15th century from a combination of Byzantine and Italian elements, and was not very widespread. The harsh modelling of the icon suggests that it should be attributed to a conservative Cretan painter at the end of the 16th century who was inspired by 15th-century models.

Conservation. F. Asimakou.

Bibliography. Vocotopoulos 1972. Chatzidakis (N.) 1983, no. 31, pp. 38, 40. Byzantine Art 1986, no. 134, pp. 130, 133. Affreschi e icone 1986, no. 90, pp. 141-142. From Byzantium to El Greco 1987, no. 60, pp. 129, 188.

P. L. V.

69

Georgios Klontzas:
Triptych with the Last Judgment
Second half of the 16th century
53×75 cm (open); 53×29.5 cm (closed)
USA. Private Collection

Tempera on gesso. The triptych (Vocotopoulos 1985, pp. 64-74, pls. IΘ΄, 1 - ΚΣΤ΄, 9 = Vocotopoulos 1987, pp. 88-95, pls. 74a-f) has the shape of a rectangle crowned by a semi-circle. The central panel has a wood-carved gold-painted frame with an architectural design: a base and two twisted colonnettes support a semi-circular arch, at the apex of which is a stylized calyx containing a pine-cone; there are two palmettes seated at the sides of the arch. The inside of the triptych has a representation of the Last Judgment as its main subject. The outer surface of the central panel has scenes from the life and the history of Mount Sinai, with the hymn 'In Thee Rejoiceth' on the left wing and scenes from the Passion and the Resurrection of Christ on the right. The group of scenes, with its wise juxtaposition of subjects, represents in condensed form the moral and cosmological philosophy of Christianity.

On the rear of the closed triptych is painted a panorama of Mount Sinai with the Monastery of St. Catherine and smaller churches in the distance, on the Sacred Mountain. The scene contains a large number of monks, some of them welcoming three official visitors, who arrive at the monastery at the left, accompanied by Bedouins. Around the border are scenes from the story of Moses (above left, Moses before the burning bush; the drowning of the Egyptians in the Red Sea at the bottom left and Moses with the army of the Jews at the right; above this Moses and the Jews offer a prayer of thanksgiving, while at the right centre is a scene showing the worship of the golden calf; above and to the left, Moses raises the Tablets of the Law in anger and breaks them;

finally, on the central peak of the mountain, Moses receives the tablets with the commandments). On the pinnacle of the mountain to the right, three angels are attending the relic of St. Catherine. The Sinaitic iconography on this panel was a popular subject in Cretan painting of the time of Georgios Klontzas, as can be seen from the Modena triptych by Domenikos Theotokopoulos (Wethey 1962, pl. 33) and other works; it offers a clue as to the original owner of the triptych, which might have been the Monastery on Sinai or one of its metochia on Crete or elsewhere, or possibly a learned monk of Sinai. Five surviving icons by Georgios Klontzas in the Monastery of Sinai (Weitzmann 1980, nos. 20 and 23. Acheimastou-Potamianou 1985-86, pp. 130ff., 132 and 135, notes 28 and 29, fig. 10) are clear evidence of the good reputation enjoyed by the painter amongst its monks.

The front of the closed triptych is adorned with a representation of the hymn 'In Thee Rejoiceth', a direct allusion to the doctrine of the Incarnation. When the triptych is open, this representation stands opposite the Passion and Resurrection of Christ on the other, right wing, which underline the doctrine of Christ's sacrifice and of redemption. The Virgin, deified, is enthroned holding Christ within a circular heavenly glory, in front of a church with five domes; she is encircled and hymned by the prophets and the angelic hosts, and is glorified by the choirs of All Saints, who are arranged hierarchically in registers below the glory. The Presentation of the Virgin in the Temple and the Presentation of Christ in the Temple at the sides, to the left and right of the Virgin, are painted here as representative scenes from the life of the Virgin and Christ, met in complete iconographic cycles, in more fully developed icons of the same subject (cf. an icon in the Byzantine Museum, Athens, from the 15th century (Chatzidakis 1969, p. 69, fig. pp. 40-41) and an icon in the Greek Institute of Venice, the work of Georgios Klontzas (Chatzidakis 1962, no. 50, pls. VI and 37). This, the main face of the triptych, bears the signature of the painter, discreetly but proudly placed in the centre of the gound at the bottom: ΧΕΙΡ ΓΕΩΡΓΙΟΥ ΚΛΟΝΤΖΑ (the hand of Georgios Klontzas). Above, next to the glory with the Virgin, was painted the coat of arms of a later owner of the triptych, a member of the Italian Spada family (Vocotopoulos 1985, p. 71 = Vocotopoulos 1987, p. 93). This addition of the escutcheon (perhaps in the 17th century) clearly shows the admiration and regard in which the owner held this fine miniature work of Cretan 16th-century painting.

When the left wing is opened, the spectator sees, on the left, the scene of Paradise, from the composition of the Last Judgment, with scenes of Paradise Lost, from the book of Genesis inserted at the sides (the creation of the animals at the right, and God reproaching Adam and Eve at the left, the exile of Adam and Eve, and the murder of Abel by Cain); juxtaposed with this on the right wing are the Passion and the Resurrection of Christ, signifying release from the bonds of original sin and opening the way for the human race to salvation and to Paradise.

The outside of the right wing is divided into three registers, the main scenes in which are the Crucifixion, Christ's Descent into Hell, according to the Byzantine type, and the Resurrection, in the Western type. This reflects the conception of the well-known Italo-Cretan icon recently acquired by the Byzantine Museum, Athens, which has the same scenes painted between the letters J H S (Jesus Hominum Salvator) and bears the signature of the 15th-century Cretan painter, Andreas Ritzos (Xyngopoulos 1957, pp. 279ff., pl. 63,2. Chatzidakis 1974 (1), pp. 176ff., pl. H´). The drama of the Crucifixion in the

broader, lowest register is intensified by the addition at the right of an agitated, multi-figural depiction of the Procession to Calvary that preceded it. To the representation in the central register of Christ's Descent to the subterranean realm of Hades have been added scenes at the sides, showing the torments of the sinners. The inscription at the bottom: Ο ΣΚΟΤΗΝΟΣ Κ(ΑΙ) ΑΚΟΡΕΣΤΟΣ. ΑΔΗΣ. ΦΟΣ ΑΝΕΤΗΛΕΝ ΣΗΜΕΡΟΝ (Dark and insatiable Hades. The light has risen today) well contrasts the concepts of dark and light that are the predominant features of the message of the Resurrection. In the semi-circle crowning the representation of the Resurrection, prominence is given to the Conqueror of Death, shown rising from the tomb in a glory of light. This culminating scene is accompanied by two scenes from the Morning Gospels: the Myrrhophores at the Tomb on the left and the Noli Me Tangere on the right. This relatively rare combination of the Resurrection with the episodes relating to the two Marias is to be found at an earlier period in a 14th-century icon of the Walters Art Gallery, Baltimore (cat. no. 26), and in a 15th-16th century wall painting in the Church of Ayios Nikolaos near the village of Trianda on Rhodes (Kollias 1986, pp. 90-97, figs. 44-48); it also occurs in two scenes of the 16th and 18th centuries (Chatzidakis 1977 (1), no. 160, pl. 194 = Chatzidakis 1985, no. 160, pl. 194. Acheimastou-Potamianou 1983, p. 195, note 142). Finally, the opening of the right wing reveals the majestic triptych of the Last Judgment, with the Judgment in the centre, Paradise at the left and Hell on the right wing. The predominant figure in the semi-circle crowning the central panel is Christ the Judge, with the venerating figures of the Virgin and St. John the Baptist at his side, and the angelic hosts around him, chanting and singing hymns to his glory, while the side leaves have the apostles seated on semi-circular benches. The angels of the Judgment are blowing trumpets and opening the books. The dead are arising from the tombs and the sea. Between them is a row of five kings, D(arius), Au(gustus), Al(exandros), Cyrus, or Nebuchadnezzar, known from the vision of Daniel and the Nebuchadnezzar's dream, and the king fourth from the left holding a cross, who is identified with Constantine the Great (cf. Vocotopoulos 1985, p. 67, note 18 = Vocotopoulos 1987, p. 91, note 18). Above the throne of the Preparation in the centre rises the cross, with Adam and Eve kneeling in veneration. Below it angels and devils, with rolls on which are written the good and evil deeds of those being judged, are weighing the souls. The righteous are being led off to the left, to Paradise, and the sinners are dragged off in chains to the right, to Hell, while others are being swallowed by the monster from the deep at the bottom of the scene. On the left wing, in the scene of Paradise, Christ is portrayed at the bottom left as the Great High Priest giving communion to the saints, who are approaching him in ranks, in successive registers. Beneath the bench with the apostles at the top is the Hand of God, holding the souls of the righteous. In the centre, the Virgin rejoices in Paradise, together with her forefather Abraham, who is holding the souls of the righteous, and with the good thief; she is surrounded by musicians and angels singing hymns.

On the right wing of the triptych, depicting Hell, the angel at the top is unrolling the scroll of the heaven. Below this is a narrow register in which the sinners are crowding together fearfully, proceeding to the left, where the avenging angel is raising his sword. The larger, lower part of the panel has a representation of the terrible kingdom of Hades, inundated by the river of fire. This chaotic environment, in which rises the Gehenna of fire and other awful buildings, is dominated by the Antichrist, with the monsters of the Apocalypse and the devils, who are inflicting a myriad tortures on the damned sinners.

Georgios Klontzas (Acheimastou-Potamianou 1985-86, pp. 132ff., with previous bibliography) was born and lived in Iraklion, Crete (c. 1540-1608). He is attested as a painter from 1564. A true representative of the cultured society of Candia in the second half of the 16th century, he was a scholar, a writer, a miniaturist and a scribe, and above all one of the most important painters of his time, perfectly capable of responding to the varied demands of his numerous, aesthetically sophisticated customers, both religious and secular, Orthodox and Catholic, in Crete and elsewhere. He had a special talent for multi-figural, miniature representations, of which the Spada triptych supplies some fine examples, and succeeded in combining the tradition of Cretan art with many elements borrowed from Western painting. Fellow-countryman and contemporary of Michael Damaskinos and the young Domenikos Theotokopoulos, of whose work he was once appointed assessor (Constantoudaki 1975, pp. 296ff.), he was one of the most representative and productive painters of 'Cretan Mannerism'. More than forty signed and unsigned works by him are known, of which eleven are triptychs, three of them signed. The Last Judgment, the Passion (cf. cat. no. 70) and Resurrection of Christ, and the 'In Thee Rejoiceth' were amongst Klontzas's favourite subjects. He painted the Last Judgment, in particular, in thirteen works, including manuscripts, triptychs and icons (Acheimastou-Potamianou 1985-86, p. 134), continuously striving for and presenting new angles on composition and interpretation.

The Spada triptych, which is probably one of the early works of Klontzas's artistic maturity (cf. Vocotopoulos 1985, p. 73 = Vocotopoulos 1987, p. 94), is linked by the details of the iconography to other triptychs and icons by him (Vocotopoulos 1985, pp. 66ff. = Vocotopoulos 1987, pp. 91ff.). Its closest resemblance, however, is with the so-called Yorkshire triptych, which also bears Klontzas's signature (East Christian Art 1987, no. 75, figs. 75a-f). With one exception, the subjects depicted in the two triptychs are the same, and the composition and iconographical treatment of them is very similar. One of the most important differences between them is that the scene of the Procession to Calvary and the Crucifixion on the outside of the right leaf of the Spada triptych is replaced in the Yorkshire triptych by the equally spectacular Slaughter of the Innocents. A vast number of other differences in the style, composition and colour, in the disposition or treatment of the detailed iconographic elements, emerge from a more extensive comparison of the two triptychs, indicating, as always, the artistic genius of Georgios Klontzas and his

flexible approach to composition and iconography. In the Spada triptych, the narrative is richer and more complete in its conceptual implications: the Yorkshire triptych is painterly and has greater facility of composition, but lacks the same stability and clarity of descriptive discourse. Analysis of the two works allows us to assign the Yorkshire triptych to a later period of Klontzas's artistic activity than the Spada triptych, and the repetition of the panorama of Mount Sinai suggests that this triptych had a similar destination.

Provenance. Formerly in a private collection in Rome.
Bibliography. Vocotopoulos 1985, pp. 64-74 = Vocotopoulos 1987, no. 74, pp. 88-95.

M. A.-P.

70

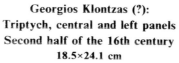

Georgios Klontzas (?):
Triptych, central and left panels
Second half of the 16th century
18.5×24.1 cm
Baltimore. The Walters Art Gallery, 37.628

The central panel has a scene of the Crucifixion, and the left wing has the Procession to Calvary on the inside and the Judgment of Caiaphas and Mocking of Christ on the outside. The lost right wing probably had scenes from the same iconographic cycle of the Passion.

The Crucifixion on the central panel is treated as a multi-figural scene with a large number of supplementary episodes. The arched shape of the panel resulted in the elevation of the cross of Christ in the centre, which is higher than those of the two thieves to the left and right, though these also follow the arched shape of the panel. A black winged daemon is taking the soul of the wicked thief at the right. Mary Magdalene kneels and embraces the cross of Christ. The mounted centurion to the left of the cross is pointing to Christ, confessing his

faith. Behind him is a group of mounted officers and women. Below the thief to the right is another multi-figural group of officers, soldiers and Jews. Finally, in the left foreground is a group of Jews with extravagant hats, with a group of soldiers to the right, throwing dice for Christ's clothes. This episode forms a contrast with that of the Virgin fainting, which is painted in the middle, just above it. The procession to Calvary on the inside of the left wing follows a winding path which cannot be seen because of the large number of episodes, leaving the impression of a unified composition. At the top left the two thieves, their hands bound, are being pushed violently by slaves with whips. At the bottom right Christ, exhausted, is sitting on the ground, and Veronica is preparing to wipe his face. In front of Christ, Simon of Cyrene is carrying the cross. The fainting of the Virgin, an episode that also occurs in the Crucifixion, is painted here too, above the group with Christ.

On the outside of the left wing the representations are less complex and have fewer figures. In the foreground Christ is being presented to Caiaphas, accompanied by soldiers. In the middleground, the scene of the Mocking of Christ is depicted beneath an arched, monumental gate.

The majority of the iconographic motifs developed on the panels of this triptych find parallels in triptychs preserved intact, or in part, in Museums in Ravenna (Constantoudaki-Kitromilides 1981), the Vatican (Muñoz 1906. Muñoz 1928), Geneva (Lazović, Frigerio-Zeniou 1985) and in private collections in Paris (Constantoudaki-Kitromilides 1985) and formerly in Rome (the Spada family triptych, see cat. no. 69). The last of these bears the signature of the Cretan painter Georgios Klontzas, and the others have been convincingly connected with his art. To the triptychs with scenes from the Passion that have been attributed to Georgios Klontzas should be added one that at the beginning of the century was in the possession of an antique dealer in Aix-les-Bains, Savoy (Willumsen 1927, I, figs. pp. 97, 99). Klontzas lived between c. 1540 and 1608, and was active in Candia (Iraklion), the capital of Crete in the period of Venetian domination.

The two panels of the Walters Art Gallery triptych can easily be attributed to Klontzas on the basis of the iconographic and stylistic similarities between it and works by Klontzas like the signed Spada triptych. In both triptychs, for example, the two episodes of the fainting of the Virgin, Simon carrying the cross, Christ in the Procession to Calvary, and Veronica, have all been depicted in exactly the same way, despite the fact that in the Spada triptych the two scenes (of the Crucifixion and the Ascent to Golgotha) have been condensed into one. The relationship between the two triptychs is shown to have been even closer by the iconographic element of the woman standing behind Veronica in the scene of the Procession to Calvary in the present triptych, who for some unaccountable reason is looking over her shoulder. This woman is also painted in the Spada triptych, where, however, she is looking over her shoulder at the group of Jews following behind her. This same element is also to be found in the Vatican triptych.

The miniature rendering of the scenes in this triptych is a further element linking it with the art of Klontzas. Klontzas is known to have been a miniature painter, and four illustrated manuscripts are associated with him (Cod. Marc. gr. Cl. VII, 22, of 1590, Paliouras 1977; Cod. Bodl. gr. Barocci 170, of 1577, Paliouras 1981 and Hutter 1978, no. 9; Cod. Vat. gr. 2137, Vocotopoulos 1985-86; unpublished codex in the Bodleian Library, information from M. Chatzidakis). In addition to the fact of being painted in miniature, the Walters Art Gallery triptych has a number of similarities of details with these manuscripts, such as the type of Caiaphas's throne (cf. also fols. 60^r, 185^v and 187^r of Cod. Marc. gr. Cl. VII, 22), the soldiers' uniforms and helmets (fols. 6^r, 10^v and 11^v in the same manuscript), the mounted figures, and their horses (fols. 7^v, 22^r and 69^r).

The wooden frame of the central panel of the triptych appears to have been treated violently at some point, and retains almost nothing of its earlier splendour. This forms a contrast with the majority of the triptychs by Klontzas, which have wood-carved frames of a very high quality (triptychs in Venice, Chatzidakis 1962, pl. 51; on Patmos, Chatzidakis 1977 (1), pl. 62; cat. no. 69; and in Ravenna, Constantoudaki-Kitromilides 1981, pls. A´, Δ´), offering incontrovertible evidence of the art of wood-carving, which was particularly flourishing in Candia at this period (Casanaki 1974). The Walters Art Gallery triptych, associated with the art of the Cretan Georgios Klontzas, is an example of the art produced in Candia, the capital of Crete during the Venetian occupation. This triptych also sheds light, in its own way, on the character and content of the civilization that flourished in Crete in the late Venetian period; it naturally sheds light more particularly on the character and content of the painting of this period which, while retaining its Byzantine background, adopted and assimilated elements from Western painting, both contemporary and earlier.

The manneristic elements, and certain Late Gothic reminiscences, taken from Western painting, are clear in this triptych, as are the Palaeologan roots of the painter.

Bibliography. Unpublished.

M. V.

71

Domenikos Theotokopoulos:
St. Luke the Evangelist
Between 1560 and 1567
41.6×33 cm
Athens. Benaki Museum, 11296
(D. Sicilianos bequest)

The Evangelist, seated on a chair of Renaissance type, with a shell containing paint in his hand, is putting the finishing touches to an icon of the Virgin on the easel in front of him. An angel descends between the painter and the easel, to crown him. A band around the angel's shoulders is blowing in the wind, revealing the inscription: ANEIKON...I...CACAN... ΥΨΩCE. Beneath the easel, the painting instruments rest on a Late Gothic stool. On the side of it is the signature, in black paint, in the form typical of Cretan icon painters: ΧΕΙΡ ΔΟΜΗΝΙΚΟΥ (the hand of Domenikos). The scene takes place inside a room drawn in perspective, with the vanishing point at the centre of the panel. The damaged area of the icon can be restored with the help of a fairly faithful copy of it in the Loverdos Collection (Xyngopoulos 1957).

At first sight, this appears to be a conventional icon of the Cretan School. This impression derives in part from the familiar pose of the Evangelist, established in the middle Byzantine period (Bergman 1973, pp. 46, 142), and in part from the fact that the Virgin Hodegetria is portrayed according to the models of the Cretan School. The modelling of the flesh on the upraised arm of the Evangelist is soft, and lit by

quick, free brush-strokes reminiscent of earlier works of Palaeologan painting. The colours in the dress, however, are now and then unusually translucent. Through them can be detected the drawing, partly incised, partly freely drawn with the brush. Luke's himation is lit by a thick white paint on the translucent red, just as in the figure of St. Paul in the Syros Dormition of the Virgin (From Byzantium to El Greco 1987, no. 63). The perspective rendering of the room and furniture creates a strong three-dimensional feeling. The Renaissance chair and Late Gothic stool, and also the Italianizing angel, are all Western loans, that serve here, just like the Renaissance candlesticks in the Syros Dormition, as incontrovertible evidence of a restless spirit in search of innovation even in a composition with known iconographic models.

Although the motif of St. Luke painting the icon of the Virgin is known in literary sources from the period of the iconoclastic controversy (Klein 1933, *passim*), it does not appear to have been used in Byzantine art before the Palaeologan period. Typical examples of it are the 14th-century wall painting at Mateić (Petković 1934, pl. CXLIV, A) and the drawing in the Patmos lectionary cod. 330, of 1427 (Spatharakis 1981, no. 287, fig. 508). The subject seems mainly to have attracted the attention of a number of Cretan painters influenced by Italian art in the second half of the 16th century, including Georgios Klontzas (Paliouras 1977, pl. 53), and probably Michael Damaskinos, to whom may be attributed a very interesting icon with this subject from the Church of Ayios Loukas on Zakynthos (Konomos 1964, p. 61). The interest taken by the westernizing Cretan painters in this unusual subject is perhaps not unrelated to the worship of St. Luke as patron saint of artists' guilds in the West from the 14th century on (Martindale 1972, p. 13). At this period we also have the first references to the guild of the painters of St. Luke at Candia (Constantoudaki 1975-76, p. 58).

The attribution of the Benaki Museum icon to Domenikos Theotokopoulos by M. Chatzidakis was disputed by students of the great painter's work (Wethey 1962, p. 246, no. X400). The arguments adduced were the omission of the surname from the painter's signature and stylistic differences between this icon and the works of Theotokopoulos then known. The

discovery of the icon of the Dormition of the Virgin on Syros, another conservative work with clear stylistic affinities with the icon of St. Luke, demonstrated beyond any doubt the soundness of the attribution of this work to Domenikos Theotokopoulos. These two icons seem to be the earliest examples of the work of the distinguished artist, and confirm the information deriving from the Venetian archives that Domenikos Theotokopoulos was a recognized painter of icons in Crete before he went to Venice, probably in 1567 (Constantoudaki 1975-76, p. 55).

Conservation. Ph. Zachariou (1956), S. Stasinopoulos (1988).
Bibliography. Chatzidakis 1956, pp. 4-5. Wethey 1962, p. 246, no. X400. Chatzidakis 1963, pp. 32-37. Chatzidakis (N.) 1983, no. 49, pp. 55-56. Chatzidakis 1987, p. 309.

L. B.

72

Domenikos Theotokopoulos:
The Adoration of the Magi
1567-1570
40×45 cm
Athens. Benaki Museum, 3048

The Virgin, seated on the stylobate of a Roman ruin, is holding out the Infant Christ to the venerating Magi, while Joseph is looking on in the background. The infant radiates light onto the figures forming a circle around him. The third Ethiopian Magus, wearing vivid red boots, a manneristic figure rendered in contrapposto. Next to him a soldier with his back turned to the spectator, and the agitated group of three horses, with lively movements in different directions, against the background of an atmospheric landscape with an unworldy light.

Although use is made of egg tempera on a wooden panel prepared with gesso on canvas, in the traditional Cre-

tan manner, the technique recalls that of oil painting. In a number of places where the paint is translucent it is possible to detect the freehand underdrawing with a light brush, especially in the figure of the Virgin and underneath the cross-vault. The figures are moulded in light and colour, with complete indifference to outlines, following the models of the Venetian School of the 16th century (Barasch 1978, pp. 90ff.). Special care is given to the rendering of the reflections of light on the metal objects and the marble architecture.

The Roman ruin, drawn in perspective with a vanishing point just above the head of the infant, creates a strong feeling of depth. The Corinthian columns are disproportionately short, and support an entablature with projections and a cross-vault with an opaion. The crepis bears the painter's signature, in black paint: ΧΕΙΡ ΔΟΜΗΝΙΚΟΥ (the hand of

Domenikos); this resembles the signatures in the Modena triptych and the icon of St. Luke (Chatzidakis 1964, pp. 79-80; and cat. no. 71), and has misled several foreign scholars, who have expressed doubt as to whether this is really the work of Theotokopoulos (Wethey 1962, p. 30).

A similar use of architectural background drawn in perspective with strong foreshortening is known in other works, that have been attributed to the early part of Theotokopoulos's period in Italy (1567-1570) (Constantoudaki 1975-76, pp. 58ff.), such as the Purification of the Temple in the National Gallery in Washington, and the Healing of the Blind in Parma (Bury 1987, pp. 388-391). From this point of view, it is interesting that Theotokopoulos possessed the manual of perspective by Daniele Barbaro, La pratica della perspettiva, printed in Venice in 1568 (Wethey 1962, I, no. 88), and the publication by Barbaro of Vitruvius's De architectura (Marías-Bustamante 1979, pp. 31-39). Domenikos Theotokopoulos seems to have returned again and again to variations of the Adoration of the Magi or the Shepherds, over a period of at least thirty years. The stable, an indispensable part of the Adoration in the Italian works of the 14th-15th centuries, was adopted by Theotokopoulos in the Modena triptych (Wethey 1962, I, pl. 33). This element was also frequently used by Cretan painters in icons in the Italian manner, such as the Adoration of the Magi by Michael Damaskinos, and that by Emmanuel Lambardos (cat. no. 74). The substitution of an ancient ruin for the stable here, perhaps inspired by an engraving, is quite common in Venetian works of the 16th century, especially paintings by Jacopo Bassano, in which the ancient ruin is often contrasted with a natural landscape, as here (The Genius of Venice 1983, p. 148).

Theotokopoulos also shared Bassano's interest in the use of an inner source of light, whether a candle or, as here, the Infant Christ; this interest is also associated with the aspirations of Correggio. These aspirations, seen here in an incipient stage, were further developed in later works by Theotokopoulos, such as the Adoration of the Shepherds in the Prado, which is dated to between 1612 and 1614 (Wethey 1962, II, pl. 161).

To recapitulate, we may say that the Adoration of the Magi is a work that reveals Theotokopoulos's assimilation of 16th-century Venetian painting, on which Titian set his seal: the use of occasionally explosive colour, an indifference to clear outlines and the use of light to give the work a distinctive atmosphere. The first art historian to accept that this was a genuine youthful work of Domenikos Theotokopoulos was A. L. Mayer (Mayer 1935, pp. 205-207).

The comparison of the signature of the painter on this work with those on the Modena triptych and St. Luke the Evangelist (cat. no. 71) acquires a new interest from the discovery of the Dormition of the Virgin on Syros (From Byzantium to El Greco 1987, no. 63). The identity of style between this last and St. Luke demonstrates that the Domenikos of the three signatures is none other than Domenikos Theotokopoulos. The Modena triptych and the Adoration of the Magi examined here should therefore be included amongst the earliest known works of Domenikos Theotokopoulos's Italian phase. The small size of it suggests that it was probably painted as a model for a larger work.

Conservation. Benaki Museum laboratories (S. Stasinopoulos - K. Milanou) (1986).
Bibliography. Wethey 1962, pp. 330ff. Chatzidakis 1963, pp. 32ff. Xydis 1964, pp. 68-70. Manzini-Frati 1969, no. 1. Gudiol 1971, no. 2. Pita Andrade 1981, no. 1. El Greco Exhibition 1986, p. 171, no. 1. Chatzidakis 1987, p. 310. From Byzantium to El Greco 1987, no. 62a, pp. 132, 190.

L. B.

73

**Emmanuel Lambardos: St. Onoufrios
End of the 16th-
Beginning of the 17th century
55.5×36.5 cm
Houston. The Menil Collection**

The hermit saint, who withdrew to live in the desert of the Thebaid in the 4th century, is depicted here full-length and frontally. He is naked, with a loin-cloth of leaves around his waist and a long white beard falling to his knees. His right hand is raised in a gesture of prayer, with the palm turned outwards, and in his left he holds an open scroll with the text ΤΥΡΒΗ ΜΑΤΑΙΑ ΚΟCΜΙΚΩΝ ΦΡΟΝ-ΤΙCΜΑΤΩΝ. His body is tall and erect, almost youthful, with correct proportions, and long thin arms and legs; it is modelled with light colours on a brown underpaint. The face is austere and tranquil, with clearly delineated characteristics and a reflective gaze, and is framed by rich hair that falls in well-drawn curls onto his shoulders. The halo is bounded by a double incised circle. The saint's body is framed by the rocky landscape with sharp, stepped rocks, behind him, which is designed to project the ascetic figure against the gold background. In the middle of the frame, at the bottom, is the signature: ΧΕΙΡ ΕΜΜΑ-ΝΟΥΗΛ ΤΟΥ ΛΑΜΠΑΡΔΟΥ (the hand of Emmanuel Lambardos). Two Cretan painters from Iraklion with the same name signed in this manner.

They are known from a large number of signed works and also from the archival sources, and were related and almost contemporary (the first is attested from 1587 to 1631 and the second from 1623 to 1644). Both belonged to the same workshop and their work is characterized by a deliberate return to the iconographic types and the style of the end of the 15th and beginning of the 16th centuries. This icon, too, repeats a type from the end of the 15th century (cf. the representation of the saint on the border of an icon by Andreas Ritzos in Tokyo). Here, however, there is no intensity; the tranquility and nobility of the head, the position of the hands, and the inscription on the scroll reveal that the painter was concentrating on the morale of the man who had been raised above worldly things rather than the saint worn out by his askesis and his toils. The volumes of the composition are well balanced and it has a distinctive accuracy and delicacy of line, a flawless technique and meticulous use of colours. The icon is probably to be attributed to the earlier of the two Cretan painters. An icon with a similar subject was reported in an Athenian collection in 1935.

Provenance. A sale at Sotheby's (1984).
Bibliography. Sotheby's 1984, no. 23, pp. 10-11.

M. C.

**Emmanuel Lambardos:
The Adoration of the Magi
16th century
46×50 cm
Athens. R. Andreadis Collection**

The scene of the Adoration is set in a typical Siennese landscape, with distant cities, trees and huge rocks. Joseph and Mary are on the left, under a wooden shelter, turning towards the

Magi, who have just dismounted and are kneeling before Christ. The signature at the left, above the heads of the two shepherds, ΧΕΙΡ ΕΜΜΑΝΟΥΗΛ ΛΑΜΠΑΡΔΟΥ, gives us the name of the famous family of 16th-century painters who worked in Candia (Iraklion) on Crete. In iconographical terms the scene is similar to that on the signed icon by Michael Damaskinos in Iraklion (Chatzidakis 1953, p.

13, pl. XVI. Borboudakis 1985, p. 146, pl. 38), and one like it in the Correr Museum in Venice (Museo Correr 1957, p. 75), which is thought to be a later copy by Michael Damaskinos. Stylistically it is similar to the icon of the Crucifixion in the Byzantine Museum, Loverdos Collection (Chatzidakis 1953, pl. XVII), signed by the same painter, though the authenticity of the signature is disputed. The elements common to both icons include the subtle contours of the features, the soft modelling of the flesh, the fine use of gold especially on the undulating gold borders of the garments, the delicate movements and the nobility of the figures. These elements exist alongside the pronounced Western influence that can be detected in the iconography and stylistic manner of both works. The fact that the present icon derived its iconography from a Western model is demonstrated by its close affinity with the Adoration of the Magi by Bartolo di Fredi in the Sienna Art Gallery (Cecchi 1928, pl. CCXXIV). It follows the Sienna model more faithfully than the icon by Damaskinos, and seems to be the earlier of the two, and since it also has a number of stylistic elements associated with early Cretan painting. If the signature is authentic, the artist in question was the Emmanuel Lambardos who also painted the Crucifixion in the Loverdos Collection and is earlier than his namesake, the Emmanuel Lambardos who painted the Venice icon of the Crucifixion at the beginning of the 17th century (Manoussakas 1971, pp. 7ff., pl. A´).

Bibliography. Baltoyanni 1986 (1), no. 19. Affreschi e icone 1986, no. 92, pp. 143, 144. From Byzantium to El Greco 1987, no. 64, pp. 134, 192.

Ch. B.

75

Michael Damaskinos:
St. John the Baptist
Second half of the 16th century
111.4×60.2 cm
Zakynthos. Museum

The winged figure of St. John the Baptist is facing to the left; his right hand is raised in a gesture of speech and he is addressing Christ, a tiny figure at the top left. His words are written in elegant capitals and with flawlessly accurate spelling on the long, unrolled scroll he is holding in his left hand: OPAC OIA ΠΑΣΧΟΥCIN... Signature: XEIP MIXAHΛ TOY ΔAMACKHNOY. The decapitated head in a bowl at the bottom is a reference to the festival of the Invention of the Head of the Baptist. In the background there are two rocky pinnacles and the axe is leaning against the foot of a tree at the bottom right. This is one of the finest icons by Damaskinos (who died in 1592), traditional in iconography and style, remarkable both for its simple colour harmony, with green, blue and blue-grey, and for the precision of the drawing; this can be seen in the treatment of the tall, aristocratic figure with its expressive gestures, and also in the gold webbing in the clothing. Elements derived by Damaskinos from 15th-century Cretan painting include in particular the perspective treatment of the scroll, and the mountains, which are reminiscent of Angelos; the manneristic arrangement of the signature, which is half hidden behind a rock is typical of his own period.

Provenance. The Church of Ayios Spyridon Flambouriaris on Zakynthos (retrieved in 1953).
Bibliography. Drandakis 1962, pp. 126ff. Babić-Chatzidakis 1983, p. 313, fig. p. 360 (in English and French). Byzantine Art 1986, no. 139, pp. 135-136. Affreschi e icone 1986, no. 95, pp. 147, 148. From Byzantium to El Greco 1987, no. 66, pp. 136, 193.

M. Ch.

St. John the Baptist
16th century
104.5×32 cm
Crete, Iraklion. Church of St. Matthew Sinaiton

This iconographic type of St. John the Baptist derives from a model dating from the Palaeologan period, which was also followed by the Cretan painters of the 15th century. The very tall figure of the saint, portrayed frontally, is wearing a melote (sheepskin) and a himation: his right hand is raised in blessing, and in his left he holds an open scroll and a long staff that terminates in a cross. The foreshortening of the left arm in this icon is a characteristic of the type. The addition of the wings, however, which are not found in the Palaeologan model and the absence of the decapitated head on the ground, are new features. The style and the modelling, in which the flesh is painted on a brown underpaint, and the freedom with which the volumes and the prominent cheekbones are rendered, are features that are also to be found in the figure of Symeon (cat. no. 77), and suggest that the icon should be attributed to Michael Damaskinos. Both icons have the same dimensions, and seem to have come from the same iconostasis.

Conservation. T. Moschos.
Bibliography. Borboudakis 1971, p. 529, pl. 544γ. Byzantine Art 1986, no. 141, pp. 137-138. Affreschi e icone 1986, no. 96, pp. 147, 148. From Byzantium to El Greco 1987, no. 67, pp. 137, 194.

M. B.

Symeon Theodochos
16th century
99×32 cm
Crete, Iraklion. Church of St. Matthew Sinaiton

This rare scene of Symeon Theodochos ('Receiver of God') with the Christ Child in his arms is thought to be an abbreviated form of the Presentation in the Temple, and derives mainly from the miniatures in the margins of illuminated manuscripts. The manner in which Symeon is holding Christ, together with the text on the scroll, are designed to focus the worshipper's attention on the holy infant. The technique used in the venerable figure of Symeon is that of Cretan painting, and the brush work is rather free; it gives him a distinctly individual, personal quality, full of strength, which is intensified by the profound, reflective gaze. The figure of Symeon is related to the figures of aged bishops in the icon of the first Ecumenical Counsil (1591) by Michael Damaskinos, and the plump figure of the young Christ is reminiscent of Christ in this same icon, in the Vision of St. Peter of Alexandria. The icon of Symeon may also be attributed to Damaskinos. A further feature common to the two is the realistic treatment of the veins on the hands and temples of the aged figures of the bishops and of Symeon, which reflects the painter's experience of Italian art.

Conservation. T. Moschos.
Bibliography. Borboudakis 1969, p. 527, pl. ΡΛΔ´. Borboudakis 1971, p. 529. Borboudakis 1985, no. 33, p. 137. Byzantine Art 1986, no. 142, p. 138. Affreschi e icone 1986, no. 97, pp. 148, 149. From Byzantium to El Greco 1987, no. 68, pp. 137, 194.

M. B.

Triptych
End of the 16th century
20×28 cm (open); 20×15 cm (closed)
Athens. City of Athens Museum

The central panel has a representation of the Deesis, with Christ in the
centre and the Virgin and St. John the
Baptist on either side. At the top are
busts of SS George and Demetrius.
Each of the side leaves has two
Church Fathers depicted frontally:
St. Gregory the Theologian and St.
John Chrysostom on the left, and SS
Basil and Spyridon on the right, accompanied by busts of SS Peter and
Paul respectively. The outside of the
two wings is decorated with the Annunciation. The painter is clearly following 15th-century models. The main
scene of the Deesis and the figures
of the Church Fathers resemble those
in the icon by Nikolaos Ritzos in
Sarajevo. Christ is holding an open
Gospel book, and the Virgin and the
Baptist are standing in attitudes of
prayer (Babić-Chatzidakis 1983, p.
321). The garments worn by the
Church Fathers also follow models
from the end of the 15th century (cf.
Byzantine Art 1986, no. 133, Affreschi e icone 1986, no. 78). The scene
of the Annunciation on the outside of
the wings, however, has no architectural background, and the Virgin is
sitting on an imposing wooden throne;
in both respects the composition dif-

fers from the usual early Cretan
iconography, and also from that used
by Theophanes in the 16th century
(Chatzidakis (N.) 1983, no. 40. Chatzidakis 1969-70, figs. 34, 68). The vigorous stride of the archangel and the
figure of the Virgin seated upon the
throne follow a model found in the
well-known bilingual, Greek-Italian
manuscript from the end of the 13th
century Par. gr. 54 (Lazarev 1967, fig.
390).

The shape of the triptych is similar to
two later ones in the Berlin Museum and the Benaki Museum, Athens
(Elbern 1979, no. 4, p. 16. Xyngopoulos 1936, no. 53, p. 76). The overall
design with the Deesis in the central
panel and the saints on the side leaves
is the same but the present work is of
a much better quality, reflected in the
careful technique and the polishing of
the gold background. The figures are
solid, and their expressions severe,
the modelling compact, using predominantly dark tones, and the
treatment of the drapery is harsher
than that in works from the end of the
15th and beginning of the 16th centuries; the triptych seems therefore to
have been painted by a fine artist
from the end of the 16th century.

Bibliography. Byzantine Art 1986, no. 147, pp.
142-143. From Byzantium to El Greco 1987,
no. 69, pp. 138, 195.

N. Ch.

79

Triptych, with the Virgin Portaitissa,
St. Paul Xiropotaminos
and St. Eleutherios
17th century
28.5×43.2 cm
Athens. Benaki Museum, 8267

Egg tempera on wood. The inside of
the triptych has a bust of the Virgin
Portaitissa in the type of the Hodegetria, flanked by two full-length saints,

Paul Xiropotaminos and Eleutherios,
on the wings. The former of these is
wearing monastic garb, while the latter is dressed in bishop's vestments.
The central panel shows a depressed
triple arch with a plain moulding. On
the outside of the wings can be detected a cross and the abbreviations
ICXC NHKA in red colour.
The Portaitissa, with the mark on the
cheek caused by an Arab pirate, is re-

lated directly to the tradition of the Iviron Monastery on Mount Athos; here, in a special chapel, is preserved what is thought to have been the model for it, one of the most important devotional icons on Mount Athos (Huber 1969, fig. 162). St. Paul Xiropotaminos, who is linked by tradition with the discovery of this icon (Smyrnakis 1903, p. 463), was an eminent spiritual figure on Mount Athos in the 10th century, and founder of the Monastery of Xiropotamou (Bompaire 1964, p. 5.) The first two figures in the triptych are directly connected with the miracle-working icon of the Iviron Monastery: St. Eleutherios, who is not usually painted on triptychs, was probably the patron saint of the person who commissioned the piece.

The tranquil, idealized expression of St. Eleutherios forms a lively contrast with the tortured, unbearded face of St. Paul, which is furrowed with wrinkles, and was probably connected with some local tradition on Mount Athos. The saint has the same expression in a Deesis icon in the chapel of Ayios Georgios in the Monastery of Ayios Pavlos (Chatzidakis 1975, pl. 48b).

The expressive power and sure drawing of the bust of the Theotokos are impressive. Christ's face, with the high forehead, the halo with the cross, the olive green shadows, the restrained use of white brush-strokes, and the white spots at the joints of the fingers are all features recalling Palaeologan models from the second half of the 14th century. Similar features are to be found in an icon of St. Demetrius in the Ekonomopoulos Collection (Baltoyanni 1986 (2), p. 19, no. 4).

However, the treatment of the wrinkles on St. Paul's face, and the austere, geometric handling of the drapery of the Virgin's deep red maphorion point to a later period, possibly in the 15th century. An even later date is indicated by the depressed triple arch (cf. Baltoyanni 1986 (2), pls. 76-77), the punched rosettes on the Virgin's halo, and the dotted decoration of the haloes of the two saints, all characteristics pointing to a Macedonian workshop centred on Thessalonike or Mount Athos, in the late 17th or 18th century (Chatzidakis 1972, p. 133). The Athonite iconography and the technical features are convincing evidence that this is an important piece from a Macedonian workshop, based on Palaeologan models.

Conservation. Ph. Zachariou (1950),
Bibliography. Chatzidakis 1965 (2), p. XXXVI, pl. 86. Kunst der Ostkirche 1977, p. 127. Chatzidakis 1980, no. 129, p. 83. Affreschi e icone 1986, no. 52, pp. 93-94.

L. B.

80

Triptych with topographical view of Mount Sinai
First half of the 17th century
35×38 cm (open)
Athens. I. Yannoukos Collection

The most striking feature of the triptych is its unusual carved wooden top, which has a topographical view of Mount Sinai. On the inside of the three panels are three miniature scenes of the life of Christ: the Transfiguration in the centre, with the Resurrection and the Crucifixion on either side. The scene of the Transfiguration is accompanied by two secondary episodes showing Christ leading his pupils to Mount Thabor and following them as they depart. The artist was clearly imitating a good Cretan model of the 15th century. The Resurrection follows the iconographic type of an icon in Venice, with the angels holding the symbols of the Passion, and the angel at the bottom chaining Hades; the same type appears in an icon by Emmanuel Tzanes on Kerkyra (Choremis 1981, pl. 5). The Crucifixion follows the type widely established by the Cretan School in the 16th century, which can be seen in an icon in the Benaki Museum attributed to Nikolaos Ritzos. In it the ends of the arms of the cross are drawn in perspective, and there is a group of four women on the right and the grieving John with Longinus on the left. In the present icon, however, the walls of Jerusalem in the background suggest a somewhat later date.

The outside of the panel with the Resurrection has a scene depicting three founders of monasticism in Egypt and Palestine, shown frontally and full-length: SS Anthony, Sabbas and Euthymios. Finally, on the outside of the triptych at the back of the Crucifixion, the figure of St. Catherine can be distinguished, despite the damage, wearing imperial robes and rendered in the Italo-Cretan type that became associated with the Monastery of Sinai from the beginning of the 17th century onwards (Weitzmann 1982 (2), p. 40). This last scene is also directly connected with the relief at the top of the triptych, which depicts Mount Sinai. In the centre of it is a scene of the Burning Bush, from behind which the angel is emerging at the left, and commanding Moses to take off his sandals (Exodus 3.5), while at the right Moses is kneeling before his flock, in order to obey. At the summit of the mountain Moses is shown for a third time, receiving the Tablets of the Law from the hand of God. On a lower peak, at the right, can be seen the relic of St. Catherine between two angels, in the same form in which it was painted by Michael Damaskinos in the icon with the Burning Bush in Iraklion, Crete. Finally, the cave of the Prophet Elijah can be seen on the left, on a third peak, behind which rises the sun, carved in relief.

The inclusion of the three founders of monasticism suggests that the triptych was probably connected with a monk. Moreover, the depiction of St. Catherine on the outside, and of Mount Sinai at the top leave no room for doubt that the triptych was connected with the Monastery of St. Catherine on Sinai. This relationship further accounts for the choice of the Transfiguration for the central panel. Mount Sinai makes its first appearance in painting in the second half of the 16th century, one of the earliest examples being the famous triptych by Domenikos Theotokopoulos in Modena, dated to c. 1567 (Wethey 1962, pl. 33). Mount Sinai is painted in similar fashion in the large icon with St. Catherine by Ieremias Palladas, which is dated to 1612 (Weitzmann 1982 (2), pl. 52). There thus seem to be known iconographic parallels for the depiction of Sinai. Its rather unusual rendering in relief, which is also to be found on another triptych, in the Monastery on Sinai, signed by Victor and dated to 1684 (Chatzidakis 1966 (2), p. 56), is probably due to Western influences.

The Italo-Cretan type of St. Catherine, with the manneristic turn of the head in the opposite direction to that of the body, the cloak with gold embroidered eagles, trimmed with ermine, and the lectionary with Renaissance style decoration, rendered in gold webbing, is also to be encountered in paintings from the beginning of the 17th century. The saint's right hand, however, which is raised in front of her breast, is not holding a palm leaf, as in the icon by Palladas, but follows the variation in the icons by Victor and by Silvestros Theocharis, on Sinai and Patmos.

These iconographic features, combined with the archaizing Christological scenes, suggest that the triptych should be attributed to a Cretan artist from the beginning of the 17th century, and possibly to Silvestros Theocharis (attested 1633-1638), one of whose triptychs (From Byzantium to El Greco 1987, no. 71) has a wood-carved base similar to that of the present work.

Bibliography. Bouras 1985, pp. 62-63. Affreschi e icone 1986, no. 100, pp. 150-152. From Byzantium to El Greco 1987, no. 70, pp. 139, 195-196.

L. B.

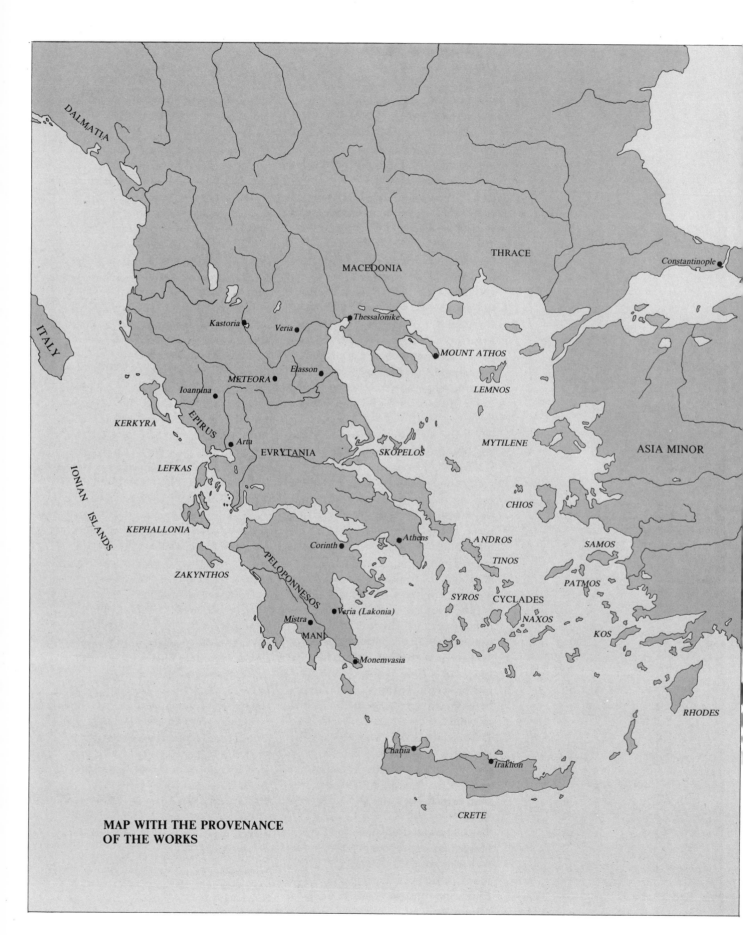

**MAP WITH THE PROVENANCE
OF THE WORKS**

DALMATIA

ITALY

MACEDONIA

THRACE

Constantinople

Kastoria

Veria

Thessalonike

MOUNT ATHOS

Elasson

LEMNOS

METEORA

Ioannina

EPIRUS

KERKYRA

Arta

EVRYTANIA

SKOPELOS

MYTILENE

ASIA MINOR

LEFKAS

IONIAN ISLANDS

CHIOS

KEPHALLONIA

Corinth

Athens

ANDROS

SAMOS

TINOS

PATMOS

ZAKYNTHOS

PELOPONNESOS

SYROS

CYCLADES

Veria (Lakonia)

NAXOS

KOS

Mistra

MANI

Monemvasia

RHODES

Chania

Iraklion

CRETE

SELECT BIBLIOGRAPHY

ABBREVIATIONS

J. BECKWITH, Early Christian and Byzantine Art, Harmondsworth 1970.

M. CHATZIDAKIS, Icônes de Saint-Georges des Grecs et de la Collection de l'Institut, Institut Grec de Venise, Neri Pozza-Venise 1962.

M. CHATZIDAKIS - V. DJURIĆ, Les icônes dans les Collections Suisses, Berne 1968.

M. CHATZIDAKIS, Icons of Patmos, National Bank of Greece, Athens 1985.

TH. CHATZIDAKIS, Exhibition Catalogue, L'art des icônes en Crète et dans les îles après Byzance, Europalia, Grèce 1982, Charleroi Palais des Beaux Arts, 3 octobre - 21 novembre 1982.

N. CHATZIDAKIS, Exhibition Catalogue, Icons of the Cretan School (15th-16th centuries), Benaki Museum, Athens 1983.

R. CORMACK, Writing in Gold, London 1985.

EXHIBITION CATALOGUE, Byzantine Icons of Cyprus, Benaki Museum, Athens 1976.

EXHIBITION CATALOGUE, Byzantine and Post-Byzantine Art, Athens, Old University (July 26th 1985 - January 6th 1986), Athens 1986.

EXHIBITION CATALOGUE, Affreschi e icone dalla Grecia (X-XVII secolo), Atene e Firenze, Palazzo Strozzi (16 Settembre - 16 Novembre 1986), Atene 1986.

EXHIBITION CATALOGUE, From Byzantium to El Greco, Greek Frescoes and Icons, Royal Academy of Arts, London (March 27th - June 21st 1987), Athens 1987.

G. GALAVARIS, The Icon in the Life of the Church, Iconography of Religions XXIV, 8, Leiden 1981.

A. GRABAR, Byzantine Painting, Geneva 1953.

P. HETHERINGTON, The Painter's Manual of Dionysius of Fourna, London 1978.

C. MANGO, The Art of the Byzantine Empire, 312-1453, New Jersey 1972.

K. WEITZMANN, The Monastery of Saint Catherine at Mount Sinai. The

AAA	Αρχαιολογικά Ανάλεκτα εξ Αθηνών
ΑΔ	Αρχαιολογικόν Δελτίον
ΔΧΑΕ	Δελτίον της Χριστιανικής Αρχαιολογικής Εταιρείας
ΕΕΒΣ	Επετηρίς Εταιρείας Βυζαντινών Σπουδών
Θησαυρίσματα	Θησαυρίσματα, Περιοδικόν του Ελληνικού Ινστιτούτου Βυζαντινών και Μεταβυζαντινών Σπουδών
Κερκυρ. Χρον.	Κερκυραϊκά Χρονικά
Κληρονομία	Περιοδικόν δημοσίευμα του Πατριαρχικού Ιδρύματος Πατερικών Μελετών
Κρητ. Χρον.	Κρητικά Χρονικά
Μακεδονικά	Μακεδονικά, Σύγγραμμα περιοδικόν της Εταιρείας Μακεδονικών Σπουδών
ΝΕ	Νέος Ελληνομνήμων
ΠΑΕ	Πρακτικά της εν Αθήναις Αρχαιολογικής Εταιρείας

ArtB	Art Bulletin
BCH	Bulletin de Correspondance Hellénique
BZ	Byzantinische Zeitschrift
CA	Cahiers Archéologiques
DOP	Dumbarton Oaks Papers
JÖB	Jahrbuch der Österreichischen Byzantinistik
PKg	Propyläen Kunstgeschichte

Icons, vol. I: From the Sixth to the Tenth Century, Princeton 1976.

K. WEITZMANN, The Icon, Holy Images, Sixth to founteenth century, Chatto and Windus, London 1978.

K. WEITZMANN, M. CHATZIDAKIS, S. RADOJČIĆ, Icons, New York 1980.

K. WEITZMANN, G. ALIBEGASVILI, A. VOLSKAJA, M. CHATZIDAKIS, G. BABIĆ, M. ALPATOV, T. VOINESCU, The Icon, Alfred A. Knopf, New York 1982.

ACHEIMASTOU 1966 = Αχειμάστου Μ., Αμφιπρόσωπες εικόνες της Ρόδου. Η εικόνα της Οδηγήτριας και του Αγίου Νικολάου, ΑΔ 21 (1966): Μελέται, pp. 62-83.

ACHEIMASTOU-POTAMIANOU 1973-74 = Αχειμάστου-Ποταμιάνου Μ., Βυζαντινά, μεσαιωνικά και νεώτερα μνημεία Ηπείρου, ΑΔ 29 (1973-1974): Χρονικά, pp. 609-614.

ACHEIMASTOU-POTAMIANOU 1983= Αχειμάστου-Ποταμιάνου Μ., Η μονή των Φιλανθρωπηνών και η πρώτη φάση της μεταβυζαντινής ζωγραφικής, Αθήνα 1983.

ACHEIMASTOU-POTAMIANOU 1985-86 = Αχειμάστου-Ποταμιάνου Μ., Η Κοίμηση της Θεοτόκου σε δύο κρητικές εικόνες της Κω, ΔΧΑΕ ΙΓ΄ (1985-1986), pp. 125-156.

AFFRESCHI E ICONE 1986 = Exhibition Catalogue, Affreschi e icone dalla Grecia (X-XVII secolo), Atene e Firenze, Palazzo Strozzi (16 Settembre - 16 Novembre 1986), Atene 1986.

ALIPRANTIS 1979 = Αλιπράντης Θ., Θησαυροί της Σίφνου, Εικόνες των ναών και των μονών, Αθήναι 1979.

ANTAL 1947 = Antal F., Florentine Painting and its Social Background. The Bourgeois Republic before Cosimo de' Medicis' advent to power, XIV and early XV centuries, London 1947[1].

BABIĆ 1968 = Babić G., Les discussions christologiques et le décor des églises byzantines au XII siècle, Frühmittelalterliche Studien, Berlin 1968, pp. 368-386.

BABIĆ-CHATZIDAKIS 1983 = Babić G. - Chatzidakis M., Le icone della penisola Balcanica e delle isole Greche (2), Weitzmann K., Alibegasvili G., Volskaja A., Babić G., Chatzidakis M., Alpatov M.,

Voinescu T., Le icone, Milano 1983, pp. 305-371.

BALTOYANNI 1984 = Μπαλτογιάννη Χρ., Παράσταση Ευαγγελισμού κάτω από νεότερη επιζωγράφηση στο βημόθυρο Τ. 737 του Βυζαντινού Μουσείου, ΑΑΑ XVII (1984), pp. 43-72.

BALTOYANNI 1985 = Μπαλτογιάννη Χρ., Εικόνες, Συλλογή Δημητρίου Οικονομοπούλου, Αθήνα 1985.

BALTOYANNI 1986 (1) = Baltoyanni Ch., Exhibition Catalogue, Icônes de collections privées en Grèce, Institut Français d'Athènes (16 janvier - 7 février 1986), Athènes 1986.

BALTOYANNI 1986 (2) = Baltoyanni Ch., Icons, Demetrios Ekonomopoulos Collection, Athens 1986.

BARASCH 1978 = Barasch M., Light and Color in the Italian Renaissance Theory of Art, New York 1978.

BELTING 1980-81 = Belting H., An Image and its Function in the Liturgy: The Man of Sorrows in Byzantium, DOP 34-35 (1980-1981), pp. 1-16.

BELTING 1981 = Belting H., Das Bild und sein Publikum im Mittelalter, Form und Funktion früher Bildtafeln der Passion, Berlin 1981.

BERENSON 1968 = Berenson B., Italian Pictures of the Renaissance, A list of the principal artists and their works with an index of plates, vol. II, London 1968.

BERGMAN 1973 = Bergman P. R., Portraits of the Evangelists in Greek Manuscripts, Illuminated Greek Manuscripts from American Collections, ed. G. Vikan, Princeton 1973, pp. 44-49.

BETTINI 1940 = Bettini S., Pitture cretesi, veneziane, slave ed italiane del Museo Nazionale di Ravenna, Ravenna 1940.

BIANCO FIORIN 1983 = Bianco Fiorin M., Nicola Zafuri, Cretese del Quattrocento, e una sua inedita 'Madonna', Arte Veneta, XXXVII (1983), pp. 164-169.

BOMPAIRE 1964 = Bompaire J., Actes de Xeropotamou, Paris 1964.

BORBOUDAKIS 1969 = Μπορμπουδάκης Μ., Βυζαντινά και μεσαιωνικά μνημεία Κρήτης, Κρητ. Χρον. ΚΒ΄ (1969), pp. 521-528.

BORBOUDAKIS 1971 = Μπορμπουδάκης Μ., Μεσαιωνικά μνημεία Κρήτης, ΑΔ 26 (1971): Χρονικά, pp. 520-533.

BORBOUDAKIS 1973 = Μπορμπουδάκης Μ., Βυζαντινά και μεσαιωνικά μνημεία Κρήτης, Κρητ. Χρον. ΚΕ΄ (1973), pp. 478-511.

BORBOUDAKIS 1975 = Μπορμπουδάκης Μ., Εικόνες του νομού Χανίων, Αθήνα 1975.

BORBOUDAKIS 1985 = Μπορμπουδάκης Μ., Ημερολόγιο 1985, κοσμημένο με κρητικές φορητές εικόνες, έκδ. Δήμου Ηρακλείου, Ηράκλειο Κρήτης 1985.

BOUGRAT 1982 = Bougrat M., L'église Saint-Jean, près de Koudoumas, Crète, CA 30 (1982), pp. 147-174.

BOURAS 1985 = Μπούρα Λ., Ένα τρίπτυχο με σιναϊτική εικονογραφία σε ιδιωτική συλλογή των Αθηνών, Πέμπτο συμπόσιο Βυζαντινής και Μεταβυζαντινής Αρχαιολογίας και Τέχνης, Περιλήψεις ανακοινώσεων, Θεσσαλονίκη 1985, pp. 62-63.

BOYD 1974 = Boyd S., The Church of the Panagia Amasgou, Monagri, Cyprus, and Its Wallpaintings, DOP 28 (1974), pp. 277-328.

BRENK 1966 = Brenk B., Tradition und Neuerung in der Christlichen Kunst des ersten Jahrtausends. Studien zur Geschichte des Weltgerichtsbildes, Wiener Byzantinische Studien, Bd. 3, Wien 1966, pp. 79-103.

BROUSKARI 1985 = Μπρούσκαρη Μ., Το Μουσείο Παύλου και Αλεξάνδρας Κανελλοπούλου, Αθήνα 1985.

BURY 1987 = Bury J., El Greco's Books, Burlington Magazine CXXIX (June 1987), pp. 388-391.

BYZANTINE ART 1964 = Exhibition Catalogue, Byzantine Art, A European Art, 9th Exhibition of the Council of Europe, Athens 1964.

BYZANTINE ART 1986 = Exhibition Catalogue, Byzantine and Post-Byzantine Art, Athens, Old University (July 26th 1985 - January 6th 1986), Athens 1986.

BYZANTINE FRESCOES 1976 = Exhibition Catalogue, Βυζαντινές τοιχογραφίες και εικόνες, Εθνική Πινακοθήκη (Σεπτέμβριος - Δεκέμβριος 1976), Αθήνα 1976.

BYZANTINE ICONS 1976 = Exhibition Catalogue, Byzantine Icons of Cyprus, Benaki Museum, Athens 1976.

BYZANTINE ICONS 1979 = Exhibition Catalogue, Byzantine, Greek and Russian Icons, London, Temple Gallery 1979, London 1979.

CARLI 1957 = Carli E., Les primitifs siennois, Paris 1957.

CASANAKI 1974 = Καζανάκη Μ., Εκκλησιαστική ξυλογλυπτική στο Χάνδακα το 17ο αιώνα. Νοταριακά έγγραφα (1606-1642), Θησαυρίσματα 11 (1974), pp. 251-283.

CATTAPAN 1972 = Cattapan M., Nuovi elenchi e documenti dei pittori in Creta dal 1300 al 1500, Θησαυρίσματα 9 (1972), pp. 202-235.

CATTAPAN 1973 = Cattapan M., I pittori Andrea e Nicola Rizo da Candia, Θησαυρίσματα 10 (1973), pp. 238-282.

CHATZIDAKIS 1956 = Χατζηδάκης Μ., Ένα νεανικό έργο του Θεοτοκόπουλου, Ζυγός 8 (1956), pp. 4-5.

CHATZIDAKIS 1960 = Χατζηδάκης Μ., Βυζαντινό Μουσείο, ΑΔ 16 (1960): Χρονικά, pp. 11-13.

CECCHI 1928 = Cecchi E., Trecentisti Senesi, Roma 1928.

CHARALAMPOUS-MOURIKI 1962-63 = Χαραλάμπους-Μουρίκη Ν., Η παράσταση της Φιλοξενίας του Αβραάμ σε μια εικόνα του Βυζαντινού Μουσείου, ΔΧΑΕ Γ΄ (1962-1963), pp. 87-114.

CHATZIDAKIS 1953 = Chatzidakis M., Contribution à l'étude de la peinture post-byzantine, L'Hellénisme Contemporain, Le Cinq-centième Anniversaire de la Prise de Constantinople, 29 mai 1953, Athènes 1953, pp. 5-31.

CHATZIDAKIS 1961 = Χατζηδάκης Μ., Δώδεκα βυζαντινές εικόνες (έκδ. Εμπορικής Τραπέζης Ελλάδος), Αθήναι 1961.

CHATZIDAKIS 1962 = Chatzidakis M., Icônes de Saint-Georges des Crecs et de la Collection de l'Institut, Institut Grec de Venise, Neri Pozza-Venise 1962.

CHATZIDAKIS 1963 = Χατζηδάκης Μ., Τα νεανικά του Θεοτοκόπουλου, Εποχές 4 (1963), pp. 32-37.

CHATZIDAKIS 1964 = Χατζηδάκης Μ., Παρατηρήσεις στις υπογραφές του Δομήνικου Θεοτοκόπουλου, Ζυγός 103-104 (1964), pp. 79-83.

CHATZIDAKIS 1964-65 = Χατζηδάκης Μ., Εικόνες επιστυλίου από το Άγιον Όρος, ΔΧΑΕ Δ΄ (1964-1965), pp. 377-403, repr. in Studies in Byzantine Art and Archaeology, Variorum Reprints, London 1972, chap. XVIII.

CHATZIDAKIS 1965 (1) = Χατζηδάκης Μ., Βυζαντινόν και Χριστιανικόν Μουσείον, ΑΔ 20 (1965): Χρονικά, pp. 11-15.

CHATZIDAKIS 1965 (2) = Chatzidakis M., Ikonen aus Griechenland, Weitzmann K., Chatzidakis M., Miatev K., Radojčić S., Frühe Ikonen, Sinai - Griechenland - Bulgarien - Jugoslavien, Wien und München 1965, pp. XXIII-XXXX.

CHATZIDAKIS 1966 (1) = Χατζηδάκης Μ., Βυζαντινόν και Χριστιανικόν Μουσείον, ΑΔ 21 (1966): Χρονικά, pp. 16-35.

CHATZIDAKIS 1966 (2) = Χατζηδάκης Μ., Ταχυδρόμος 24.12.1966, p. 56.

CHATZIDAKIS 1966-69 = Χατζηδάκης Μ., Η χρονολόγηση μιας εικόνας της Καστοριάς, ΔΧΑΕ Ε΄ (1966-1969), pp. 303-307.

CHATZIDAKIS 1967 = Chatzidakis M., Aspects de la peinture murale du XIII siècle en Grèce, L'art byzantin du XIIIe siècle, Symposium de Sopočani 1965, Beograd 1967, pp. 59-73, repr. in Studies in Byzantine Art and Archaeology, Variorum Reprints, London 1972, chap. XIII.

CHATZIDAKIS 1968 = Chatzidakis M., Griechenland, PKg, Bd. 3, von W. F. Volbach und J. Lafontaine-Dosogne, Berlin 1968, pp. 231-241.

CHATZIDAKIS-DJURIĆ 1968 = Chatzidakis M. - Djurić V., Les icônes dans les Collections Suisses, Berne 1968.

CHATZIDAKIS 1969 = Chatzidakis M., Musée Byzantin d'Athènes, Icônes, Athènes 1969.

CHATZIDAKIS 1969-70 = Chatzidakis M., Recherches sur le peintre Théophane le Crétois, DOP 23-24 (1969-1970), pp. 39-352.

CHATZIDAKIS 1972 = Χατζηδάκης Μ., Περί Σχολής Κωνσταντινουπόλεως ολίγα, ΑΔ 27 (1972): Μελέται, pp. 121-137.

CHATZIDAKIS 1973 = Chatzidakis M., Ikonostas, Reallexikon zur byzantinischen Kunst (1973), III, col. 343.

CHATZIDAKIS 1974 (1) = Chatzidakis M., Les débuts de l'école crétoise et la question de l'école dite 'italogrecque', Μνημόσυνον Σοφίας Αντωνιάδη, Βενετία 1974, pp. 169-211.

CHATZIDAKIS 1974 (2) = Chatzidakis M., Essai sur l'école dite 'italogrecque' précédé d'une note sur les rapports de l'art vénitien avec l'art crétois jusqu'à 1500, Venezia e il Levante fino al secolo XV, Firenze 1974, pp. 69-124.

CHATZIDAKIS 1974 (3) = Χατζηδάκης Μ., Βυζαντινό Μουσείο, Τα Ελληνικά Μουσεία, Εκδοτική Αθηνών, Αθήνα 1974.

CHATZIDAKIS 1974 (4) = Chatzidakis M., Classicisme et tendances populaires au XIV siècle. Les recherches sur l'évolution du style, Actes du XIVe Congrès International des Etudes Byzantines (Bucarest, 6-12 septembre 1971), Bucarest 1974, pp. 153-188.

CHATZIDAKIS 1975 = Chatzidakis M., Note sur le peintre Antoine de l'Athos,

Studies in Memory of D. Talbot-Rice, Edinburgh 1975, pp. 83-93.

CHATZIDAKIS 1976 = Chatzidakis M., L'évolution de l'icône au 11e-13e siècles et la transformation du templon, XVe Congrès International d'Etudes Byzantines, Rapports, III. Art et Archéologie, Athènes 1976, pp. 159-191.

CHATZIDAKIS 1977 (1) = Χατζηδάκης Μ., Εικόνες της Πάτμου. Ζητήματα Βυζαντινής και Μεταβυζαντινής ζωγραφικής, Εθνική Τράπεζα της Ελλάδος, Αθήνα 1977.

CHATZIDAKIS 1977 (2) = Chatzidakis M., La peinture des 'madonneri' ou 'vénétocrétoise' et sa destination, Venezia Centro di Mediazione tra Oriente e Occidente (secoli XV-XVI). Aspetti e problemi, Atti del II Convegno Internazionale di Storia della Civiltà Veneziana (1973), II, Firenze 1977, pp. 675-690.

CHATZIDAKIS 1979 (1) = Chatzidakis M., L'évolution de l'icône au 11e-13e siècles et la transformation du templon, Actes du XVe Congrès International d'Etudes Byzantines, Athènes - Septembre 1976, I, Athènes 1979, pp. 333-366.

CHATZIDAKIS 1979 (2) = Chatzidakis M., Weitzmann K., Radojčić S., Le grand livre des icônes, Agence internationale d'édition, Paris 1979.

CHATZIDAKIS 1980 = Chatzidakis M., The Icons of Greece, Weitzmann K., Chatzidakis M., Radojčić S., Icons, New York 1980, pp. 63-136.

CHATZIDAKIS 1981 = Chatzidakis M., Mystra, Ekdotike Athenon, Athens 1981.

CHATZIDAKIS 1985 = Chatzidakis M., The Icons of Patmos, Ekdotike Athenon, Athens 1985.

CHATZIDAKIS (Th.) 1982 = Chatzidakis Th., Exhibition Catalogue, L'art des icônes en Crète et dans les îles après Byzance, Europalia, Crèce 1982, Charleroi Palais des Beaux Arts, 3 octobre - 21 novembre 1982.

CHATZIDAKIS (N.) 1983 = Chatzidakis N., Exhibition Catalogue, Icons of the Cretan School (15th-16th centuries), Benaki Museum, Athens 1983.

CHATZIDAKIS-BABIĆ 1983 = Chatzidakis M. - Babić G., Le icone della Penisola Balcanica e delle isole Greche (1), Weitzmann K., Alibegasvili G., Volskaja A., Babić G., Chatzidakis M., Alpatov M., Voinescu T., Le icone, Milano 1983, pp. 129-199.

CHATZIDAKIS 1987 = Χατζηδάκης Μ., Έλληνες ζωγράφοι μετά την Άλωση

(1450-1830), με εισαγωγή στην ιστορία της ζωγραφικής της εποχής, Κέντρο Νεοελληνικών Ερευνών Ε.Ι.Ε., 33, Αθήνα 1987.

CHOREMIS 1981 = Χωρέμης Α., Νέο εικονογραφικό σύνολο του Τζάνε στην Κέρκυρα, Κερκυρ. Χρον. 25 (1981), pp. 217-227.

CONSTANTOUDAKI 1975 = Constantoudaki M., Dominicos Théotocopoulos (El Greco). De Candie à Venise. Documents inédits (1566-1568), Θησαυρίσματα 12 (1975), pp. 292-308.

CONSTANTOUDAKI 1975-76 = Κωνσταντουδάκη Μ., Ο Δομήνικος Θεοτοκόπουλος (El Greco). Από το Χάνδακα στη Βενετία. Ανέκδοτα έγγραφα (1566-1568), ΔΧΑΕ Η΄ (1975-1976), pp. 55-71.

CONSTANTOUDAKI - KITROMILIDES 1981 = Κωνσταντουδάκη-Κιτρομηλίδου Μ., Τρίπτυχο με σκηνές από το Πάθος του Χριστού στη Δημοτική Πινακοθήκη της Ραβέννας, Θησαυρίσματα 18 (1981), pp. 145-176.

CONSTANTOUDAKI-KITROMILIDES 1985 = Κωνσταντουδάκη-Κιτρομηλίδου Μ., Τρίπτυχο του Γεωργίου Κλόντζα (;), άλλοτε σε ξένη ιδιωτική συλλογή, Πεπραγμένα του Ε΄ Διεθνούς Κρητολογικού Συνεδρίου (Άγιος Νικόλαος 1981), Β΄, Ηράκλειο 1985, pp. 209-249.

CZERWENKA-PAPADOPOULOS 1984 = Czerwenka-Papadopoulos K., Eine Wiener Ikone aus dem Umkreis des Andreas Ritzos, Βυζάντιος, Festschrift für Herbert Hunger, Wien 1984, pp. 203-212.

DELIVORRIAS 1980 = Δεληβορριάς Α., Οδηγός του Μουσείου Μπενάκη, Αθήνα 1980.

DEMUS 1949 = Demus O., The Mosaics of Norman Sicily, London 1949.

DEMUS 1975 = Demus O., The Style of the Kariye Djami and its Place in the Development of Palaeologan Art, The Kariye Djami, 4, Ed. P. A. Underwood, Princeton 1975, pp. 109-160.

DJURIĆ 1961 = Djurić V., Les icônes de Yougoslavie, Belgrade 1961.

DJURIĆ 1964 = Djurić J. V., Fresques médiévales à Chilandar, Actes du XIIe Congrès International d'Etudes Byzantines (Ohride, 10-16 septembre 1961), III, Beograd 1964, pp. 59-98.

DJURIĆ 1975 = Djurić V., Mali Grad - Sv. Atanasije u Kostury-Borje, Zograf 6 (1975), pp. 31-49.

DRANDAKIS 1962 = Δρανδάκης Β. Ν., Ο Εμμανουήλ Τζάνε Μπουνιαλής, θεωρούμενος εξ εικόνων του σωζομένων κυρίως εν Βενετία, Εν Αθήναις 1962.

DRANDAKIS 1969 = Δρανδάκης Β. Ν., Εικονογραφία των Τριών Ιεραρχών, Ιωάννινα 1969.

EAST CHRISTIAN ART 1987 = Exhibition Catalogue, East Christian Art. A 12th anniversary exhibition (catalogue compiled and edited by Y. Petsopoulos), London 1987.

ELBERN 1979 = Elbern V., Das Ikonenkabinett der Frühchristlich-Byzantinischen Sammlung in der Skulpturengalerie Berlin, Bilderheft der Staatlichen Museen Preussischer Kulturbesitz-Berlin, Heft 34/35, Berlin 1979.

EL GRECO EXHIBITION 1986, Exhibition Catalogue, El Greco, Tokyo 1986.

EMBIRICOS 1967 = Embiricos A., L'école crétoise, Dernière phase de la peinture byzantine, Paris 1967.

EXHIBITION FOR THE CENTENARY OF CH.A.E. 1984 = Exhibition Catalogue, Έκθεση για τα 100 χρόνια της Χριστιανικής Αρχαιολογικής Εταιρείας (1884-1894), Βυζαντινό και Χριστιανικό Μουσείο Αθηνών (6 Οκτωβρίου 1984-30 Ιουνίου 1985), Αθήνα 1984.

FELICETTI-LIEBENFELS 1956 = Felicetti-Liebenfels W., Geschichte der byzantinischen Ikonenmalerei, Olten-Lausanne 1956.

FRINTA 1965 = Frinta M., An Investigation of the Punched Decoration of Mediaeval Italian and Non-Italian Panel Paintings, ArtB XLVII, 2 (1965), pp. 261-265.

FRINTA 1981 = Frinta M., Raised Gilded Adornment of the Cypriot Icons and the Occurrence of the Technique in the West, Gesta 20 (1981), pp. 333-347.

FROM BYZANTIUM TO EL GRECO 1987 = Exhibition Catalogue, From Byzantium to El Greco, Greek Frescoes and Icons, Royal Academy of Arts, London (27th March - 21st June 1987), Athens 1987.

GALAVARIS 1980-81 = Galavaris G., An Icon with the 'Epinikios' Hymn in the Benaki Museum, ΔΧΑΕ Ι´ (1980-1981), pp. 85-95.

GOUMA PETERSON 1984-85 = Gouma Peterson T., A Byzantine Anastasis Icon in The Walters Art Gallery, The Journal of The Walters Art Gallery, 42/43 (1984-1985) pp. 48-61.

GROZDANOV 1980 = Grozdanov Cv., Ohridskoto zidno slikarstvo od XIV veka, Beograd 1980.

GUIDE TO THE BENAKI MUSEUM 1935 = Οδηγός, Μουσείον Μπενάκη, Αθήνα 1935.

GUDIOL 1971 = Gudiol J., Doménikos Theotokópoulos: El Greco, 1541-1614, Barcelona 1971.

HADERMANN-MISGUICH 1975 = Hadermann-Misguich L., Kurbinovo, Les fresques de Saint-Georges et la peinture byzantine du XII siècle, Bruxelles 1975.

HADERMANN-MISGUICH 1983 = Hadermann-Misguich L., Pelagonitissa et Kardiotissa: Variantes extrêmes du type Vierge de Tendresse, Byzantion LIII (1983), pp. 9-16.

HUBER 1969 = Huber P., Athos, Leben Glaube Kunst, Zürich 1969.

HUTTER 1978 = Hutter I., Corpus der byzantinischen Miniaturenhandschriften, vol. 2, Stuttgart 1978.

ICONES 1975 = Icônes grecques et russes, Galerie Nikolenko, Paris 1975.

ICONES 1977 = Icônes grecques et russes, Galerie Nikolenko, Recklinghausen 1977.

ICONS 1980 = Icons and East Christian Works of Art, ed. M. van Rijn, Amsterdam 1980.

IOANNOU 1959 = Ιωάννου Α., Βυζαντινές τοιχογραφίες της Εύβοιας, Α´. Δέκατου τρίτου και δέκατου τέταρτου αιώνα, Αθήνα 1959.

IRAKLION 1971 = Το Ηράκλειον και ο νομός του, έκδ. Νομαρχίας Ηρακλείου, Ηράκλειον 1971.

KALOKYRIS 1973 = Kalokyris C., The Byzantine Wall-paintings of Crete, New York 1973.

KARAKATSANI 1980 = Καρακατσάνη Α., Εικόνες, Συλλογή Γεωργίου Τσακύρογλου, Αθήνα 1980.

KARAMAN 1932 = Karaman L., Notes sur l'art byzantin et les Slaves Catholiques de la Dalmatie, L'art Byzantin chez les Slaves, Receuil dédié à la mémoire de Théodore Uspenskij, II, Paris 1932, pp. 332-380.

KARTSONIS 1986 = Kartsonis D. A., Anastasis, The Making of an Image, Princeton, New Jersey 1986.

KLEIN 1933 = Klein D., Sankt Lukas als Maler der Maria, Berlin 1933.

KOLLIAS 1986 = Κόλλιας Η., Δύο ροδιακά ζωγραφικά σύνολα της εποχής της Ιπποτοκρατίας, Ο Άγιος Νικόλαος στα Τριάντα και η Αγία Τριάδα (Ντολαπλί Μετζίντ) στη Μεσαιωνική Πόλη, Διδακτορική διατριβή, Αθήνα 1986.

KONOMOS 1964 = Κονόμος Ντ., Ναοί και μονές στη Ζάκυνθο, Αθήνα 1964.

KOSHI 1973 = Koshi K., Über eine kretische Ikone des 15. Jahrhunderts von Andreas Ritzos im Nationalmuseum für Westliche Kunst in Tokio, Bulletin annuel du Musée National d'Art Occidental, Tokyo 1973, pp. 37-57.

KOUTELAKIS 1981 = Κουτέλακης Μ. Χ., Τήνος, Ιστορία-Τέχνη-Αρχαιολογία, Αθήνα 1981.

KREIDL-PAPADOPOULOS 1970 = Kreidl-Papadopoulos K., Die Ikonen im Kunsthistorischen Museum in Wien, Jahrbuch der Kunsthistorischen Sammlungen in Wien, 66 (1970), pp. 49-134.

KUNST DER OSTKIRCHE 1977 = Kunst der Ostkirche, Katalog, Stift Herzogenburg, Wien 1977.

LAFONTAINE-DOSOGNE 1965 = Lafontaine-Dosogne J., Iconographie de l'enfance de la Vierge dans l'empire byzantin et en Occident, I, Brussels 1965.

LAFONTAINE-DOSOGNE 1984 = Lafontaine-Dosogne J., L'illustration de la première partie de l'Hymne Akathiste et sa relation avec les mosaïques de l'Enfance de la Kariye Djami, Byzantion LIV (1984), pp. 648-702.

LAMBROS 1907 = Λάμπρος Σ., Λακεδαιμόνιοι βιβλιογράφοι και κτήτορες κωδίκων κατά τους μέσους αιώνας και επί Τουρκοκρατίας, ΝΕ Δ´ (1907), pp. 176-179.

LAZAREV 1967 = Lazarev V., Storia della pittura bizantina, Torino 1967.

LAZARIDIS 1964 = Λαζαρίδης Π., Αρχαιότητες και μνημεία Θεσσαλίας, ΑΔ 19 (1964): Χρονικά, pp. 241-293.

LAZOVIĆ - FRIGERIO-ZENIOU 1985 = Lazović M. et Frigerio-Zeniou S., Les icônes du musée d'art et d'histoire Genève, Genève 1985.

LEXICON 1972 = Lexicon der Christlichen Iconographie, Rom, Freiburg, Basel, Wien, vol. 4 (1972), col. 513-516.

LIGHTBOWN 1986 = Lightbown R., Mantegna with a Complete Catalogue of the Paintings, Drawings and Prints, Oxford 1986.

MAKRIS 1982 = Μακρής Α. Κ., Χουρμουζιάδης Γ., Ασημακοπούλου-Ατζακά Π., Μαγνησία, Το Χρονικό ενός πολιτισμού, Αθήνα 1982.

MALTEZOU 1973 = Μαλτέζου Χρ., Άγνωστη εικόνα του Εμμανουήλ Τζάνε (1661), Η Παναγία η Καρδιώτισσα και ο αφιερωτής της Ιωάννης Μέγγανος, Θησαυρίσματα 10 (1973), pp. 283-290.

MALTEZOU 1986 = Μαλτέζου Χρ., Βενετική μόδα στην Κρήτη (τα φορέματα μιας Καλλεργοπούλας), Byzantium, Tribute to Andreas Stratos, vol. I, Athens 1986, pp. 139-147.

MANOUSSAKAS 1971 = Μανούσακας Μ., Ο ζωγράφος, οι αφιερωταί, και η χρονολόγησις της 'Σταυρώσεως' του Αγίου Γεωργίου Βενετίας (Εμμανουήλ Λαμπάρδος - Μάρκος και Αντώνιος Πάντιμος), Θησαυρίσματα 8 (1971), pp. 7-16.

MANZINI-FRATI 1969 = Manzini G. - Frati T., L'opera completa del Greco, Milano 1969.

MARÍAS-BUSTAMANTE 1979 = Marías F. - Bustamante A., Le Greco et sa théorie de l'architecture, Revue d'Art 46 (1979), pp. 31-39.

MARTINDALE 1972 = Martindale A., The Rise of the Artist in the Middle Ages and Early Renaissance, London 1972.

MARTINELLI 1982 = Martinelli Angiolini P., Le icone della collezione classense di Ravenna, Bologna 1982.

MASSIGNON 1961 = Massignon L., Le culte liturgique et populaire des VII dormants martyrs d'Ephèse (All-Al-Kalif), repr. from Studia Missionaria, Pontificia Universitas Gregoriana, Rome 1961.

MASTOROPOULOS 1983 = Άγνωστες χρονολογημένες βυζαντινές τοιχογραφίες 13ου και 14ου αι. από τη Νάξο και τη Σίκινο, ΑΑΑ XVI (1983), pp. 121-131.

MAVROPOULOU-TSIOUMI 1985 = Μαυροπούλου-Τσιούμη Χρ., Οι τοιχογραφίες της Μονής Βλατάδων. Αφιέρωμα στα 2300 χρόνια της Θεσσαλονίκης, Θεσσαλονίκη 1985.

MAYER 1935 = Mayer A. L., Una obra juvenil de Greco, Archivo Español de Arte y Arqueologia 32 (1935), pp. 205-207.

MEISS 1978 = Meiss M., Painting in Florence and Siena after the Black Death. The Arts, Religion and Society in the Mid-Fourteenth Century, Princeton, New Jersey 1951', repr. 1978.

MILJKOVIĆ-PEPEK 1972 = Miljković-Pepek P., Sur les peintres le métropolite Jovan et l'hiéromoine Makarije, L'école de la Morava et son temps, Symposium de Rešava 1968, Beograd 1972, pp. 239-248.

MILLET 1916 = Millet G., Recherches sur l'iconographie de l'Evangile au XIVe, XVe et XVIe siècles d'après les monuments de Mistra, de la Macédoine et du Mont-Athos, Paris 1916.

MILLET 1927 = Millet G., Monuments de l'Athos, I. Les peintures, Paris 1927.

MILLET-FROLOW 1962 = Millet G. - Frolow A., La peinture du Moyen-Age en Yougoslavie (Serbie, Macédoine, Monténégro), III, Paris 1962.

MILLET-VELMANS 1969 = Millet G. - Velmans T., La peinture du Moyen-Age en Yougoslavie (Serbie, Macédoine, Monténégro), IV, Paris 1969.

MIRKOVIĆ 1936 = Mirković L., Die italo-byzantinische Ikonenmaler-Familie Rico, Actes du IVe Congrès International des Etudes Byzantines, Bulletin de l'Institut Archéologique Bulgare, X, Sofia 1936, pp. 133-134.

MOURIKI 1968 = Mouriki D., A Deësis Icon in the Art Museum, Record of the Art Museum, Princeton University 27 (1968), pp. 13-28.

MOURIKI 1970 = Μουρίκη Ντ., Αι βιβλικαί προεικονίσεις της Παναγίας εις τον τρούλλον της Περιβλέπτου του Μυστρά, ΑΔ 25 (1970), Μελέται, pp. 217-251.

MOURIKI 1970-72 = Mouriki D., The Theme of the 'Spinario' in Byzantine Art, ΔΧΑΕ ΣΤ' (1970-1972), pp. 53-66.

MOURIKI 1978 = Mouriki D., Stylistic Trends in Monumental Painting of Greece at the Beginning of the Fourteenth Century, L'art byzantin au début du XIVe siècle, Symposium de Gračanica 1973, Beograd 1978, pp. 55-83.

MOURIKI 1980-81 = Mouriki D., The Mask Motif in the Wall-paintings of Mistra, Cultural implications of a classical feature in late Byzantine painting, ΔΧΑΕ Ι' (1980-1981), pp. 307-338.

MUÑOZ 1906 = Muñoz A., L'art byzantin à l'exposition de Grottaferrata, Roma 1906.

MUÑOZ 1928 = Muñoz A., I quadri bizantini della Pinacoteca Vaticana, Roma 1928.

MURARO 1970 = Muraro M., Paolo da Venezia, University Park and London 1970.

MURARO 1972 = Muraro M., Varie fasi di influenza bizantina a Venezia nel Trecento, Θησαυρίσματα 9 (1972), pp. 180-201.

MUSEO CORRER 1957 = Il Museo Correr di Venezia, Dipinti dal XIV secolo, Venezia 1957.

NAUMANN-BELTING 1966 = Naumann R. - Belting H., Die Euphemia-Kirche am Hippodrom zu Istanbul und ihre Fresken, Berlin 1966.

PALIOURAS 1977 = Παλιούρας Α., Ο ζωγράφος Γεώργιος Κλόντζας (1540 ci.-1608) και αι μικρογραφίαι του κώδικος αυτού, Αθήνα 1977.

PALIOURAS 1981 = Παλιούρας Α., Οι μικρογραφίες του χρησμολογικού κώδικα 170 Barozzi, Πεπραγμένα του Δ' Διεθνούς Κρητολογικού Συνεδρίου (Ηράκλειο 1976), Β', Αθήνα 1981, pp. 318-328.

PAPADOPOULOS 1968 = Papadopoulos A. S., Essai d'interprétation du thème iconographique de la paternité dans l'art byzantin, CA XVIII (1968), pp. 121-136.

PAPADOPOULOS-KERAMEUS 1909 = Παπαδόπουλος-Κεραμεύς Α. εκδ., Διονυσίου του εκ Φουρνά, Ερμηνεία της ζωγραφικής τέχνης, Πετρούπολις 1909.

PAPAGEORGIOU 1969 = Papageorgiou A., Icons of Cyprus, London 1969.

PAPAZOTOS 1980 = Παπαζώτος Θ., Εικόνα Παναγίας Οδηγήτριας από το ναό του Χριστού Βεροίας, Μακεδονικά 20 (1980), pp. 167-174.

PAVAN 1979 = Pavan G., Icone dalle collezioni del Museo Nazionale di Ravenna, Ravenna 1979.

PELEKANIDIS 1953 = Πελεκανίδης Στ., Καστορία, I. Βυζαντιναί τοιχογραφίαι, Πίνακες, Θεσσαλονίκη 1953.

PELEKANIDIS 1973 = Πελεκανίδης Στ., Καλλιέργης, όλης Θετταλίας άριστος ζωγράφος, Εν Αθήναις 1973.

PELEKANIDIS-CHATZIDAKIS 1984 = Πελεκανίδης Σ. - Χατζηδάκης Μ., Καστοριά, Αθήνα 1984 (English edition, Athens 1985).

PETKOVIĆ 1934 = Petković R. V., La peinture Serbe du Moyen Age, Beograd 1934.

PITA-ANDRADE 1981 = Pita-Andrade M. S., El Greco, Milano 1981.

POGLAYEN-NEUWALL 1943-49 = Poglayen-Neuwall St., Die Pietà-Ikone in der Pinacoteca Vaticana und ihr Kreis (zum Ursprung der Pietà-Ikone), BZ 42 (1943-1949), pp. 186-192.

PRIJATELJ 1974 = Prijatelj K., L'icona della Pietà nella Galleria di Split, Zograf 5 (1974), pp. 55-57.

RIZZI 1972 = Rizzi A., Le icone bizantine e postbizantine delle chiese veneziane, Θησαυρίσματα 9 (1972), pp. 250-29.

ROBB 1936 = Robb D., The Iconography of the Annunciation in the Fourteenth and Fifteenth Centuries, ArtB XVIII, 4 (1936), pp. 480-526.

— 243 —

ROBERTSON 1968 = Robertson G., Giovanni Bellini, Oxford 1968.

ROOZEMUND 1981 = Roozemund R. and H., Divine Beauty, Echtheld 1981.

ŠEVČENKO 1983 = Ševčenko P. N., The Life of Saint Nicholas in Byzantine Art, Torino 1983.

SKOUVARAS 1967 = Σκουβαράς Ε., Ολυμπιώτισσα, Αθήναι 1967.

SMYRNAKIS 1903 = Σμυρνάκης Γ., Το Άγιον Όρος, Αθήναι 1903.

SOTHEBY'S 1984 = Sotheby's Catalogue of Icons, London 1984 (June auction).

SOTHEBY'S 1985 = Sotheby's Icons and East Christian Works of Art, London (14th November 1985).

SOTIRIOU 1927 = Σωτηρίου Α. Γ., Μονή Ολυμπιωτίσσης, ΕΕΒΣ Δ΄ (1927), pp. 327-331.

SOTIRIOU 1931 = Σωτηρίου Γ., Οδηγός του Βυζαντινού Μουσείου, Αθήναι 1931.

SOTIRIOU 1937 = Σωτηρίου Α. Γ., Κειμήλια του Οικουμενικού Πατριαρχείου, Πατριαρχικός Ναός και Σκευοφυλάκιον, Εν Αθήναις 1937.

SOTIRIOU 1956 = Σωτηρίου Α. Γ., Οδηγός του Βυζαντινού Μουσείου Αθηνών, Αθήναι 1956.

SOTIRIOU 1962 = Sotiriou G., Guide of the Byzantine Museum, Athens 1962.

SPATHARAKIS 1981 = Spatharakis I., Corpus of Dated Illuminated Greek Manuscripts to the Year 1453, Leiden 1981.

SPLENDEUR DE BYZANCE 1982 = Exhibition Catalogue, Splendeur de Byzance, Musées Royaux d'Art et d'Histoire, Europalia, Grèce, Bruxelles 1982.

STOYOGLOU 1971 = Στογιόγλου Γ. Η., Η εν Θεσσαλονίκη πατριαρχική μονή των Βλατάδων, Θεσσαλονίκη 1971.

SUBOTIĆ 1980 = Subotić C., Ochridska slikarska skola od XV veka, Beograd 1980.

TALBOT RICE 1937 = Talbot Rice D., The Icons of Cyprus, London 1937.

TALBOT RICE 1959 = Talbot Rice D., The Art of Byzantium, London 1959 (French edition, Paris-Bruxelles 1959).

TALBOT RICE 1963 = Talbot Rice D., Art of the Byzantine Era, London 1963.

TALBOT RICE 1968 = Talbot Rice D., Byzantine Painting: The Last Phase, London 1968 (German edition, Frankfurt am Main 1973).

TEMPLE 1982 = Temple R., Icons: A Search for Inner Meaning, London 1982.

THE GENIUS OF VENICE 1983 = Exhibition Catalogue, The Genius of Venice, 1500-1600, Royal Academy of Arts, London 1983.

TOURTA 1977 = Τούρτα Α., Αμφιπρόσωπη εικόνα στη μονή Βλατάδων, Κληρονομία 9 (1977), pp. 133-153.

TOURTA 1982 = Τούρτα Α., Εικόνα με σκηνές Παθών στη μονή Βλατάδων, Μακεδονικά 22 (1982), pp. 154-179.

TRIANTAFYLLOPOULOS 1977 = Τριανταφυλλόπουλος Δ., Βυζαντινά, μεσαιωνικά και νεώτερα μνημεία Ηπείρου, ΑΔ 32 (1977): Χρονικά, pp. 157-180.

TSIGARIDAS 1972 = Τσιγαρίδας Ν. Ε., Βυζαντινά και μεσαιωνικά μνημεία Μακεδονίας και Θράκης, ΑΔ 27 (1972): Χρονικά, pp. 548-573.

TSIGARIDAS 1978 = Τσιγαρίδας Ν. Ε., Τοιχογραφίες και εικόνες της Μονής Παντοκράτορος Αγίου Όρους, Μακεδονικά 18 (1978), pp. 181-204.

TSIGARIDAS 1980-81 = Τσιγαρίδας Ν. Ε., Εικόνα Παναγίας Ελεούσας από την Καστοριά, ΔΧΑΕ Ι΄ (1980-1981), pp. 273-287.

TSIGARIDAS 1985-86 = Τσιγαρίδας Ε., Έρευνες στους ναούς της Καστοριάς, Μακεδονικά 25 (1985-1986), pp. 379-389.

TSITOURIDOU 1986 = Τσιτουρίδου Α., Ο ζωγραφικός διάκοσμος του Αγίου Νικολάου Ορφανού στη Θεσσαλονίκη, Θεσσαλονίκη 1986.

UNDERWOOD 1966 = Underwood A. P., The Kariye Djami, 3, New York, N.Y. 1966.

VASSILAKES-MAVRAKAKES 1981 = Βασιλάκη-Μαυρακάκη Μ., Ο ζωγράφος Άγγελος Ακοτάντος, Θησαυρίσματα 18 (1981), pp. 290-298.

VASSILAKI 1985-86 = Βασιλάκη Μ., Εικόνα του Αγίου Χαραλάμπους ΔΧΑΕ ΙΓ΄ (1985-1986), pp. 247-259.

VERDIER 1966 = Verdier P., The Riches of Byzantium, Apollo 84, no. 58 (1966), pp. 38-44.

VOCOTOPOULOS 1972 = Βοκοτόπουλος Λ. Π., Ημερολόγιον Ιονικής και Λαϊκής Τραπέζης, Αθήναι 1972.

VOCOTOPOULOS 1977-79 = Βοκοτόπουλος Λ. Π., Μια πρώιμη κρητική εικόνα της Βαϊοφόρου στη Λευκάδα, ΔΧΑΕ Θ΄ (1977-1979), pp. 309-321.

VOCOTOPOULOS 1985 = Βοκοτόπουλος Λ. Π., Ένα άγνωστο τρίπτυχο του Γεωργίου Κλόντζα, Πεπραγμένα του Ε΄ Διεθνούς Κρητολογικού Συνεδρίου (Άγιος Νικόλαος 1981), Β΄, Ηράκλειο Κρήτης 1985, pp. 64-74.

VOCOTOPOULOS 1985-86 = Βοκοτόπουλος Λ. Π., Οι μικρογραφίες ενός κρητικού χειρογράφου του 1600, ΔΧΑΕ ΙΓ΄ (1985-1986), pp. 191-207.

VOCOTOPOULOS 1987 = Vocotopoulos L. P., A Hitherto Unknown Triptych by George Klontzas, Exhibition Catalogue, East Christian Art, London 1987, pp. 88-95.

WACKERNAGEL 1981 = Wackernagel M., The World of the Florentine Renaissance Artist. Projects and Patrons, Workshop and Art Market, Leipzig 1938[1], English trans., New Jersey 1981.

WEHLE 1940 = Wehle B. H., A Catalogue of Italian, Spanish and Byzantine Paintings, Metropolitan Museum, New York 1940.

WEITZMANN 1963 = Weitzmann K., Thirteenth Century Crusader Icons on Mount Sinai, ArtB XLV, 3 (1963), pp. 179-203, repr. in Studies in the Arts at Sinai, Essays by K. Weitzmann, Princeton, New Jersey 1982, chap. XI, pp. 291-324.

WEITZMANN 1964-65 = Weitzmann K., Fragments of an Early Saint Nicholas Triptych on Mount Sinai, ΔΧΑΕ Δ΄ (1964-1965), pp. 17-18.

WEITZMANN 1966 = Weitzmann K., Icon Painting in the Crusader Kingdom, DOP 20 (1966), pp. 49-83.

WEITZMANN 1968 = Weitzmann K., Chatzidakis M., Miatev K., Radojčić S., Icons from South Eastern Europe and Sinai, London 1968.

WEITZMANN 1973 = Weitzmann K., Illustrated Manuscripts at Saint Catherine's Monastery on Mount Sinai, St. John University Press, Collegeville, Minnesota 1973.

WEITZMANN 1976 = Weitzmann K., The Monastery of Saint Catherine at Mount Sinai. The Icons, vol. I, Princeton 1976.

WEITZMANN 1980 = Weitzmann K., Ikonen aus dem Katharinenkloster auf dem Berge Sinai, Berlin 1980.

WEITZMANN 1982 (1) = Weitzmann K., Alibegasvili G., Volskaja A., Chatzidakis M., Babić G., Alpatov M., and Voinescu T., The Icon, London 1982.

WEITZMANN 1982 (2) = Weitzmann K., Loca Sancta and the Representational Arts of Palestine, Studies in the Arts at Sinai, Princeton, New Jersey 1982, chap. II.

WEITZMANN 1983 (1) = Weitzmann K., The Saint Peter Icon of Dumbarton Oaks

(Byzantine Collection Publications no. 6), Washington DC 1983.

WEITZMANN 1983 (2) = Weitzmann K., Le icone di Constantinopoli, Weitzmann K., Alibegasvili G., Volskaja A., Babić G., Chatzidakis M., Alpatov M., Voinescu T., Le icone, Milano 1983, pp. 11-83.

WETHEY 1962 = Wethey E. H., El Greco and his School, I-II, Princeton, New Jersey 1962.

WILLUMSEN 1927 = Willumsen F. J., La jeunesse du peintre El Greco. Essai sur la transformation de l'artiste byzantin en peintre européen, I-II, Paris 1927.

WINFIELD 1972 = Winfield D., Hagios Chrysostomos, Trikomo, Asinou: Byzantine Painters at Work, Πρακτικά του Α΄ Διεθνούς Κυπρολογικού Συνεδρίου (Εταιρεία Κυπριακών Σπουδών), Nicosia 1972, II, pp. 283-291.

XYDIS 1964 = Ξύδης Α., Η Προσκύνηση των Μάγων, Ζυγός 103-104 (1964), pp. 68-70.

XYNGOPOULOS 1936 = Ξυγγόπουλος Α., Μουσείον Μπενάκη. Κατάλογος των εικόνων, Εν Αθήναις 1936.

XYNGOPOULOS 1939 = Ξυγγόπουλος Α., Μουσείον Μπενάκη, Κατάλογος των εικόνων, Συμπλήρωμα, Αθήναι 1939.

XYNGOPOULOS 1948 = Xyngopoulos A., Une icône byzantine à Théssalonique, CA III (1948), pp. 114-128.

XYNGOPOULOS 1951 = Ξυγγόπουλος Α., Συλλογή Ελένης Σταθάτου, Περιγραφικός κατάλογος των εικόνων, Αθήναι 1951.

XYNGOPOULOS 1953 = Ξυγγόπουλος Α., Η ψηφιδωτή διακόσμησις του ναού των Αγίων Αποστόλων Θεσσαλονίκης, Θεσσαλονίκη 1953.

XYNGOPOULOS 1957 = Ξυγγόπουλος Α., Σχεδίασμα ιστορίας της θρησκευτικής ζωγραφικής μετά την Άλωσιν, Αθήναι 1957.

XYNGOPOULOS 1964 = Ξυγγόπουλος Α., Οι τοιχογραφίες του Αγίου Νικολάου Ορφανού Θεσσαλονίκης, Αθήναι 1964.

XYNGOPOULOS 1964-65 = Ξυγγόπουλος Α., Νέαι προσωπογραφίαι της Μαρίας Παλαιολογίνας και του Θωμά Πρελιούμποβιτς, ΔΧΑΕ Δ΄ (1964-1965), pp. 53-70.

XYNGOPOULOS 1967 = Xyngopoulos A., Icônes du XIIIe siècle en Grèce, L'art byzantin du XIIIe siècle, Symposium de Sopočani 1965, Beograd 1967, pp. 75-82.

XYNGOPOULOS 1970 = Ξυγγόπουλος Α., Ο εικονογραφικός κύκλος της ζωής του Αγίου Δημητρίου, Θεσσαλονίκη 1970.

ZAKYTHINOS 1975 = Zakythinos A. D., Le Despotat grec de Morée, Vie et institutions/Histoire politique, Edition revue et augmentée par Chr. Maltézou, Variorum Reprints, London 1975.

ZIAS 1966-69 = Ζίας Ν., Εικόνες του Βίου και της Κοιμήσεως του Αγίου Νικολάου, ΔΧΑΕ Ε΄ (1966-1969), pp. 275-298.

ZIAS 1971 = Ζίας Ν., Βυζαντινά και νεότερα μνημεία Νήσων Αιγαίου, ΑΔ 26 (1971): Χρονικά, p. 483.

ŽIVKOVIĆ 1970 = Živković Bz., Arilje, Beograd 1970.

ICONOGRAPHICAL INDEX

INDEX OF NAMES